OBSESSIVE COMPULSIVE DISORDER
DISORDER

38

2 0 MAY

The Wiley Series in

CLINICAL PSYCHOLOGY

J. Mark G. Williams *School of Psychology, University*
(Series Editor) *of Wales, Bangor, UK*

Further titles in preparation: *A list of earlier titles in the series follows the index*

OBSESSIVE COMPULSIVE DISORDER

A Cognitive and Neuropsychological Perspective

Frank Tallis
Charter Nightingale Hospital, London, UK

JOHN WILEY & SONS
Chichester • New York • Brisbane • Toronto • Singapore

Other Wiley Editorial Offices

John Wiley & Sons, Inc., 605 Third Avenue,
New York, NY 10158-0012, USA

Jacaranda Wiley Ltd, 33 Park Road, Milton,
Queensland 4064, Australia

John Wiley & Sons (Canada) Ltd, 22 Worcester Road,
Rexdale, Ontario M9W 1L1, Canada

John Wiley & Sons (SEA) Pte Ltd, 37 Jalan Pemimpin #05-04,
Block B, Union Industrial Building, Singapore 2057

British Library Cataloguing in Publication Data

A catalogue record for this book is available from the British Library

ISBN 0-471-95775-5 (cased)
ISBN 0-471-95772-0 (paper)

Typeset in 10/12pt Palatino by Laser Words, Madras, India
Printed and bound in Great Britain by Bookcraft (Bath) Ltd
This books is printed on acid-free paper responsibly manufactured from sustainable
forestation, for which at least two trees are planted for each one used for paper production.

MR OCD

When did it start, when will it stop,
When will I ever be free?
When will they find a 'wonder cure' for this bloody OCD?
It may start with a plug, it might be a switch
It could be the number 3,
He'll just tap on your head and barge right in,
That Mr OCD.
He'll sit on your shoulder and shout in your ear,
'Go on, do it again and again',
He's deaf to your protests, stubborn and cruel,
And totally blind to your pain.
He'll disguise himself as a 'habit',
'It's no more than that you'll say',
Then you realise this so called habit
Is taking up most of your day.

B. King (Hillingdon OCD support group, UK)

CONTENTS

ABOUT THE AUTHOR

Frank Tallis   *Charter Nightingale Hospital,*
11–19 Lisson Grove, London
NW1 6SH, UK

Frank Tallis was for several years a Lecturer in Clinical Psychology at the Institute of Psychiatry, University of London, and now works at the Charter Nightingale Hospital, London. He has published widely in research journals and now combines clinical work with research on OCD.

SERIES PREFACE

The aim of the Wiley Series in Clinical Psychology is to provide a comprehensive collection of texts which together illustrate the range of ways in which the science of psychology may be applied to problems in mental health and abilities. This volume by Frank Tallis is an excellent example of such application. In it, he considers the many kinds of explanation that have been offered for obsessive compulsive disorder (OCD), including biological, psychodynamic and learning theories. He traces the development of the field, bringing the reader up to date with the latest neurological and experimental cognitive work. Tallis shows how current explanations may be drawn together into a coherent and testable account. The book sets this current work helpfully in the historical context, and provides numerous clinical examples to illustrate the theoretical or practical point being made. In this way, he is able to address the central issues of OCD: its relation to affect (including controversies about its link with anxiety and depression); the problem of co-morbidity; how the concept of 'insight' may best be understood in OCD; its association with neurocognitive deficits. He is able to illustrate the way in which such knowledge of causes and mechanisms may help in determining therapy strategies. Both academic and clinical psychiatrists and psychologists will find this book an extremely helpful map of a complex area. Students of psychopathology will find a model for how experimental cognitive psychology can build bridges between biological, psychological and phenomenological accounts of a disorder. Finally, cognitive behaviour therapists will be able to update their practice in the light of the latest findings from the experimental work reviewed in this book.

J. Mark G. Williams
Series Editor

PREFACE

Obsessive compulsive disorder (OCD) has recently undergone a dramatic change in status. Once considered a relatively rare example of the neuroses (Rudin, 1953), it now occupies a central position in contemporary psychiatry. The National Institute of Mental Health (NIMH) Catchment Area Survey, initiated in the 1970s, yielded results which startled the academic community. Obsessive compulsive disorder was found to be 50 to 100 times more common than previously believed, making it the fourth most common psychiatric disorder after phobias, substance abuse, and major depression (Myers et al., 1984; Robins et al., 1984). In addition to the NIMH study, two areas of research have rekindled interest in OCD over the last decade. The first is concerned with determining the biological substrates of OCD, while the second is concerned with cognition and cognitive processes.

The success of clomipramine and the more selective serotonin reuptake inhibitors in the treatment of OCD, combined with the results of numerous brain-imaging studies (Baxter et al., 1987; Baxter et al., 1992; Swedo et al., 1992b; McGuire et al., 1994) suggest the presence of abnormalities in several brain systems. These findings have inevitably prompted some theorists to challenge the present location of OCD among the anxiety disorders, preferring instead to claim it as a near relative of neurological conditions such as Tourette's syndrome (Pauls, 1992).

At the same time, research into cognition and cognitive processes has yielded equally interesting results. Neuropsychological investigations suggest the presence of specific cognitive deficits in OCD (Boone et al., 1991; Zielinski, Taylor & Juzwin, 1991; Christensen et al., 1992), while research more closely linked with clinical practice has resulted in a much clearer understanding of the phenomenology of OCD (McFall & Wollersheim, 1979; Salkovskis, 1985; Rachman, 1994). Both the neuropsychological and clinical lines of investigation have already begun to influence treatment methods (Tallis, 1993; van Oppen, Hoekstra, and Emmelkamp, in press).

To dedicate a whole volume to cognition within the context of OCD is justifiable for several reasons. Clinical psychology has recently undergone a fundamental transformation. This has largely been due to the ascendence and expansion of cognitive clinical psychology. The 'cognitive revolution', as it is sometimes described, has resulted in academic interest in 'information-processing' models of psychopathology, and a complementary development of cognitive therapy techniques. A close examination of cognitive factors in OCD is therefore entirely consistent with current trends. Moreover, this field of interest is now sufficiently developed to warrant review.

Unfortunately, biological and cognitive research traditions have developed somewhat independently. This has led to increasingly polarised views with respect to the exact nature of OCD. On the one hand there are those who view OCD as the result of a disturbance in biological systems, while on the other hand there are those who consider OCD the result of learning history and the formation of associated beliefs; however, OCD is a complex phenomenon. It is unlikely, therefore, that any single theoretical perspective will provide an entirely satisfactory account of the problem. It is perhaps more useful to conceptualise OCD as the *common end with respect to several different pathways and factors*. Moreoever, each pathway and factor may be of differential significance in any given individual. The purpose of this volume is, therefore, two-fold. First and foremost, its aim is to provide the reader with a comprehensive guide to cognitive aspects of OCD; however, in addition, a secondary objective is to forge closer links between biological and cognitive research. To that end, the final chapter borrows a conceptual framework from the area of cognitive neuropsychology as a meeting place.

Frank Tallis
London, January 1995

ACKNOWLEDGEMENTS

I would like to thank a number of colleagues who kindly read the earlier drafts of this book; David Veale, Paul Burgess, Adrian Wells, Roz Shafran, Roger Baker, and Nicola Fox.

I would also like to thank Edward Stonehill, Lewis Clein, Robert Cawley, Michael Best, and particularly Anthony Isaacs, for providing access to patients suffering from OCD, many of whom stimulated much of the following.

Finally, I would like to thank all of the patients who have been in my care with a diagnosis of OCD. It would not have been possible to write this book without their inadvertent help and guidance.

Section I

BACKGROUND

Chapter 1

PHENOMENOLOGY: FUNDAMENTAL FEATURES

PHENOMENOLOGY, COGNITION, AND BEHAVIOUR

The word 'phenomenology', a philosophical term, is usually employed to denote enquiry into one's own conscious processes (Thines, 1987). The word is derived from the Greek *phainein*, 'to appear', and it is the appearance of OCD, especially from within, that forms the main subject matter of this chapter. The phenomenological features of OCD are also given further consideration in Chapters 2, 9, 10 and 11. Clearly, the phenomenology, or conscious experience of OCD, is described most meaningfully in a cognitive discourse. Particular emphasis will be given to cognitive events (e.g. intrusive thoughts) and structures (e.g. deep seated beliefs) in Chapters 9, 10 and 11. Finally, from a slightly different vantage, much can be learned of the experience of OCD by considering the content and factor structure of formal assessment instruments; these are described and discussed in Chapters 7 and 8.

It should be noted from the outset that, in the present context at least, cognitive accounts of OCD are not to be considered in opposition to behavioural accounts. The division between cognitive and behavioural psychologies is somewhat artificial, reflecting historical and academic prejudices rather than an 'actual' divide. There are numerous arguments that can be marshalled in favour of this position; however, a few fundamental points are presented in lieu of an extended discussion.

First, with the exception of 'radical behaviourists', behavioural psychologists have become increasingly willing to acknowledge the role of cognitive factors in determining behaviour; to infer the presence of cognitive representations even in the 'minds' of laboratory animals is no longer considered unacceptable (Dickinson, 1980; Mackintosh, 1983). Second, cognition is frequently considered to be a kind of 'behaviour'; for example, neuropsychological models of behavioural organisation recognise both cognitive and motor schemata (cf. Norman & Shallice, 1980). Third, recent models of psychopathology explicitly recognise the close relationship between learning history, thoughts, and behaviour, by employing the composite 'cognitive-behavioural' designation or heading (Hawton et al., 1989).

OCD has high levels of Axis I and Axis II comorbidity (Yaryura-Tobias & Neziroglu, 1983; Baer & Jenike, 1992). The phenomenology of OCD is therefore predictably complex. Although a number of mood- and trait-related features of obsessional thinking will be considered, an effort will be made to limit consideration to mental events closely associated with OCD as an Axis I phenomenon. There are, however, some notable omissions; namely, 'perfectionism' and 'the need to control', two constructs frequently linked with obsessional states. Patients with OCD often exhibit perfectionist tendencies. Moreover, many of the symptoms of OCD can be viewed as attempts to exercise unrealistic levels of control over the environment. However, issues relating to perfectionism and control are the 'daily bread' of clinical practice. Perfectionism has been linked with alcoholism, anxiety, anorexia nervosa, bulimia, chronic pain, depression, and Type A behaviour (Hewitt, Flett & Blankstein, 1991). Moreover, 'control' is one of the essential elements of emotion, according to dimensional analyses (Barlow, 1988). Given that perfectionism and control issues are so intimately related to a broad range of psychopathological states, the value of discussing them with specific reference to OCD is questionable.

THE NATURE OF OBSESSIVE AND COMPULSIVE SYMPTOMS

Obsessions are persistent thoughts, impulses, or images that are unwanted, causing anxiety and distress, whereas compulsions are repetitive behaviours that usually occur in response to obsessions and can be overt (e.g. hand washing) or covert (e.g. counting). Obsessional thoughts are largely involuntary and interrupt ongoing conscious activity.

Compulsions, on the other hand, are largely voluntary, but are often associated with an intention to 'resist'. The degree to which an individual resists (or acquiesces) is more often than not determined by environmental factors. Lewis, in 1967, observed that: 'If an unobtrusive gesture or unspoken phrase can avert ... discomfort, this phrase or gesture will be indulged in without any reluctance: but if ... [it] is such as to arouse ridicule or censure ... it may be ineffectually resisted, or half-heartedly yielded to, or wholly abstained from' (p. 158). High levels of resistance are more frequently reported in the early stages of an obsessional illness.

Chronicity may result in individuals giving up 'the struggle' and capitulating more swiftly with respect to compulsive urges (cf. Stern & Cobb, 1978; Rachman & Hodgson, 1980). This pattern of behaviour is recognised in measurement instruments like the Yale–Brown Obsessive Compulsive Scale (Y-Bocs) (Goodman et al., 1989b; Goodman et al., 1989c), where active resistance is construed as a healthy sign (see Chapter 7).

It was suggested above that compulsions are largely voluntary; however, it should be noted that the vast majority of compulsive behaviour is associated with diminished control. Rachman & Hodgson (1980) quite rightly suggest that it is more accurate to speak of the *extent* of voluntary control, rather than to categorise behaviour as voluntary or involuntary. The same argument applies, though to a less significant degree, to obsessions.

Although compulsive behaviour usually serves to reduce anxiety, anxiety reduction does not always occur. This phenomenon is particularly common in individuals who compulsively check (especially in the form of 'retracing') or 'ask questions'. They often suggest that maximum relief is accomplished after the first check (or question); subsequent repetitions may serve only to increase anxiety and doubt (Case 1.1). Lewis (1967) goes so far as to suggest that the anxiety engendered by compulsive behaviour can prompt secondary compulsions, the purpose of which are to reduce the anxiety produced by the primary compulsion (p. 158). When repetitions serve to increase, rather than decrease, anxiety, patients frequently describe ritualising until exhausted. Compulsive behaviour is abandoned because of fatigue, rather than because of the achievement of 'satisfaction' criteria.

Case 1.1

Jim was a 40-year-old general manager. Although always cautious and conscientious, obsessional symptoms did not emerge until a stressful period at work precipitated a range of checking behaviours. Jim found it extremely difficult to leave his house in the morning without making sure that all the windows were closed and that household appliances and lights were switched off. He began to worry excessively about being responsible for a domestic accident or mishap. These worries caused extreme distress if he considered that an act of negligence on his part would cause harm to his wife or their neighbours. A particularly disturbing image that entered Jim's mind was of his wife entering the kitchen, turning on the electric light, and then being burnt to death in a gas explosion. Jim imagined that a spark from the light switch could easily cause such an explosion if he were 'foolish' enough to leave the unlit gas cooker turned on. For Jim, leaving the house in the morning to go to work became more and more difficult as his rituals would take over an hour to complete. This necessitated rising earlier than was necessary. Unfortunately, the more Jim checked light switches, the gas cooker, and water taps etc., the less sure he was that his safety precautions had been successfully accomplished. He became plagued by doubts, and often returned home after starting his journey for 'just one more check'.

In addition to these symptoms, Jim began to worry about being responsible for injuring someone while driving. He took to driving very slowly and would stop the car if he saw a cyclist for fear of inadvertently 'knocking the cyclist over'. Every time Jim heard a noise that he could not immediately explain he worried that someone had been hurt. Eventually, Jim began to retrace his journeys in order to see if he had been the cause of an accident. Even though he never found any evidence confirming his fears, he would still return to the probable location of the 'accident' several times. Once Jim had started to retrace, he found it virtually impossible to stop. He would only return home when completely exhausted. After one of these evenings spent retracing, he was on the verge of 'giving himself up' as a 'hit and run' driver at his local police station. His wife had great trouble dissuading him from this course of action.

SYMPTOMS AND HOMOGENEITY

OCD appears to be characterised by a wide range of mental and behavioural phenomena. The most common symptoms are checking compulsions (usually accompanied by pathological doubting), and washing compulsions (usually accompanied by contamination fears). Other obsessional symptoms are, in descending order of frequency, a need for symmetry, unwanted aggressive thoughts, and unwanted sexual thoughts. Other compulsive symptoms include counting, the need to ask or confess, order rituals, and hoarding (Rasmussen & Eisen, 1991). Some have argued that this 'surface' heterogeneity is misleading. Patients often present with multiple obsessions and compulsions; therefore, although a washer might at first sight seem very different from a checker, both individuals may have a third compulsion in common. Similarly, it is not unusual for patients to report both washing and checking as principal symptoms, but at different times. Thus washers can become checkers and vice versa. The relatively clear line that was once drawn confidently between washers and checkers (cf. Rachman, 1976a) is now treated with some caution. A complex case of OCD, showing a range of symptoms occurring at different times, is described below (Case 1.2).

Case 1.2

Laura was a 31-year-old woman reporting a range of obsessional symptoms. Her OCD had an insidious onset dating back to early childhood; however, at the age of 13 symptoms became more significant. When Laura experienced a 'bad thought' (which could be as innocuous as 'I might fail my exams'), she would have to retrace her steps to the point at which the thought had occurred and replace the bad thought with a 'good thought'. When prevented from retracing to neutralise bad thoughts, Laura might experience anxiety/discomfort for up to three days. When writing, words written at the time of having a bad thought would have to be crossed out or 'written over' while thinking a good thought. Similarly, while reading, the occurrence of a bad thought would necessitate passages being reread with a good thought in mind. In addition, certain words had to be avoided in speech, in order to avoid 'something bad happening'. In late adolescence, thinking the names of people she disliked would require the recollection of the names of her friends.

At the age of 21, the above problems remitted completely; however, they were replaced by contamination fears. Laura recalled writing a letter to a friend, who was employed as a nurse. At that time, Laura had a cold and feared that blowing her nose would leave 'germs' on the letter. These germs could be passed on to vulnerable patients. Soon after this incident, Laura's contamination fears resulted in extensive washing rituals. Within a year, Laura began to worry about knocking people over in the street. Moreover, a number of checking behaviours emerged, particularly relating to home safety. Laura once took 30 minutes to leave a bathroom; during this time, she adjusted and readjusted a bath mat, fearing that someone might trip up on it resulting in injury. A year later, Laura unblocked a sink using chemicals from a container marked with a skull and cross-bones. She formed the impression that she had contaminated the door handle, and this fear of contamination soon spread to everything else in the house. Ten years later, she still believes that some of her possessions dating back to that time are contaminated.

At the age of 30, Laura's washing and checking problems became less significant, and her 'bad thoughts' returned. These still require neutralising.

A further point of interest is that some checking behaviour can be extremely subtle. In Case 1.3, an example is given of an individual who checked the integrity of his current mental state by retrieving memories of past mental states for the purpose of comparison. Individuals who present as relatively clear-cut 'washers' may engage in a number of covert activities which are functionally equivalent to checking.

Case 1.3

Paul was a 23-year-old undergraduate who had no previous history of obsessional illness. His ruminations began after taking cannabis for the first time in a nightclub. At that time, he became confused and repeatedely asked a friend where they were. Reflecting on his own behaviour, Paul became quite alarmed. He began to monitor his mental processes. This sometimes took the form of 'checking' past mental states, and comparing them with his present mental state in order to detect discrepancies. Monitoring, and repeated retrieval of index memories, frequently interrupted routine mental functions. The effect of this was to confirm beliefs that his mental functioning was impaired and that he was developing a serious mental illness such as schizophrenia. Subsequent panic attacks reinforced his fears, resulting in a state of continuous rumination, mental checking, and distress.

Finally, it should be noted that certain key obsessional symptoms can arise within the context of a seemingly unrelated, though equally obsessional belief system. For example, washing is commonly associated with contamination fears; however, the author has seen patients whose washing is extended, because a certain *number* of hand movements are required to avert potential personal catastrophes. Similarly, another patient washed extensively in order to feel clean, because unacceptable thoughts were 'polluting' his mind (cf. Rachman, 1994). The fact that certain 'classical' symptoms emerge in unusual contexts strengthens the notion that OCD is a largely homogeneous phenomenon.

Chapter 2

PHENOMENOLOGY: TRAITS AND MOOD DISTURBANCE

DOUBT AND DOUBT-RELATED PHENOMENA

In addition to the 'symptoms' described in Chapter 1, OCD has been associated with a range of personality traits. Many of these have also been described from a cognitive perspective, as representing the 'formal characteristics' of obsessional thinking (Reed, 1968). On the whole, recent evidence does not support the traditional view that OCD is more likely to develop in individuals with preexisting 'obsessional' personalities (See Chapter 3); notwithstanding this criticism, it may be the case that specific personality traits are associated with specific symptoms.

Although many trait-like characteristics have been described, the vast majority of these seem to be conspicuously related, suggesting a 'core cluster'. Lack of inner conviction, difficulty in choosing, uncertainty, incompletion, inconclusion, indecision, procrastination, and pathological doubting, have all been described in conjunction with the symptoms of OCD since the dawn of psychiatry (Reed, 1985).

In 1638, Richard Younge provided the following description of an afflicted individual: 'Like an empty Balance with no weight of Judgement to incline him to either scale ... he does nothing readily' (cited by Hunter & Macalpine, 1963, p. 116). Esquirol (1838) suggested that obsessional symptoms emerged from a 'scrupulous type of character', while Janet (1903) described the 'psychaesthenic' as 'continually tormented by an inner sense of imperfection' (see Pitman, 1987a, 226–227). The deliberative nature of the obsessional patient is also described by Maudsley (1895) in terms of 'terrible and incredible ... petty vacillations and paltry irresolutions'. For Freud (1909), doubt and uncertainty were intimately related: 'It is ... doubt that leads the patient to uncertainty about his protective measures, and to his continual repetition of them in order to banish that uncertainty ...' (p. 121).

These early observations have been reinforced by a more recent phenomenological investigation of OCD (Akhtar et al., 1975). This study found doubts to be the most prominent feature of the disorder, prompting the authors to reconsider the propriety of the earlier diagnostic term 'manie du doute'. Pathological doubting in OCD is also described by Rapoport (1989b), who suggests that obsessional patients may have lost a unique function: the ability to know if they know something. She describes this as 'a defect in knowing' or 'epistemological sense'.

The possibility that obsessional doubting might be subserved, at least in part, by a memory deficit, is implicit in the clinical descriptions of Janet: 'They suffer a sort of continual "amnesia", e.g. not remembering whether they made their beds or salted their food' (Pitman, 1987a, p. 227). Freud (1909) also gives memory functioning considerable importance: 'In obsessional neuroses the uncertainty of memory is used to the fullest extent as a help in the formation of symptoms' (pp. 112–113). He goes on to suggest that when an obsessional patient recognises 'the untrustworthiness of memory ... the discovery enables him to extend his doubt over everything' (p. 122). More recently, Rachman (1973), suggests that the obsessional ruminator shows a 'lack of confidence in his ability to recall events'. Further, 'This memory deficit is generally specific to the content of the ruminations' (p. 72). With regard to their sample of checkers, Rachman & Hodgson (1980), suggest that this group experienced 'trouble remembering whether they have completed their rituals correctly' (p. 125), and spend 'hours simply thinking about whether or not they had checked correctly' (p. 127). The mnestic deficit hypothesis, and its relationship to doubting, is given more detailed consideration elsewhere (Chapters 13 and 15).

The characteristics described above are clearly evident in existing measures of obsessional illness. For example, the Maudsley Obsessional Compulsive Inventory (MOCI) includes a doubting and conscientiousness subscale (Hodgson & Rachman, 1977). In the Padua Inventory (PI) (Sanavio, 1988), items reflecting persistent doubt (e.g. item 11), difficulty making decisions (26), and worries about memory (43) are all represented. Similarly, Cooper & Kelleher's (1973) principal component analyses of the Leyton Obsessional Inventory (LOI) (Cooper, 1970) items consistently produced a second factor that closely resembled Janet's (1903) 'sentiment d'incompletude'.

Collectively, the clinical descriptions and psychometric investigations described above suggest the presence of phenomena that are, to a greater or lesser extent, related to the experience of doubt. Although Reed (1985) has attempted to provide concise definitions of the various phenomena that are subsumed under the 'doubt' heading here, there is little empirical evidence to suggest their independence, especially with respect to OCD; subsequently, in the absence of empirical evidence, Reed begins his discussion with recourse to an English dictionary (p. 170).

The tendency to doubt or question the validity of one's own experience seems to be best construed as a pervasive trait. The reader is reminded of Freud's contention (cited above) that obsessional doubt might spread 'over everything'; however, in OCD, uncertainty and doubt are closely related to symptoms. A checker might ask 'Is the door really closed?', whereas a washer might ask 'Are my hands really clean?'. Neither will routinely ask the question 'Is this really an orange in my hand?' or 'Am I really sitting on a chair?'. The situational exacerbation of doubt is consistent with Hodgson & Rachman's (1977) contention that doubt should be considered a symptom, rather than a trait. However, the debate as to whether doubting is a trait or a symptom is perhaps less important than the fact that there is a consensus regarding its *actual* presence in OCD.

The situational specificity of doubt might be explained with recourse to biological factors. Brain scan investigations have shown that cortical blood flow is reduced in patients with OCD when anxious, perhaps compromising higher order information-processing skills (Zohar et al., 1989). In addition, there is some evidence to suggest that the basal ganglia, structures that possibly function abnormally in OCD, are important with respect to the processing of non-verbal information (Boone et al., 1991; Boller et al., 1984; Chiu et al., 1986). Doubt-related phenomena may arise because of verification failures in this system. The presence of a 'limbic loop' (Martin, 1989) may go some way towards explaining why doubt is exacerbated in patients with OCD during acute episodes of anxiety. This issue is given further consideration in Chapter 22.

POOR TOLERANCE OF UNCERTAINTY

Rasmussen & Eisen (1990) include a need for certainty or completeness as a core feature of OCD. Clearly, there is some conceptual overlap here with the doubt-related phenomena described above. Notwithstanding this criticism, it can be argued that poor tolerance of uncertainty can be distinguished from doubt at the symptomatic level. A non-clinical individual may experience doubt about the successful accomplishment of a previously performed behaviour; however, he or she will not feel compelled to ameliorate discomfort through checking, being able to comfortably tolerate the uncertainty.

The degree to which poor tolerance of uncertainty can be considered a core, or exclusive, feature of OCD, is debatable. Many individuals with other anxiety disorders and depression will claim that they cannot tolerate uncertainty; however, the link between poor tolerance of uncertainty and some of the symptoms of OCD appears to be more direct. For example, many retracing obsessional motorists return to the location where they feel that they may have injured a pedestrian, not because they feel that this is very likely, but because they cannot tolerate the aversive emotional state associated with 'not knowing for sure'. As such, poor tolerance of uncertainty is a key motivational factor with respect to engendering compulsive behaviour. Again, this feature of OCD is reflected in formal measures, most notably the Inventory of Beliefs Related to Obsessions (IBRO) (Freeston et al., 1991), which contains items such as 'uncertainty is a source of concern' and 'to be uncertain about having caused possible harm is unbearable even if the possibility is very unlikely'.

An extraordinary feature of poor tolerance of uncertainty in the context of OCD is its specificity. It is often the case that an obsessional individual will be able to tolerate the uncertainty associated with everyday contingencies without experiencing any distress: for example, the possibility of developing heart disease or being hit by a car while crossing the road. However, the same individual might be completely unable to tolerate uncertainty within a restricted and idiosyncratic domain. Case 2.1 is given as an example.

Case 2.1

Robert was a 55-year-old factory owner. He suffered from ruminations and intermittent retracing to ensure that he had not caused an accident. He was excessively concerned that his insurance policies did not provide him with adequate financial cover; especially with respect to accidents in the workplace. He would read and reread his insurance documentation several times every evening and call his agent in order to resolve perceived ambiguities in the text. He would also ask his wife to read the same documentation in order to verify his understanding of the terms. When a particular reading of his documents left him uncertain about the extent of his cover, he was completely unable to resist rereading the documentation, calling his agent, or seeking reassurance from his wife. He described the state of uncertainty as 'intolerable', requiring resolution at the earliest opportunity.

A further interesting feature of some patients with OCD is that the 'uncertainty' itself is often perceived as being more aversive than the actual occurrence of the related negative outcome. It is the author's impression that many patients with pronounced tolerance difficulties will suggest that, at times, they wish the feared catastrophe would actually occur. This would be preferable to continued uncertainty.

OVERCONSCIENTIOUNESS

Although overconscientiousness and perfectionism are similar constructs, in the context of OCD, high standards of behaviour are usually set within some kind of moral framework. This aspect of obsessional thinking is clearly reflected in a number of measures. The LOI (Cooper, 1970) includes seven 'overconscientiousness and lack of satisfaction' questions, and the MOCI (Hodgson & Rachman, 1977) contains a 'doubting and conscientiousness' subscale. Examples of the latter include items such as 'I am more concerned than most people about honesty' and 'I have a very strict conscience'. In addition to the above, it should be noted that assessment areas on the Y-Bocs (Goodman et al., 1989b; Goodman et al., 1989c) symptom checklist capture many phenomena associated with the violation of 'moral code', for example, aggressive obsessions, sexual obsessions, and obsessions to do with blasphemy.

The relationship between overconscientiousness and rumination has been underscored by numerous theologians. In 1660, Jeremy Taylor (cited by Suess & Halpern, 1989) suggests that the scrupulous' ... repent when they have not sinned ...'. This observation is strengthened by modest evidence suggesting a relationship between religiosity and OCD (Suess & Halpern, 1989; Steketee et al., 1991). However, overconscientiousness does not only occur within the context of strongly held religious beliefs. An individual may develop a sensitivity to moral issues because of over-critical parenting. Rachman (1976a), suggests that compulsive checking is most likely to arise in families where parents set high standards and are overcritical. In psychoanalytic terms, such parenting might result in the development of a highly influential superego.

Overconscientiousness, unlike doubting, appears to be a more pervasive characteristic, suggesting the presence of a genuine trait-like phenomenon. It is not uncommon to find patients in the clinic whose conscientiousness, with respect to causing harm, is reflected in many other areas of life, for example excessive devotion to work. In such cases, devotion to work is usually influenced by 'ethical' considerations (e.g. 'It would be wrong to slack'). Moreover, in some individuals, even trivial activities, such as housework, can be invested with some moral significance.

Although there have not been any systematic investigations of overconscientiousness in other anxiety disorders, there is considerable clinical evidence suggesting that moral sensitivity is more evident in patients suffering from OCD (Freud, 1909; Rachman & Hodgson, 1980). Moreover, it is relatively easy to see how overconscientiousness could result in the negative appraisal of many classes of intrusive thought (e.g. sexual or blasphemous). Such negative appraisals might result in the frequent experience of guilt. This issue will be considered in greater detail in the next section.

MOOD DISTURBANCE: ANXIETY, DEPRESSION AND GUILT

OCD has long been associated with mood disturbance (Legrand du Saulle, 1875); however, there has been considerable debate as to its exact nature (Insel, Zahn & Murphy, 1985). OCD is generally classified as an anxiety disorder. From a cognitive perspective, a key feature of anxiety is abnormal risk assessment. This processing feature was underscored in one of the first contemporary 'cognitive' theories of obsessional illness, proposed by Carr in 1970, who suggested that 'in all situations the compulsive neurotic has an abnormally high subjective estimate of the probability of occurrence of the unfavourable outcome' (p. 289). Abnormal risk assessment is also described as a 'core' feature of OCD in more recent phenomenological accounts of the disorder (Rasmussen & Eisen, 1991).

Clearly, abnormal risk assessment is an important contributory factor with respect to threat appraisal and the subsequent experience of anxiety; however, it is by no means the only one. The perceived imminence of a negative outcome, its perceived aversiveness, and 'coping resource' estimates, will also influence the appraisal process (cf. Lazarus, 1966; Paterson & Neufeld, 1987; Tallis & Eysenck, 1994). Nevertheless, recent research suggests that abnormal risk assessment is central to the experience of anxiety (Butler & Mathews, 1983; Butler & Mathews, 1987) and associated phenomena such as worry (MacLeod et al., 1991; MacLeod, 1994). Although depressed subjects also show abnormal risk estimation (Butler & Mathews, 1983), this might be attributable to comorbid anxiety problems.

Carr (1974), suggested that: 'because the compulsive neurotic *always* makes an abnormally high subjective estimate of the probability of the undesired outcome, then all situations that have any potential harmful outcome, however minimal, will generate a relatively high level of threat with its consequent anxiety' (p. 316). This is, to a greater or lesser extent, true; however, it is also true of *all* the anxiety disorders. An individual with contamination fears is as likely to overestimate the probability of viral infection, as a panic patient is likely to overestimate the probability of cardiac arrest. Abnormal risk assessment is indeed a core feature of OCD, but it is not unique to OCD in the same way that the 'doubting' phenomena described above are.

Although OCD is classified as an anxiety disorder, some commentators have suggested that anxiety is not always present in OCD (Insel, Zahn & Murphy, 1985). In addition, it may be the case that a classical anxiety state is less common in individuals with predominantly checking compulsions, who tend to describe a more diffuse emotional state characterised by general 'discomfort' (Rachman & Hodgson, 1980). Notwithstanding these observations, it should be noted that, with the exception of some chronic cases, the number of symptomatic individuals who present *without any* anxiety is vanishingly small. Moreover, anxiety in OCD almost invariably arises from an abnormal risk assessment, in which the probability of a negative outcome is clearly inflated.

Depression is the most common comorbid Axis I complication of OCD (e.g. Rosenberg, 1968; Swedo & Rapoport, 1989); moreover, there is some evidence to suggest substantial overlap with respect to the biological substrates of both conditions (Carrol et al., 1981; Insel et al., 1982); however, recent investigations suggest that most affective disturbance observed in OCD is secondary to a more fundamental obsessional problem (Rasmussen & Eisen, 1992), which is consistent with earlier clinical observations and studies (Lewis, 1966; Wilner et al., 1976).

There have been no investigations seeking to determine phenomenological differences between depression *per se*, and depression within the context of OCD; however, the implications of Lewis's (1966) suggestion that obsessional patients are depressed because 'their illness is a depressing one' (p. 1200) are readily appreciated. Ideation on themes relating to restricted freedom, the prospect of unemployment, domestic conflict, loss of self-esteem, and a subsequent pessimistic view of the future, are all typical of secondary depression in OCD. Issues relating to the biological overlap between OCD and depression and issues relating to differential diagnosis are given more detailed consideration in Chapter 4.

There is some evidence to suggest that guilt, evoked directly, or perhaps mediated indirectly through depression, is of special significance in OCD.

Rosen (1975) suggested that guilt has an important role in the motivation of compulsive behaviour. Indeed, Rachman & Hodgson (1980) have suggested that compulsive checking can be construed, at least in part, as an attempt to avoid the experience of guilt. They also suggest that intrusive thoughts are more likely to be a problem for individuals with strict moral backgrounds, that is those in whom feelings of guilt will be more easily evoked.

There is a growing body of evidence favouring these suggestions. Steketee, Grayson & Foa (1987) found that feelings of guilt were more prominent in patients with OCD, compared with other anxiety disorders. This finding has been complemented by studies on non-clinical populations. Niler & Beck (1989) found that the frequency of intrusive thoughts and impulses, their tenacity, and associated levels of distress were best predicted by levels of guilt, rather than levels of anxiety and depression. Rosen, Tallis & Davey (submitted), found that guilt was a significant predictor of checking, as measured by the MOCI (Hodgson & Rachman, 1977), even after the effects of depression and anxiety had been removed. Finally, Frost et al. (1994) found that individuals scoring above arbitrary cut-off points on a number of standardised measures of OCD, experienced more guilt than those scoring below. Although one study conducted on a non-clinical population (Reynolds & Salkovskis, 1991) failed to find a strong relationship between guilt and intrusive thoughts, this has so far proved to be an exception.

From a cognitive perspective, guilt will arise when the individual violates an 'inner rule' reflecting a desired standard of moral conduct (cf. Burns, 1980). Such rules may be violated by omission, as well as commission. Therefore, a failure 'to do something I *should* have', may have the same effect as doing something 'I *shouldn't* have'. Clearly, the higher the standard is set (and the more inflexible the associated belief system), the more frequently transgressions will occur and engender feelings of guilt. This formulation may go some way towards explaining the clinical observation that feelings of guilt in OCD tend to be associated with the trait of overconscientiousness. However, recent attempts to examine the structure of guilt provide some independent supportive evidence. Kugler & Jones (1992) conducted a factor analysis of 63 items from a range of guilt inventories. Analyses revealed four factors: regret, self-hate, guilt experiences, and conscience. The relationship between guilt and the specific symptoms of OCD are given further consideration in due course (see Chapter 10).

In sum, OCD is associated with a range of different cognitive and behavioural symptoms that frequently coincide. In addition, a number of doubt-related phenomena are particularly common. Although doubt-related phenomena can occur in other neurotic spectrum disorders, they occupy a more central position in the anatomy of OCD. In addition to doubt, poor tolerance of uncertainty may also be an important feature. It is more predominant in obsessional illness than other anxiety disorders, and is a logical prerequisite for the emergence of many symptoms. Overconscientiousness is another personality feature that appears to be more closely related to OCD than other neurotic spectrum disorders. Unlike perfectionism, overconscientious behaviour appears to arise within the context of moral sensitivity.

The vast majority of patients with OCD experience mood disturbance. The most common manifestation of mood disturbance is anxiety, which arises as a result of an abnormal risk assessment. The overestimation of risk is a fundamental cognitive substrate of all anxiety states. Although depression is the most common comorbid Axis I diagnosis, it tends to develop as a secondary feature of OCD. Subsequently, thought content tends to reflect the impact of obsessional illness. There is some evidence to suggest that feelings of guilt are more systematically associated with OCD than any other anxiety disorder. This association between guilt and OCD might be mediated by factors such as a strict moral attitude and/or overconscientiousness.

Chapter 3

HISTORY

DEVELOPMENT

Although obsessional phenomena had been noted before modern times (Hunter and Macalpine, 1963; Yaryura-Tobias & Neziroglu, 1983) it was not until 1799 that Wartburg employed the term 'obsession' (see Monserrat-Esteve, 1971) signalling the beginnings of a modern conception of OCD. Berrios (1989) describes two important developments occurring during the course of the 19th century. First, obsessions were recognised as being qualitatively different from delusions (in so far as insight was present) and thus obsessional illness was separated from 'insanity'. Second, compulsions were recognised as being qualitatively different from 'impulsions', a broad class of paroxysmal and irresistible behaviours. This second process of separation took considerably longer than the first and it is interesting to note that the current vogue for neurological accounts of OCD might herald the reversal of this process (Baxter et al., 1990; Baxter et al., 1992).

After the 1860s organic theories of obsessional illness implicated several physical abnormalities; these included autonomic nervous system dysfunction, problems with respect to cortical blood supply and cerebrospinal pathology (Berrios, 1989). Psychological theories, on the other hand, implicated volitional (Esquirol, 1838), emotional (Morel, 1866), or intellectual (Westphal, 1877) impairment. In addition to promoting the 'intellectual' theory of OCD, Westphal was also the first psychiatrist to use the term 'compulsion' to describe compulsive behaviours; however, by 1900 it was the emotional theory of OCD that was most widely endorsed (indeed, by that time it had become fashionable to describe nearly all mental disorders in terms of emotional impairment). After considerable argument OCD had become established as an example of the newly formed class of neuroses.

In the latter half of the 19th century, the most perceptive clinical descriptions of OCD are provided by Legrand du Saulle (1875). He noted that obsessional problems were often associated with depression and other conditions that would now come under the anxiety disorders rubric. He recognised that OCD could start in childhood, might have an insidious onset and a fluctuating course and that symptoms could change with time. Moreover, he suggested that OCD was more likely to affect individuals from the higher social classes and especially those with certain personality characteristics. With respect to symptoms, Legrand du Saulle describes irresistible thoughts (often accompanied by feelings of doubt), engendering elevated levels of anxiety. This heightened emotional state was, he suggested, causally related to the emergence of ritualistic behaviour. He observed that severe cases may be housebound and that OCD could be associated with attempted suicide. Moreover, he suggests that depression or other conditions might be the reason for hospital admission. Most, if not all, of these observations have been substantiated to a greater or lesser extent by research conducted over the past 25 years. Of particular interest is Legrand du Saulle's precocious recognition of childhood OCD (cf. Adams, 1973; Rapoport, 1989a).

It was not until the new century that previous concepts were consolidated and refined by Janet (1903) in his seminal work, *Les Obsessions et la Psychaesthenie*. For Janet, obsessional illness progressed through three stages. The first was described as the 'psychaesthenic state', which corresponds closely with the modern concept of obsessive compulsive personality disorder (OCPD). It is characterised by feelings of incompleteness, doubt, an inner sense of imperfection, a need for uniformity and order, pedantry, a restricted range of emotional experience, excessive cleanliness, poor thought control, and a fondness for collecting things (including money). The second stage is characterised by 'forced agitations'. These might take the form of order and symmetry rituals, compulsive checking, and/or ruminations. These 'agitations' are functional, in so far as they compensate for the lack of certainty at the heart of the psychaesthenic state. Thus, Janet stressed a common underlying psychopathology that unified a heterogeneous group of symptoms. Tics were also typical of this second stage; however, Janet's clinical descriptions resemble harm avoidance rituals more than neurological abnormalities (Pitman, 1987a). The third and final stage of the illness was that of 'obsessions and compulsions'. These terms were only used to describe thoughts and impulses that were easily evoked and had come to dominate the patient's life. Obsessions were typically concerned with blasphemous, violent, and sexual themes and attempts to resist impulses increased anxiety. Implicit in Janet's stages is the existence of an obsessional continuum, ranging from normal obsessional behaviour, through personality disorder, to symptomatic neurosis.

The psychaesthenic state was clearly the blueprint for the emerging concept of the anancastic* or obsessional personality. The European diagnostic scheme for anancastic personality is closely associated with Janet's psychaesthenia (Rasmussen & Eisen, 1992) with its implicit endorsement of an obsessional continuum (cf. *International Classification of Diseases-10th Revision* [ICD-10]) (World Health Organisation, 1992).

Janet's distinction between the 'psychaesthenic state' and 'obsessions and compulsions' was reflected five years later in the writings of Freud (1913a), who also distinguished the 'anal erotic character' from obsessive compulsive neurosis (i.e. symptomatic OCD). The central features of the anal erotic character are obstinacy, parsimony, and orderliness (Freud, 1908). Freud suggested that the anal erotic character predisposed towards the development of OCD. The contemporary diagnostic category of obsessive compulsive personality disorder (OCPD), as described in the fourth edition of the *Diagnostic and Statistical Manual of Mental Disorders* (DSM-IV) (American Psychiatric Association [APA], 1994) captures the cardinal features of both psychaesthenic and anal erotic personality types (Table 1).

The relationship between personality variables and symptoms is both complex and controversial. The notion that individuals with OCD have premorbid obsessional personality types is a legacy bequeathed principally by Freud and Janet, although it should be noted that Freud and later influential commentators such as Lewis (1936) did not see the progression as inevitable. Current evidence is inconsistent with the premorbid obsessional personality hypothesis. After reviewing the literature, Baer & Jenike (1992) conclude that the majority of patients with OCD have at least one personality disorder; however, OCPD is in the minority, often occurring less frequently than mixed, dependent, avoidant, and histrionic types (DSM-III) (APA, 1980) and DSM-III-R (APA, 1987). A typical example of a recent study is that reported by Black et al., (1989), who investigated the personality profiles of 21 individuals with OCD. Although seven of these subjects met the diagnostic criteria for a diagnosis of at least one DSM-III personality disorder, none of these subjects met the diagnostic criteria for a diagnosis of 'compulsive personality' (OCPD in DSM-III-R and DSM-IV).

It should be noted that none of the studies investigating the relationship between OCD and OCPD control for mood. This is important, as the presence of mood disturbance might obscure specific relationships. Recently, Rosen & Tallis (1995) addressed this issue by administering

---

* However, it should be noted that the term 'anancasmus' (from the Greek meaning destiny or fated) was first used by Donath (1897) to describe obsessions without phobia.

Table 1 The DSM-IV criteria for obsessive-compulsive personality disorder

A pervasive pattern of preoccupation with orderliness, perfection, and mental and interpersonal control, at the expense of flexibility, openness, and efficiency, beginning by early adulthood and present in a variety of contexts, as indicated by four (or more) of the following:

1. Is preoccupied with details, rules, lists, order, organisation, or schedules to the extent that the major point of the activity is lost.

2. Shows perfectionism that interferes with task completion (e.g. is unable to complete a project because his or her own overly strict standards are not met).

3. Is excessively devoted to work and productivity to the exclusion of leisure activities and friendships (not accounted for by obvious economic necessity).

4. Is overconscientious, scrupulous, and inflexible about matters of morality, ethics, or values (not accounted for by cultural or religious identification).

5. Is unable to discard worn-out or worthless objects even when they have no sentimental value.

6. Is reluctant to delegate tasks or to work with others unless they submit to exactly his or her way of doing things.

7. Adopts a miserly spending style toward both self and others; money is viewed as something to be hoarded for future catastrophes.

8. Shows rigidity and stubbornness.

Reproduced by permission of the American Psychiatric Association from *Diagnostic and Statistical Manual of Mental Disorders*, Fourth Edition, 1994, Washington, DC. Copyright © 1994 American Psychiatric Association.

a range of questionnaire measures to 83 non-clinical college students. These included the Personality Diagnostic Questionnaire (PDQ-R; Hyler & Rieder, 1987), the MOCI (Hodgson & Rachman, 1977), and measures of depression (Beck et al., 1961) and anxiety (Spielberger et al., 1980).

Statistical analyses showed that obsessional symptoms, as measured by the MOCI, were significantly correlated with PDQ-R scores for 9 out of the 12 personality disorders; however, when the effects of anxiety and depression were removed, only the relationship between obsessional symptoms and OCPD remained significant. Although this study could be criticised for employing non-clinical subjects, the choice of a community sample may have reduced the effects of mood disturbance to an absolute minimum, thus reducing the influence of confounding variables.

Although the *specific* relationship between obsessional personality types and OCD is still the subject of debate, there is a considerable amount of evidence favouring the validity of the obsessional personality (cf. Pollak, 1979). Moreover, the failure to demonstrate a specific relationship between OCPD and OCD in clinical populations does not diminish the likelihood of certain personality variables being more frequently associated with OCD than others (cf. Frost & Gross, 1993; Tallis, 1995). As Rachman and Hodgson (1980) suggest, specific traits (perhaps appearing under different personality disorder headings) may be related to specific symptom profiles. Finally, some recent criticism does not seek to challenge the association between OCD and obsessional personality characteristics, but instead seeks to challenge the notion of 'priority'. Berg et al. (1989), for example, have suggested that obsessional characteristics might develop after the onset of OCD, and that obsessional personality features might represent an adaptive effort to cope with OCD symptoms. There is some evidence in support of this view. Ricciardi et al. (1992) found that nine out of ten patients who responded to medication and/or behavioural therapy no longer met criteria for personality disorder. Obsessive-compulsive personality disorder was the most frequent personality disorder found prior to treatment.

In sum, the contemporary diagnosis of OCD has a long history. Indeed, many of the symptoms of OCD have been recognised for over a hundred years. Although the concept of the obsessional personality appears to be a valid one, current evidence does not suggest a special relationship between OCPD and OCD. However, there is some evidence to suggest that studies yielding negative results suffer from a significant methodological flaw; namely, a failure to control for the influence of mood.

Chapter 4

DIAGNOSIS AND DIFFERENTIAL DIAGNOSIS

DIAGNOSIS

The current diagnostic criteria for OCD (DSM-IV) are shown in Table 2 (APA, 1994). OCD is placed among the anxiety disorders. To receive a diagnosis of OCD, an individual must be troubled by either obsessions or compulsions; however, it should be noted that the vast majority of patients presenting at clinics suffer from both (Akhtar et al., 1975; Rettew et al., 1992 [unpublished data cited by Swedo, Leonard & Rapoport, 1992a]). There is some evidence to suggest that the presence of both obsessions and compulsions is a marker of severity, in so far as the NIMH study found that only 8.6% of individuals in the community reported both obsessions and compulsions (Myers et al., 1984; Robins et al., 1984).

Obsessions are persistent thoughts, impulses, or images that are unwanted, causing anxiety and distress. Compulsions are repetitive behaviours that usually occur in response to obsessions and can be overt (e.g. handwashing) or covert (e.g. counting). Although the purpose of compulsive behaviour is (at least initially) to reduce anxiety, compulsions may not be connected in a realistic way with anxiety reduction. An individual may, for example, attempt to prevent a member of the family being killed in an accident by repeating a particular word a specified number of times. Harm avoidance rituals may, therefore, have a superstitious quality. Most individuals with OCD recognise that the obsessions and compulsions they suffer from are unreasonable, and acknowledge moderate to marked levels of interference with respect to everyday functioning. However, there is increasing awareness of individuals who claim to have little or no insight into their behaviour. It has been claimed that this is specially true of children (Rapoport, 1989a), although it should be noted that insight is compromised in many examples of child psychopathology.

The DSM-IV diagnostic scheme highlights several contentious issues; however, the most important of these is the validity of locating OCD

Table 2 The DSM-IV criteria for obsessive-compulsive disorder

A. Either obsessions or compulsions

Obsessions as defined by (1), (2), (3), and (4):

1. Recurrent and persistent thoughts, impulses, or images that are experienced, at some time during the disturbance, as intrusive and inappropriate, and cause marked anxiety or distress.

2. The thoughts, impulses, or images are not simply excessive worries about real-life problems.

3. The person attempts to ignore or suppress such thoughts, impulses or images, or to neutralise them with some other thought or action.

4. The person recognises that the obsessional thoughts, impulses, or images are a product of his or her own mind (not imposed from without as in thought insertion).

Compulsions as defined by (1) and (2):

1. Repetitive behaviours (e.g. handwashing, ordering, checking) or mental acts (e.g. praying, counting, repeating words silently) that the person feels driven to perform in response to an obsession, or according to rules that must be applied rigidly.

2. The behaviours or mental acts are aimed at preventing or reducing distress or preventing some dreaded event or situation; however, these behaviours or mental acts either are not connected in a realistic way with what they are designed to neutralise or prevent or are clearly excessive.

B. At some point during the course of the disorder, the person has recognised that the obsessions or compulsions are excessive or unreasonable. *Note:* this does not apply to children.

C. The obsessions or compulsions cause marked distress, are time-consuming (take more than 1 hour a day), or significantly interfere with the person's normal routine, occupational (or academic) functioning, or usual social activities or relationships.

D. If another Axis I disorder is present, the content of the obsessions or compulsions is not restricted to it (e.g. preoccupation with food in the presence of an eating disorder; hair pulling in the presence of trichotillomania; concern with appearance in the presence of body dysmorphic disorder; preoccupation with drugs in the presence of a substance use disorder; preoccupation with having a serious illness in the presence of hypochondriasis; preoccupation with sexual urges or fantasies in the presence of a paraphilia; or guilty ruminations in the presence of major depressive disorder).

E. The disturbance is not due to the direct effects of a substance (e.g. a drug of abuse, a medication) or a general medical condition.

Specify if:

With poor insight: if, for most of the time during the current episode, the person does not recognise that the obsessions and compulsions are excessive or unreasonable.

among the anxiety disorders. Insel et al. (1985) point out that anxiety is not always present in OCD. Moreover, when it is present, substantial phenomenological differences between OCD and other anxiety disorders are apparent. Although individuals with predominantly washing compulsions report an anxiety state similar to that described by simple phobics (Rachman, 1976a), individuals with predominantly checking compulsions describe a more diffuse emotional state more accurately described by the term 'discomfort' (Rachman & Hodgson, 1980).

The most common complicating problem associated with OCD is depression (Rosenberg, 1968; Goodwin, Guze, & Robins, 1969; Swedo & Rapoport, 1989; Rasmussen & Eisen, 1992) and OCD patients have exhibited biological abnormalities characteristic of depressed, rather than anxious groups; for example, non-suppression on the dexamethasone suppression test (Carrol et al., 1981; Insel et al., 1982), shortened latency to rapid eye movement sleep, and diminished stage 4 sleep (Insel et al., 1982). In addition, OCD patients fail to respond to anxiogenic agents that generally exacerbate anxiety disorders; for example lactate (Gorman et al., 1985), yohimbine (Rasmussen et al., 1987), CO_2 inhalation (Griez et al., 1990) and caffeine (Zohar et al., 1987). Finally, various types of anti-depressant medication, for example monoamine oxidase inhibitors (MAOIs) (Joffe & Swinson, 1990), trycyclics (Pato et al., 1988) and selective serotonin reuptake inhibitors (SSRIs) (Jenike et al., 1990) have proved effective as treatments for OCD, whereas the efficacy of anxiolytic medication remains uncertain (cf. Rickels, 1978; Waxman, 1977; Rabavilas et al., 1979). Insel, Zahn & Murphy (1985) conclude that the classification of OCD as an anxiety disorder is 'misleading' and that the condition might legitimately be considered an independent diagnostic entity that overlaps with a number of other psychiatric syndromes.

Although the above evidence suggests that the biological substrates of OCD overlap more with depression than with anxiety, not all of the data are consistent. For example, Monteiro et al. (1986) found that OCD subjects had normal dexamethasone suppression test results, unless diagnoses were complicated by factors such as alcoholism, depression, anorexia nervosa, cancer, or a reversed diurnal rhythm. In addition, the distinction between anxiolytic and anti-depressant drugs may be rather artificial. Several so-called 'anti-depressant' drugs have proven effective with respect to anxiety disorders; for example, imipramine has been found to improve the outcome of behaviour therapy with patients suffering from panic (Zitrin et al., 1983). Moreover, in a recent study conducted by Clark et al. (1994), panic patients were significantly improved at six months undertaking cognitive-behavioural therapy or taking imipramine.

The DSM system acknowledges that the categorical approach to diagnoses is limited and that individuals often meet criteria for several Axis I diagnoses. This is particularly true of OCD (Rasmussen & Eisen, 1992). In addition to depression, obsessional patients consistently present with a wide range of other psychiatric problems. Yaryura-Tobias & Nerizoglu (1983) suggest that this should be more explicitly recognised by making a distinction between primary (obsessions and compulsions) and secondary symptoms (e.g. anxiety, phobias, sexual disturbances). The implications of high comorbidity rates have been noted elsewhere. For example Pitman (1987a) suggests that the development of strict diagnostic criteria has been influenced more by research objectives, such as achieving sample homogeneity, than clinical observation. Although earlier concepts such as psychaesthenia are undoubtedly overinclusive, they may reflect something of a clinical reality that is only partially captured by DSM-IV criteria. A broader conception of OCD would be consistent with Insel and colleagues' argument for an independent diagnostic entity.

With the advent of DSM-IV, it is now necessary to specify if patients with OCD have poor insight. Up until the 1850s, obsessional phenomena were viewed as a type of insanity. However, after the 1850s obsessional phenomena were described under the heading 'folie avec conscience', or insanity with insight (Berrios, 1989). Recognition of the presence of insight facilitated the conceptual transition of OCD from psychotic illness to neurosis. Indeed, absence of insight remains the principal means of distinguishing psychotic illness (with its clear biological associations) and neurotic illness. By recognising a class of obsessional phenomena characterised by compromised insight, DSM-IV weakens the position of OCD among the anxiety disorders. Clearly, the absence of insight also strengthens the position of those who view OCD as a neurological condition.

The term 'insight' usually refers to the affected individual's ability to recognise the irrationality of his or her obsessions and compulsions. In DSM-IV the clinician is asked to specify if, for most of the time, the person does not recognise that the obsessions and compulsions are excessive and unreasonable. Unfortunately, this level of description does not give sufficient emphasis to the effect of state variables such as anxiety and depression. It is often the case that, when very anxious or depressed, individuals with OCD have a strong belief in abnormal risk assessments and the efficacy of harm avoidance rituals, however implausible. This should be considered within the context of biological evidence suggesting that higher cognitive functions are compromised during acute anxiety episodes due to a reduction in cortical blood flow (Zohar et al., 1989).

The strength of 'irrational' beliefs may decrease when mood improves. The value of considering insight as a relatively stable feature of a clinical presentation is therefore questionable.

In sum, the present exclusive location of OCD among the anxiety disorders is by no means certain. Inconsistent biological evidence, high rates of psychiatric comorbidity, and varying degrees of insight suggest that a broader conceptualisation, possibly an independent spectrum of obsessional disorders, might provide a more accurate reflection of the clinical reality.

DIFFERENTIAL DIAGNOSIS

As suggested above, the symptoms of OCD are likely to exist within the context of several other psychiatric problems. It is unlikely, therefore, that an exclusive diagnosis will be readily established. However, a correct diagnosis of OCD is necessary if appropriate treatment, either pharmacological, psychological, or a combination of both, is to be provided. In this respect differential diagnosis is important.

The cognitive and behavioural components of OCD are often confused with a wide spectrum of disorders. These range from neurotic symptoms such as extreme worry in generalised anxiety disorder (Barlow, 1988) to symptoms with putative neurological bases such as stereotypies in childhood autism (cf. Baron-Cohen 1989). In addition, a number of disorders have been compared with OCD, in so far as they share some similarities. These include hypochondiasis (Salkovskis & Warwick, 1986; Tynes, White & Steketee, 1990), body dysmorphic disorder (Brady, Austin & Lydiard, 1990; Hollander et al., 1989) and trichotillomania (Swedo et al., 1990). However, the most common misdiagnoses, by a substantial order, are schizophrenia and depression (Yaryura-Tobias & Neziroglu, 1983). The majority of OCD patients have a relatively well-circumscribed presentation, even if set against a background of comorbid problems; however, where irrational beliefs are strongly held and/or compulsions are absent, covert, or subtle, diagnostic confusion may well arise.

Depression

The confusion of depression and OCD is in part historical. For example, Maudsley (1895) made no distinction between the two, preferring instead to include obsessional features as part of depressive illness. Even earlier, obsessions and depression were inextricably linked in the form of scrupulosity and religious melancholia (Jeremy Taylor, 1660; cited in Hunter &

Macalpine, 1963). It has already been argued that OCD and depression share common features, many of which may be biological. Although such evidence challenges the location of OCD among the anxiety disorders, it is not so compelling as to suggest that OCD can be subsumed under the depression heading. Moreover, 33% of OCD patients fail to report depressed mood over the course of a lifetime (Rasmussen & Eisen, 1992).

With respect to differential diagnosis, it is important to establish whether depression is primary or secondary, a distinction advocated by Lewis (1966). The reader is reminded that Lewis pointed out that 'in most cases' obsessional patients are 'depressed', because 'their illness is a depressing one' (p. 1200). Recent investigations suggest that the majority of OCD patients report secondary depression (Rasmussen & Eisen, 1992) and this is consistent with earlier work, for example that of Wilner et al. (1976) who noted that the transition from OCD to depression was three times more common than the reverse.

Misdiagnosis might be more likely to occur when depression masks the underlying obsessional problem. Indeed, the occurrence of depression can lead to the complete remission of compulsive symptoms (Gittleson, 1966), most probably due to the effect of psychomotor retardation. Misdiagnosis may also occur when patients fail to report their obsessional symptoms because of embarrassment. Obsessional patients are notoriously secretive in this respect (Rapoport, 1989a; Tallis 1992; Clarizio, 1991) and may find it more acceptable to describe the secondary depression than report its primary cause. As Legrand du Saulle noted in 1875, depression is the most likely cause of hospital admission. Finally, it should be noted that some cases might legitimately receive either of the two diagnoses. In Case 4.1, the diagnosis might be determined according to the examining clinician's subjective assessment of to what degree repeated confession can be described as 'compulsive'.

Case 4.1

David was a 28-year-old man who reported depressed mood and continuous rumination on themes of guilt and worthlessness. He also conducted a number of harm avoidance rituals which had a superstitious quality. Questioning revealed that his guilt had arisen largely because of thoughts about having sexual intercourse with women other than his partner. In an effort to atone for these perceived transgressions, he would repeatedly confess these thoughts to his partner.

The principal function of diagnosis is to guide treatment. Where depression is clearly secondary and of moderate severity, obsessional symptoms should be targeted. Successful treatment of obsessional symptoms will result in the spontaneous remission of affective problems (Yaryura-Tobias & Nerizoglu, 1983); however, a primary diagnosis of OCD does not guide psychological treatment if the secondary depression is severe. There is some evidence to suggest that severe depression will result in poor compliance with respect to behavioural interventions such as exposure and response prevention (Rachman & Hodgson, 1980; Foa, 1979). In such circumstances, the depression must at least be partially treated — perhaps with medication — before behavioural work can be undertaken (Abel, 1993).

Schizophrenia and Delusional Disorder

As with depression, the reasons why schizophrenia and OCD are often confused might be attributable to the vestigial influence of historical factors; the reader is reminded that up until the mid-19th century, obsessional phenomena were regarded as typical of psychotic illness. In addition, a conceptual link was forged between schizophrenia and OCD in the writings of Stengel (1945), who observed that obsessive-compulsive symptoms tended to retard the disintegration of personality in schizophrenia. He suggested that OCD was a 'defence' against psychotic experience, and that the longer obsessional symptoms were evident before the emergence of a psychotic illness, the less severe that illness would be.

Irrespective of this historical legacy, there is, in fact, little evidence to suggest a special relationship between the two problems (Black, 1974). The transition from OCD to schizophrenia is considered rare, occurring in only 0.6 to 6 percent of cases (Pollitt, 1957; Rosen, 1957; Ingram, 1961; Kringlen, 1965; Lo, 1967). Nevertheless, the forging of possible links between OCD and schizophrenia continues to interest the academic community from both biological (Austin et al., 1991) and information-processing perspectives (Enright & Beech, 1990).

On the whole, the presence of hallucinations and severely impaired social functioning will readily distinguish the individual with schizophrenia from the individual with OCD; however, where the diagnosis of schizophrenia has been determined almost exclusively by the presence of delusional thinking the likelihood of misdiagnosis is increased. This is largely because certain types of obsessional thinking can be described as having a 'delusional quality'. Indeed, this is so marked in some cases that the clinical vocabulary has been expanded to accommodate the phenomenon; as in 'overvalued ideation' (Foa, 1979), a term commonly employed to describe strongly held beliefs that obsessional fears are realistic. Some have suggested that such patients occupy a position on a theoretical continuum, extending from typical OCD to 'obsessive compulsive psychosis' (Ballerini & Stanghellini, 1989; Insel & Akiskal, 1986).

The boundary between psychotic illness and OCD is blurred even further in delusional disorder (DSM-IV) (APA, 1994), especially when designated somatic type. This problem is characterised by delusional thinking which occurs largely in the absence of other psychotic symptoms. Consider an individual who, while living hundreds of miles from a nuclear power source, is persistently fearful of radioactive contamination and is firmly convinced that such fear is reasonable. As noted in the section on depression, an ambiguous case might legitimately receive one of two diagnoses and the subjective biases of the assessing clinician will be the ultimate determinant. It should also be noted that, although rare, severe depression can transform obsessions into delusions (Lewis, 1966; Ingram, 1961). For example, doubts about having been the cause of harm coming to others might evolve into a rigid belief that harm was irrefutably done. In extreme cases the patient might be convinced that he or she has committed a murder (Gittleson, 1966).

It is of some interest to note that patients can respond to the occurrence of intrusive thoughts and compulsive behaviour by developing 'explanatory' and semi-delusional theories. In the absence of appropriate knowledge about the nature of OCD, certain mental phenomena may appear particularly 'odd' or unusual. Maher (1988) has argued that delusions are in fact rational theories developed in order to explain abnormal or anomalous experiences. The clinician must take great care to discriminate between genuine delusions, and the patient's idiosyncratic, and perhaps culturally influenced response to obsessional phenomena. An example is given in Case 4.2.

Case 4.2

Raymond was a 23-year-old university student. He recalled performing compulsive touching rituals between the ages of 8 and 11, and 20 and 21. These were essentially harm-avoidance rituals of a superstitious nature. At the age of 22 he began to experience internal 'contradictions' to everyday thoughts and actions. For example, he would begin to open a door and experience the intrusive thought, 'don't open the door'. He formed the opinion that these contradictions were of some spiritual significance. Further, if he disobeyed them, he might not go to heaven.

When Raymond saw the number '4' after the occurrence of an internal contradiction, he considered this somehow confirmed his views. Although Raymond only rated his degree of belief in the spiritual significance of these 'contradictions' at the 2% level, he was excessively concerned that his interpretation of these phenomena might be true.

In sum, OCD has relatively high levels of comorbidity with other types of disorder and several Axis I diagnoses may be required. The most common misdiagnoses are depression and schizophrenia. With depression, the distinction between primary and secondary depression should guide diagnosis; however, this will not necessarily guide treatment. Overvalued ideation can mimic some of the symptoms of schizophrenic illness and delusional disorder. If overvalued ideas exist in the absence of significant distress or mood disturbance, it is unlikely that an unequivocal distinction between psychotic illness and OCD can be made. This fact has led some commentators to suggest that obsessional patients with overvalued ideas should be placed in a separate diagnostic category of their own (Perse, 1988).

Chapter 5

EPIDEMIOLOGY, DEMOGRAPHY, AND CLINICAL FEATURES

EPIDEMIOLOGY

The occurrence of both adult and childhood OCD in inpatient and outpatient psychiatric populations is relatively low, ranging from 0.5–4% (Pollitt, 1957; Kringlen, 1965; Ingram, 1961; Lo, 1967; Hollingsworth et al., 1980; Coryell, 1981; Rasmussen & Tsuang, 1984); however, results from a more recent study (reported by Rasmussen & Eisen, 1992), undertaken in a private outpatient clinic, suggest that 10% of subscribing patients exhibited obsessive compulsive symptoms (according to DSM-III criteria). This latter figure is more consistent with the prevalence rates reported in the general population as part of the NIMH Epidemiologic Catchment Areas Survey (ECA). OCD was found to have a six-month point prevalence of 1.6% (Myers et al., 1984) and a lifetime prevalence of 2.5% (Robins et al., 1984). These figures indicate that there may be up to 5 million individuals with OCD in the United States and possibly 1 million individuals with OCD in the UK (Rapoport, 1989a).

It has been suggested that the results of the NIMH ECA study are inaccurate; non-professional interviewers were employed to collect data and a liberal interpretation of diagnostic criteria for OCD might account for elevated prevalence estimates. However, this is unlikely, since similar prevalence rates have been found in several independent studies conducted in Finland (Vaisaner, 1975), Africa (Orly & Wing, 1979), Canada (Bland et al., 1988), and Taiwan (Hwuh, Chang et al., 1989).

DEMOGRAPHY

Sex Ratio

Men and women are affected by OCD in equal numbers (Black, 1974; Karno et al., 1988); however, gender may be unequally distributed with respect to presenting symptoms. For example, among adults there is a tendency for more women than men to suffer from contamination fears accompanied by washing and cleaning rituals, whereas more men than women suffer from obsessional slowness (Marks, 1987, p. 424). When OCD occurs in childhood and adolescence, males outnumber females by more than two to one (Hollingsworth et al., 1980; Swedo & Rapoport, 1989). In addition, obsessions about numbers are particularly common in boys. Of the 18 cases reported in the NIMH sample with an onset age of between 2–7 years, only three were female (Swedo & Rapoport, 1989). However, some doubt must be entertained as to the accuracy of differential diagnosis in this very early onset group, especially with respect to autism.

Notwithstanding this criticism, other work is consistent with the NIMH results. For example, Noshirvani et al. (1991) found that among 307 adults with OCD, early onset (5–15 years) was more common in men than women. Moreover, early onset was associated with the presence of checking compulsions rather than washing compulsions.

Ordinal Position

Several studies have investigated the influence of ordinal position on the development of OCD; however, results are inconclusive (Tsuang, 1966; Kayton & Borge, 1967; Coryell 1981). Although Kayton & Borge (1967) found that OCD patients were more likely to be first-born or only children when compared with a control group, this finding has not been replicated; however, it is of some interest to note that first-born relatives of OCD patients have more obsessional symptoms than those born later (McKeon, 1983). Investigation of birth order may seem, at first sight, of limited value, especially since increased levels of psychopathology in first-born children is a well-recognised clinical phenomenon (Rutter, 1989). However, from the vantage of cognitive appraisal theories of OCD (Salkovskis, 1985; Rachman, 1993), the social environment occupied by the first-born child may increase his or her sense of 'responsibility'; a construct given central importance by this group of theorists (see Chapter 10).

Marital Status

Up to 47% of individuals with OCD lead a celibate life (Rudin, 1953; Costa Molinari et al., 1971) and a higher percentage of individuals with OCD remain single compared with age-matched controls (Rudin, 1953; Costa Molinari et al., 1971). Yaryura-Tobias & Neziroglu (1983) suggest, quite plausibly, an inverse relationship between marriage and illness severity.

It is generally believed that marital conflict is a common feature of OCD (Rachman & Hodgson, 1980), and indeed, recent evidence suggests an association between obsessional illness, separation, and divorce (Karno et al., 1988). Moreover, it has been suggested that, if the illness develops after marriage, marital discord may occur in almost half of cases (Yaryura-Tobias and Neziroglu, 1983). Individuals with obsessions only are more likely to be married or living with a partner compared with individuals with obsessions and accompanying compulsions (Arts et al., 1993). This might be attributable to the presence of a more severe illness in individuals exhibiting both obsessions and compulsions.

Religion

Freud (1913b) was perhaps the first to comment on the parallels that can be drawn between religious ceremony and obsessional rituals. Both can reduce anxiety associated with subjectively perceived moral transgressions, and both serve to ward off catastrophes. Since Freud's commentary, there has been continued speculation as to how religious practice and OCD might be related.

There is some evidence to suggest that OCD may be associated with certain religions more than others; however, it is more likely that intensity of belief is of greater importance than denomination. Catholicism and Judaism are usually selected for special attention (Suess & Halpern, 1989) although the first recorded description of obsessional behaviour can be found in a Pali scripture, and concerns the obsessional cleaning behaviour exhibited by a Buddhist monk (de Silva & Rachman, 1992).

In numerous commentaries Catholicism has been associated with scrupulosity and guilt, both of which are found, to a greater or lesser extent, in obsessional illness. A scrupulous thinking style is indeed reflected in many of the traits ascribed to individuals with either OCD or OCPD: for example, perfectionism, indecision, and doubting (Reed, 1985). Moreover, there is considerable evidence suggesting that guilt is a significant phenomenological feature of OCD (see Chapter 2). It is of some interest to note that Gaitonde (1958), conducting a study in Bombay, found that all his obsessional subjects were Catholic. Similar findings have been found in Jewish communities. For example, Greenberg (1984) found that half of the obsessional patients attending a psychiatric clinic in an orthodox area of Jerusalem reported experiencing OCD problems related to the practice of Judaism at some time in their lives. With the exception of one patient in this group, the onset of OCD was reliably triggered by increased religious commitment.

Steketee, Quay & White (1991) did not find any specific association between denomination and OCD. Moreover, obsessional patients were not found to be more religious or guilty than anxious controls. However, the severity of OCD symptoms was positively correlated with religiosity and guilt. In addition, greater religious devotion was associated with more guilt in OCD, but not with other anxiety disorders.

Fitz (1990) has reviewed religious factors in the aetiology of OCD, but suggests that the evidence is inconclusive. He suggested that research methods should be refined, to the extent that specific family environments, particular dimensions of religion, and different subtypes of OCD are all taken into account. It may be the case that certain features of spiritual belief systems are associated with certain symptoms of OCD, in the same way that specific personality traits might plausibly be related to specific OCD symptoms. Such a suggestion would be consistent with Hoffnung et al. (1989) who report phenomenological analyses of two cases. The symptoms of these patients were predominantly distortions and exaggerations of rituals practised in their own religious subculture. An example of the blurring of religious practice and OCD is given in Case 5.1.

Case 5.1

Harry was a 28-year-old Jewish man. His orthodox practice required the recitation of prayers at certain times of the day. Harry became excessively concerned that he was 'speaking' the words without giving due consideration to their meaning. Lapses of concentration, or the occurrence of intrusive thoughts during recitation would render the prayer invalid. This would necessitate a complete repetition from the beginning. He was unable to resist restarting, and a single three-minute prayer might take up to 30 minutes. As a result of this compulsive behaviour, Harry avoided praying in public. In addition, he would doubt in the evening whether he had said his morning prayers. In order to reduce doubt, he would place slips of paper in his prayer book to indicate successfully completed prayers.

CLINICAL FEATURES

Age of Onset

The age of onset in OCD is variable; however, it is likely that most cases first occur in late adolescence or in the early twenties. This is of course consistent with several other disorders on the neurotic spectrum, for example simple and social phobia (DSM-III-R) (APA, 1987). In addition, there is some evidence to suggest the presence of an early onset group who are predominantly male (see above). It is possible that several adolescent onset cases could be placed in this latter category; patients were simply able to conceal their symptoms through childhood. Indeed, Swedo & Rapoport (1989) suggest that early onset symptoms may be present in children four to six months before parents become aware of the problem. Irrespective of early onset cases, the average time elapsing between onset and first clinical presentation is approximately seven to eight years (Pollitt, 1957; Yaryura-Tobias & Neziroglu, 1983), underscoring the severe embarrassment suffered by individuals with an obsessional illness. Finally, there is some evidence supporting the existence of a late onset subgroup, characterised by obsessions only (Arts et al., 1993); an intriguing complement to the very early onset group who are predominantly compulsive.

Precipitating Events

Research into precipitating factors in OCD has yielded mixed results. Some studies have found that in 30–50% of cases no precipitants are reported (Goodwin, Guze & Robins, 1969; Black, 1974), whereas others suggest that between 56% and 90% of patients with OCD can recall a precipitant (Lo, 1967; Ingram, 1961; Rudin, 1953; Pollitt, 1957; Bridges, Goktepe & Maratos, 1973; Kringlen, 1965; Rassmussen & Eisen, 1992).

Precipitants usually take the form of some kind of emotional stress in the domestic or work environment, although any life change resulting in increased levels of responsibility may also be significant (Rachman and Hodgson, 1980). Recent research (Khanna et al., 1988) has found that OCD subjects experience a significant excess of life events in the six months prior to illness, particularly undesirable, uncontrolled events in the areas of health and bereavement.

An acute onset is typically more marked in women (Rasmussen & Eisen, 1992), for example during pregnancy, after a termination, or after the birth of a first child. Indeed, in one study, 69% of female OCD patients linked onset or worsening of OCD symptoms with pregnancy and childbirth (Buttolph & Holland, 1990). Individuals with predominantly cleaning compulsions are more likely to report a precipitating event than those with predominantly checking compulsions, which are associated with a more gradual onset (Rachman and Hodgson, 1980).

Mood disturbance may also be an important factor. There is some evidence to suggest that a reactive or neurotic depression can precipitate obsessional problems (Kiloh & Garside, 1963). Also Gittleson (1966), found that of those subjects without obsessions prior to a depressive illness, 25% developed obsessional symptoms during its course.

Course

The course of OCD is variable. It is not uncommon to find patients who have experienced episodes of varying length that remit before the disorder becomes chronic (Marks, 1987); however, a complete remission is rare. In three studies summarised by Black (1974), the initial course of OCD was static or steadily worsening in 57% of subjects, phasic in 13% of subjects, and fluctuating in 30%. More recently, Gojer, Khannu & Channabasavanna (1987) reported that after discharge, 66% of patients showed a deteriorating course, 17% fluctuated, 11% remained the same, and only 2% improved.

Although a broad division is often made between the most common manifestations of OCD, namely washing and checking, there is an increasing recognition that the relationship between these two forms may be complex. Clearly, washing and checking compulsions often coexist in the same individual; however, the predominance of either symptom may change with time (see Case 1.2). This phenomenon has also been noted in children. As a rule, paediatric OCD consists of both obsessions and compulsions; however, the focus of obsessional ideation, and the subsequent compulsive behaviour, may change over time in 95% of cases (Rettew et al., 1992; cited by Swedo, Leonard, & Rapoport, 1992a). The rate at which primary symptoms change varies from individual to individual. Such transitions may take place on a time scale of weeks to years.

After remission, relapse may be precipitated by a number of factors, particularly 'fatigue, depression, any cause of anxiety, and recurrence of conditions that initially triggered the problem' (Marks, 1987, p. 426).

CONCLUSION

In sum, OCD is an extremely common disorder, the prevalence of which seems relatively constant irrespective of culture and geographical location. It affects both sexes equally, although males may be overrepresented when onset is very early. There is some evidence to suggest that the manifest symptoms of OCD may be unequally distributed with respect to gender.

Like many other neurotic conditions, OCD is likely to begin in adolescence or early adulthood. Precipitants include negative life events, changes of circumstance associated with increased responsibility, and reactive depression. Acute onset is relatively common in individuals suffering from contamination fears and washing compulsions. The course of the illness is variable, and primary symptoms may change over time.

Religiosity may influence the development of OCD, although the exact relationship is at present unclear. Further, there is evidence to suggest that individuals with OCD experience problems forming and maintaining intimate relationships.

Chapter 6

BIOLOGICAL FACTORS

INTRODUCTION

Evidence for a biological substrate of OCD is derived from several sources: studies showing an association between OCD and mass lesions or infarcts (Brickner, Rosner & Munroes, 1940; Hillbom, 1960; McKeon, McGuffin & Robinson, 1984; Cambier et al., 1988; Tonkonogy & Barriera, 1989; Seibyl et al., 1989; Weilberg et al., 1989); studies suggesting that OCD may develop following infection (Jellife, 1929; Swedo et al., 1989); studies suggesting an association between OCD and metabolic disorders (George, Kellner & Fossey, 1989; Lees et al., 1989); and studies suggesting an association between OCD and epilepsy (Kettle & Marks, 1986; Yaryura-Tobias & Neziroglu, 1983). In addition to the above, single articles have suggested that OCD can arise in the context of diabetes insipidus (Barton, 1965), hypogylcaemia (Riperre, 1984), manganese poisoning (Mena et al., 1967), and after a wasp sting (La Plane et al., 1981). There are numerous studies suggesting that patients with OCD show 'abnormal' electroencephalography (Flor-Henry et al., 1979; Ceiseilski, Beech & Gordon, 1981; Beech, Ceiseilski & Gordon , 1983; Insel et al., 1983; Shagass et al., 1984), and the outcome of psychosurgery procedures is widely held to implicate a biological basis for OCD (see Chiocca & Martuza, 1990, for a review).

A more detailed discussion of the above evidence is beyond the scope of this volume; however, three more literatures are worthy of detailed discussion on account of their current importance with respect to contemporary biological theories of OCD: first, the genetics literature; second, studies implicating the serotonergic system; and finally the results of brain scan investigations.

GENETICS

Several investigations have investigated familial inheritance (Luxenburger, 1930; Lewis, 1936; Brown, 1942; Rudin, 1953; Kringlen, 1965;

Alanen et al., 1966; Lo, 1967; Rosenberg, 1967; Carey, 1978; Rasmussen & Tsuang, 1986; McKeon & Murray, 1987). In spite of these studies employing different diagnostic systems and different sampling techniques, they show a remarkable level of agreement. OCD appears to affect 4.6% and 10% of parents in most earlier studies, and the same is true for two out of three recent studies (Macdonald, Murray & Clifford, 1992).

In addition to the above, Lenane et al. (1990) interviewed 145 first degree relatives of 46 children and adolescent OCD probands. Thirty per cent of probands had at least one first-degree relative with OCD. Indeed, 25% of fathers and 9% of mothers received this diagnosis. Lenane and colleagues point out that symptoms of probands and their parents were usually different, suggesting data could not be accounted for by cultural transmission (i.e. children simply mimicking their parents' symptoms).

Evidence for the heritability of OCD has also been derived from twin studies showing high concordance rates in monozygotic (MZ) pairs (Woodruff & Pitts, 1964; Parker, 1964; Inouye, 1965; Marks et al., 1969). However, it should be noted that this literature is relatively small. Carey (1978) estimated that only 30 concordant and 13 discordant MZ pairs, and no concordant but 14 discordant dizygotic (DZ) pairs had been reported in the world literature at that time. Moreover, these figures have to be treated with some caution, as in many cases, both the diagnosis and zygosity are in doubt.

Carey & Gottesman (1981) found that 87% of MZ twins were concordant for OCD, compared with only 47% of DZ pairs. These individuals were taken from the Maudsley register, which ensures both reliable zygosity and diagnosis. A follow-up study was conducted including most twin pairs from this series, and additional pairs were added over the subsequent 10 years. Preliminary results (Macdonald & Murray, 1989) confirm earlier findings of increasing MZ and DZ concordance as inclusion criteria are broadened towards obsessional traits or any neurotic disorder. The authors conclude that these, and other data, suggest the inheritance of a general predisposition to neurotic illness, rather than the inheritance of OCD *per se*.

The degree to which general predispositions are inherited is, itself, still subject to considerable debate. Although some studies (Shields, 1962) have provided compelling evidence favouring a strong genetic determinant of neuroticism, other studies suggest a less significant contribution (Langinvaino et al., 1984; Pedersen et al., 1984). Torgersen (1990) concludes his review of the evidence by suggesting that 'neuroticism or anxiousness may be modestly influenced by genetic factors . . . . However, by far the most important source of variance seems to be individual environmental factors' (p. 285).

In spite of the above, and similar conclusions drawn by other commentators (e.g. M.W. Eysenck, 1992), interest in the genetics of OCD remains a key topic of interest. Perhaps this is attributable to the recent suggestion that Gilles de la Tourette's Syndrome (GTS) and OCD are alternative phenotypic expressions of the same underlying genetic trait. Indeed, efforts have been made to locate candidate genes, especially those that modulate both serotonergic and dopaminergic systems (Leckman & Chittenden, 1990).

THE SEROTONERGIC SYSTEM

There are several lines of evidence that suggest the presence of a specific serotonin metabolism abnormality in OCD. First, only potent serotonin reuptake inhibitors appear to have a *specific* anti-obsessional effect (The Clomipramine Collaborative Study Group, 1991; Jenike, Hyman & Baer, 1990; Price et al., 1987). The precise mechanism of action remains unclear, but a decrease in responsiveness to endogenous serotonin seems likely after long-term administration (Insel & Winslow, 1990). Although treatment results are strongly suggestive of a serotonin abnormality, outcome studies can only provide indirect evidence. The traditional arguments are still applicable: although an analgesic might alleviate pain, one cannot conclude that pain is attributable to the absence of analgesic compounds.

Three classes of investigation have sought to demonstrate a specific abnormality in the serotonergic system of untreated OCD patients employing more direct methodologies: studies of blood serotonin, studies of cerebrospinal fluid (CSF) concentrations of 5-hydroxyindoleacetic acid (5-H1AA; the primary serotonin metabolite), and a challenge strategy employing the serotonin agonist m-chlorophenylpiperazine (mCPP).

The first of these methodologies, studies of blood serotonin, have yielded inconsistent results (Yaryura-Tobias & Bhagavan, 1977; Flament et al., 1987). Investigations of CSF 5-H1AA have provided more promising results, in so far as higher concentrations of CSF 5-H1AA have been found in patients suffering from OCD (Insel et al., 1985; Thoren et al., 1980a). Moreover, decrease in obsessional symptoms after treatment with clomipramine was correlated with decreased levels of CSF 5-H1AA, implicating the inhibition of uptake in the anti-obsessional effect (Thoren et al., 1980b). However, it should be noted that CSF 5-H1AA is notoriously difficult to interpret, and conclusions drawn from this work are, at best, tentative (Insel & Winslow, 1990).

Zohar et al. (1987b) have investigated behavioural and endocrine effects after activating the serotonergic system by administering the serotonin agonist (m-chlorophenylpiperazine [mCPP]) to untreated patients with OCD. Agonists are substances that produce a direct measurable response by interacting with receptors. Relative to healthy controls, untreated patients with OCD became significantly more anxious, depressed, and showed greater increases in 'altered self-reality' (e.g. feeling out of touch, mistrustful, having unusual thoughts, feeling unreal or strange). Moreover, following mCPP, but not placebo, untreated patients with OCD experienced a transient but marked exacerbation of OCD symptoms. Five of the group described emergence of new obsessions, or the return of obsessions that had not been present for several months. In a follow-up study, mCPP and placebo were administered to patients before and after treatment with clomipramine (Zohar et al., 1988). Readministration of mCPP after four months' treatment with clomipramine did not increase obsessional symptoms and anxiety to a significant degree. Finally, further evidence suggests that all mCPP changes can be reversed by the serotonin receptor antagonist metergoline (Benkelfat et al., 1989).

The *classical* serotonergic hypothesis, as formulated by Yaryura-Tobias et al. (1977), suggests that OCD is due to a deficiency of serotonin. This conclusion was based on accounts of the clinical improvement observed after administration of clomipramine. The inhibition of reuptake makes more serotonin available to postsynaptic receptors. Consistent with this notion, administration of the serotonin precuror l-tryptophan, can reduce obsessional symptoms (Yaryura-Tobias & Bhagavan, 1977), and augment the anti-obsessional effects of clomipramine (Rasmussen, 1984).

If the classical theory were accurate, then administration of mCPP should reduce, rather than exacerbate, symptoms. This anomaly has prompted a revision of the classical theory. It has now been suggested that it is *increased serotonergic responsiveness*, rather than deficiency, that is associated with OCD. Increased serotonergic responsiveness should result in a worsening of symptoms during initial treatment with SSRIs, as SSRIs cause an increase of serotonin content in the synaptic cleft before down-regulation of the receptors occurs. This prediction is supported by data from patient diaries collected by Zohar and colleagues (unpublished findings cited in Zohar & Zohar-Kadouch, 1991). The mechanisms associated with SSRI mediated improvement with respect to classical and revised serotonin theories are shown in Figure 1.

Although the serotonin theory has been influential, it is unlikely that a single neurotransmitter imbalance can account for the rich phenomenology and symptom profile associated with OCD. Inevitably, many other neurotransmitters will be involved. Jenike, Hyman & Baer

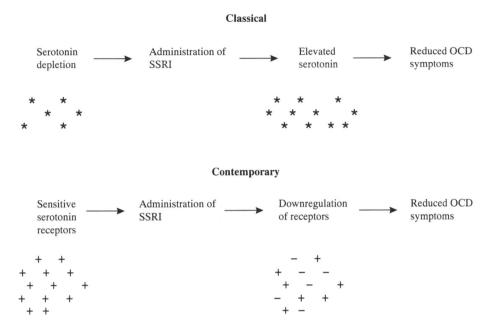

Figure 1 Putative mechanisms subserving the efficacy of the selective serotonin reuptake inhibitors (SSRIs): classical and contemporary accounts

(1990) examined data from several controlled and open trials of the various SSRIs and conducted a meta-analysis to determine effect size. Calculations showed that clomipramine was the most effective, followed by fluoxetine, fluvoxamine, and setraline. It is interesting to note that the order of decreasing effectiveness is inversely related to the medications selectivity for serotonin reuptake inhibition.

BRAIN SCAN INVESTIGATIONS

The strongest evidence for a biological substrate of OCD has been derived from brain-imaging studies (Behar et al., 1984; Luxenberg et al., 1988; Baxter et al., 1988; Swedo et al., 1989; Nordahl et al., 1989; Martinot et al., 1990; Sawle et al., 1991; Machlin et al., 1991; Rubin et al., 1992; McGuire et al., 1994). The technologies employed provide information on brain structure (e.g. X-ray computed tomography, CT; magnetic resonance imaging, MRI) and biochemical functioning (Xenon 133 — measured blood flow, Xe-flow; positron emission tomography, PET). Although some results have been inconclusive or inconsistent, there is a growing consensus that a fronto-striatal abnormality is present in OCD. Readers unfamiliar with neuroanatomy are reminded that the striatum is comprised of three structures: the caudate nucleus, the putamen, and nucleus accumbens.

Out of the range of scanning technologies available, PET has proved the most popular in the study of OCD. It can be used to measure neuroanatomically localised cerebral glucose metabolic rates. Glucose is considered to be a very sensitive indicator of cerebral functioning. Baxter et al. (1987) compared three groups: patients with OCD, normal controls, and unipolar depressives. Absolute glucose metabolic rates for the whole cerebral hemispheres, caudate nuclei, and orbital gyri were significantly elevated in OCD compared with control groups. In addition, metabolic rates in the left orbital gyrus were found to be significantly higher than those found in normal controls. Similar results were also reported by Baxter et al. (1988), in a study comparing OCD subjects and normal controls. The patient group displayed significantly higher glucose metabolic rates for the whole of the cerebral hemispheres, the head of the caudate nucleus, and the orbital gyri.

Swedo et al. (1989b) also compared OCD patients and normal controls, and found increased glucose metabolism in the left orbital and right sensorimotor regions, and bilaterally in the anterior cingulate gyri and lateral prefrontal areas.

Normalised values were significantly increased in right lateral prefrontal and left anterior cingulate regions only. Of greater interest was a correlation between absolute and normalised right orbital glucose metabolic activity and a measure of symptom severity. Finally, patients who failed to respond to clomipramine had significantly higher anterior cingulate and right orbital levels of metabolism. Nordhal et al. (1989) found that normalised regional brain metabolic rates were high in OCD patients in both orbital gyri relative to non-clinical control subjects.

Sawle et al. (1991) conducted an investigation of oxygen metabolism in patients with obsessional slowness; however, their slowness could be attributed to time-consuming rituals, checking behaviour and other compulsions (cf. Veale, 1993). Findings suggested focal hypermetabolism in the orbital frontal, premotor, and mid frontal cortex.

Zohar et al. (1989) conducted a Xe flow study of patients with OCD. The major disadvantage of this method of investigation is that images are of a low resolution, and no information is provided with respect to deep brain structures. Patients were all scanned in three conditions: relaxation, imaginal flooding, and *in vivo* exposure. Cerebral blood flow significantly increased in the imaginal flooding condition compared to the relaxation condition, but only in the temporal cortex. Cerebral blood flow significantly *decreased* in all other cortical regions. The authors suggest that this may reflect the fact that anxiety states are associated with a decrease in higher order processing, while lower subcortical structures become more active.

The study conducted by Zohar et al. (1989) emphasises the importance of state effects. A further investigation of the relationship between state effects and cerebral blood flow was conducted by McGuire et al. (1994). PET technology was employed on 12 separate occasions, where each scan was paired with a stimulus eliciting a different level of symptom intensity. Results showed significant positive correlations between symptom intensity and blood flow in the right inferior frontal gyrus, caudate nucleus, putamen, globus pallidus and thalamus, and the left hippocampus and posterior cingulate gyrus. Negative correlations were evident in the right superior prefrontal cortex, and the tempero-parietal junction, particularly on the right side. The authors conclude that increases in cerebral blood flow in the orbitofrontal cortex, striatum, globus pallidus and thalamus were related to urges to perform rituals, while those in the hippocampus and posterior cingulate cortex corresponded to the anxiety that accompanied them.

Perhaps the most compelling evidence favouring the fronto-striatal hypothesis is derived from studies that show the resolution of regional anomalies after treatment (Baxter et al., 1992; Benkelfat et al., 1990; Hoehn-Saric et al., 1991; Swedo et al., 1992b). The Baxter et al. (1992) study serves as an excellent example, as two treatment modalities were employed: medication (fluoxetine) or behavioural therapy. After treatment, blood flow in the head of the right caudate nucleus was decreased significantly compared with pretreatment values in patients who responded to both drug and behaviour therapy. Non-responders showed no change. Percentage change in OCD symptom ratings correlated significantly with percent of right caudate change with drug therapy, and a trend ($p = 0.09$) was observed with respect to behaviour therapy. When all responders were grouped together, right orbital cortex metabolism was significantly correlated with ipsilateral caudate and thalamus metabolism before treatment, but not after. Moreover, the differences before and after treatment were significant.

In many of the studies cited above, only small numbers of subjects were employed. Data could therefore be expected to have a high degree of variance. Yet most of the scanning studies so far undertaken show remarkably similar results. Notwithstanding this point, it should be noted that there are some inconsistent findings. For example, Martinot et al. (1990) conducted a PET scan investigation of 16 non-depressed OCD patients and 8 normal controls. Results demonstrated global grey matter hypometabolism and normalised prefrontal lateral cortex hypometabolism; the exact reverse of the hypermetabolism observed in other investigations. The authors suggest several reasons for this discrepancy; these include the fact that their patient sample was somewhat older compared to other samples, and the duration of their illness was longer (mean 18 years). However, also included in the Martinot et al. (1990) study was an investigation of treatment effects. Recovered patients were scanned again, and it was found that whole cortex glucose metabolism had increased. One of this group later relapsed and a third scan showed a complementary decrease in glucose metabolism.

The implications of these investigations with respect to a fronto-striatal theory of OCD are given further consideration in Chapters 21 and 22.

CONCLUSION

In sum, there are a wide range of studies suggesting that OCD is determined, at least in part, by biological factors. The evidence for the genetic inheritance of OCD is not compelling, although interest in a common genetic origin for both GTS and OCD may stimulate further research. Abnormalities in the serotonin metabolism have been implicated as a contributory factor in OCD, and the strongest direct evidence for this position has been derived from observing the effects of mCPPP (a serotonin agonist) administration. The strongest evidence for a biological substrate in OCD comes from brain scan investigations, the results of which suggest the presence of hypermetabolism in the frontal lobe and the caudate nucleus of the basal ganglia.

Chapter 7

ASSESSMENT: GENERAL MEASURES

INTRODUCTION

In this chapter, a number of general measures for OCD are described. These provide an index of symptom severity and/or subscale scores which reflect a symptom profile. Most of these measures are widely used and their strengths and weaknesses will be critically evaluated. A complementary chapter (Chapter 8) is devoted to instruments with a specific cognitive bias. The majority of these are relatively new, and insufficient data are available to provide a critical evaluation at this stage; however, given the principal subject matter of this volume their inclusion could be considered a necessity. Although a distinction is made between general measures and specific cognitive measures, it should be noted that most of the general measures are also, to a greater or lesser extent, measures of cognition. Even a relatively behaviour-orientated instrument like the MOCI (Hodgson & Rachman, 1977) contains items such as 'I frequently get nasty thoughts and have difficulty getting rid of them'. Finally, although OCD is associated with a range of emotional experiences, most notably depression and anxiety, the clinical literature and cognitive appraisal theories of OCD suggest that guilt may be of particular significance (Rachman, 1993). There are many well-established measures of depression and anxiety (Beck et al., 1961; Spielberger et al., 1980; Beck & Steer, 1987); however, few measures of guilt are widely known. For this reason, a brief description of selected guilt measures is provided.

Most of the measures described below are 'self-report'; however, some examples of 'observer-rated' instruments are also included. Both methods are, to some extent, limited by the fact that OCD patients do not always readily volunteer a complete account of their symptoms. In addition, observer-rated instruments will inevitably be influenced by the examining clinician's familiarity with OCD and his or her clinical skills.

Self-report and observer-rated assessment instruments are not employed for diagnostic purposes. Diagnosis is usually undertaken after a psychiatric interview has been conducted, and the reader is referred to *Psychiatric Examination* (Institute of Psychiatry and Maudsley Hospital, 1987) for an excellent text. Familiarity with the standard diagnostic systems, such as ICD-10 (WHO, 1992) and DSM-IV (APA, 1994) is usually assumed. A thorough psychiatric examination can be supplemented by provocation tests, for example, requesting patients with contamination fears to touch feared objects or substances. Subsequent discomfort can then be gauged by asking patients to rate emotional disturbance on a 0–8 or 0–10 point scale representing subjective units of distress (Wolpe, 1982). However, not all individuals with an obsessional illness are readily provoked, and in some cases, the mere presence of an examining clinician can ameliorate anxiety completely. This is especially true in individuals whose symptoms are related to inflated responsibility (cf. Chapter 10), in whom diffusion of responsibility is likely to result in reduced discomfort. Behavioural assessment might also extend to consideration of the incidental correlates of obsessional behaviour. This is especially true with respect to washers and cleaners, where the purchase of domestic and personal hygiene products will covary with severity (Salkovskis, 1989b).

As has been suggested, OCD is commonly associated with several other Axis I and Axis II diagnoses. It is beyond the scope of the present section to recommend assessment instruments for all the potential comorbid Axis I problems. However, because of the small number of Axis II measures, a few can be recommended. The first, The Structured Clinical Interview for DSM-III-R Personality Disorders (SCID-II) (Spitzer et al., 1987) is, as the name suggests, a structured clinical interview. The second, The Personality Diagnostic Questionnaire-Revised (PDQ-R) (Hyler & Rieder, 1987), is a self-report measure for screening patients for DSM-III-R personality disorders. Although the latter is not a substitute for a structured interview, it shows high sensitivity and moderate specificity for most Axis II disorders (Hyler et al., 1992).

In the following section, a number of general measures are described. These include the Leyton Obsessional Inventory (LOI) (Cooper, 1970), the Maudsley Obsessive Compulsive Inventory (MOCI) (Hodgson & Rachman, 1977), the Padua Inventory (PI) (Sanavio, 1988), the NIMH Global Obsessive Compulsive Scale (NIMH-GOCS) (Rapoport, Elkins & Mikkelsen, 1980; Insel et al., 1983b), and the Yale Brown Obsessive Compulsive Scale (Y-Bocs) (Goodman et al., 1989b; Goodman et al., 1989c). The NIMH-GOCS and Y-Bocs are observer-rated scale.

Assessment instruments of the kind described in this and the subsequent chapter are commonly employed to assess the content, frequency, and/or severity of symptoms and traits. If such an instrument possesses sound psychometric properties, the effects of either psychological or medical interventions can be more meaningfully quantified. Although such quantification may only bestow modest advantage compared with clinical judgement, any improvements in accuracy of measurement should of course be welcomed.

THE LEYTON OBSESSIONAL INVENTORY

The LOI (Cooper, 1970) is a 69-item self-report measure which is administered in the form of a card sort. It is used to assess a wide range of obsessional symptoms and traits (Table 3) and yields additional scores for resistance and interference. The measure was originally developed using a population of houseproud housewives; however, means and standard deviations (in parentheses) are reported for 17 obsessional patients: symptom $\mu = 3.3$ (7.7), trait $= 11.0$ (3.2), resistance $= 36$ (11.2), and interference $= 36.7$ (18.4).

In spite of well-recognised weaknesses (Goodman & Price, 1992; Yaryura-Tobias & Nerizoglu, 1983) it remains one of the most widely used assessment measures for OCD.

The most problematic feature of the LOI is its lengthy and complex administration. The patient is asked to work through a pile of cards on which are written questions, for example, 'Do you hate dirty things?'. Positive or negative responses are registered after each card has been placed into a 'Yes' or 'No' postbox. The 'Yes' aperture must be placed directly above the 'No' aperture in order to avoid a handedness response bias. A possible maximum of 41 endorsed cards are then rated for resistance and interference; a procedure which involves use of two further

Table 3   Symptoms and traits assessed using the Leyton Obsessional Inventory (Cooper, 1970)

Symptoms	Traits
Thoughts	Hoarding
Checking	Cleanliness
Dirt and contamination	Meanness
Dangerous objects	Irritability and moroseness
Personal cleanliness and tidiness	Rigidity
Household cleanliness and tidiness	Health (concerns)
Order and routine	Regularity
Repetition	Punctuality
Overconscientiousness and lack of satisfaction	
Indecision	

sets of 'rating' cards. Resistance is expressed according to how strongly the patient wishes to stop a particular obsessional activity, while interference is expressed according to what extent that activity impairs everyday functioning. It should be noted that two different sets of question cards are used depending on the gender of the patient. Moreover, the clinician may be required to check the validity of certain answers and modify the score sheet during testing.

Administration difficulties have resulted in several attempts to adapt the LOI as a pen and paper questionnaire. For example Allen & Tune (1975) used 20 of the original LOI items in a revised form in the Lynfield Obsessive-Compulsive Questionnaire. Perhaps the most successful modification of this type is that described by Snowdon (1980). This version consists of 70 questions, the first 40 of which are supplemented by resistance and interference scales. All 70 questions are answered first before the subject provides resistance and interference ratings. Questions are equally applicable to both genders. No significant differences were found between written and postbox forms using 100 medical students as subjects.

In addition to the above, a postbox form of the LOI has been developed for use with children (Berg, 1989). The LOI-CV (child version) has 44 items and thus requires less focused concentration to complete. Content has been modified to increase relevance for younger respondents and items can be found under headings such as 'school work' and 'magic games'. Preliminary work suggests that the psychometric properties of the measure are good (Berg, 1989). Finally, a 20-item written form of the LOI has been developed for use with adolescents. Only interference ratings are taken to supplement symptom endorsement. Again, psychometric properties are promising (Berg, 1989).

Cooper and Kelleher (1973) conducted several principal component analyses on LOI data. Common to all analyses were three components: first, concern with being clean and tidy; second, a feeling of incompleteness; and third, checking and repetition. It is interesting to note that the incompleteness component of the LOI bears a strong resemblance to Janet's (1903) 'sentiment d'incompletude'.

The LOI differentiates between obsessional patients and non-clinical individuals with little overlap (Cooper, 1970). Moreover, test–retest reliability is satisfactory for symptom and trait scores, although data are only reported for a depressed, rather than obsessional group (Cooper, 1970). There is some debate as to whether the LOI is sensitive to the effects of medication. Some studies suggest that the LOI is capable of detecting such changes (Allen & Rack, 1975; Ananth et al., 1979; Prasad, 1984) whereas others suggest the contrary (Insel et al., 1983b; Thoren et al., 1980b). There is also some doubt as to whether the measure is sensitive to change brought about by behaviour therapy (e.g. Rachman, Hodgson & Marks, 1972).

There are a number of problems with the LOI. The first of these, administration, has been addressed through the development of questionnaire versions, particularly the written LOI developed by Snowden (1980). A second problem relates to content. Although a wide range of symptoms and traits are included, the LOI does not include questions that would detect obsessions on aggressive, violent, or blasphemous themes. There is also no reference to compulsive behaviours such as retracing. A third conceptual difficulty relates to the distinction made between symptoms and traits. For example, although an inability to discard possessions is recognised as an obsessional personality characteristic, most contemporary theorists would regard hoarding, an LOI trait, as a symptom of OCD (Frost & Gross, 1993; Rapoport, 1989a). Similarly, the LOI overconscientiousness items might tap individual differences at the trait level rather than the symptom level. Finally, reliability and validity data are incomplete and inconsistent (Goodman & Price, 1992; Yaryura-Tobias & Nerizoglu, 1983).

In spite of the above, the LOI has several advantages. It measures a relatively comprehensive range of symptoms and traits and has gained wide acceptance in the academic community.

THE MAUDSLEY OBSESSIONAL COMPULSIVE INVENTORY

The MOCI (Hodgson & Rachman, 1977), is a 30-item self-rated questionnaire. Only those items able to discriminate obsessional patients from a matched anxiety group were selected for inclusion. Respondents are requested to indicate whether self-referent statements are either True or False. A principal component analysis produced four orthoganal factors which accounted for 43% of the total variance: checking, cleaning, slowness, and doubting. A fifth factor only captured two rumination items and was subsequently ignored. The MOCI yields a total score, and/or four subscale scores. Hodgson & Rachman (1977) report means and standard deviations for one hundred heterogeneous obsessional patients: total $\mu = 18.86$ (4.92), checking $\doteq 6.10$ (2.21), cleaning $= 5.55$ (3.04), slowness $= 3.63$ (1.93), and doubting $= 5.39$ (1.6). Alpha coefficients of the subscales are within the 0.7–0.8 range and good test–retest reliability is reported for 50 non-clinical adults (Kendall's Tau of 0.8). Recently, non-clinical norms for the MOCI were reported by Dent & Salkovskis (1986).

The items included in the MOCI do not reflect the full range of obsessional symptoms. Although the most common obsessional phenomena, excessive doubt, washing and checking compulsions, are well represented, many other phenomena on the OCD spectrum are not. A further problem with the MOCI is the absence of a severity rating. A patient disabled by an idiosyncratic monosymptomatic obsession can easily score in the 'normal' range. In addition, some patients find responding to the double negative items difficult, for example, answering True or False to 'Neither of my parents was very strict during my childhood'. Results might be contaminated by subject error with these items. Finally, the MOCI cannot be used on children with OCD and there is no modified version.

Although the MOCI is described as a measure of obsessional symptoms (or complaints), it is possible that the doubting subscale is in fact measuring a personality trait. Hodgson & Rachman (1977) marshal arguments against this suggestion, though perhaps unnecessarily. Doubting is a relatively ubiquitous obsessional trait (cf. Akhtar et al., 1975). Unlike those traits included on the LOI, there is more consensus regarding the central position of doubt in obsessional illness (Janet, 1903; Freud, 1909; Lewis, 1936; Reed, 1985; Rapoport, 1989a). If the MOCI measures a key trait, in addition to key symptoms, this does not compromise the instrument's utility.

The MOCI is an extremely convenient measure on account of its brevity. It has also gained wide acceptance in the academic community and has been employed in numerous studies (Zielinski et al., 1991; Tallis & de Silva, 1992; McNally & Kohlbeck, 1993; Persons & Foa, 1984; Sher, Frost & Otto, 1983). The MOCI shows some sensitivity to drug effects (Goodman et al., 1989a; Perse et al., 1987) and appears to be sensitive to change after behavioural therapy (Rachman & Hodgson, 1980). There is some evidence to suggest that the MOCI is more sensitive than the LOI when used on adolescents (Clark & Bolton, 1985).

THE PADUA INVENTORY

The PI (Sanavio, 1988) is a 60-item questionnaire; each is rated on a 0–4 point scale for degree of disturbance. The psychometric properties of the PI were determined on a large normal population. Inventory consistency (0.9–0.94) and test–retest reliabilities (0.78–0.83) are good. Means and standard deviations are reported for 35 male $\mu = 83.6$ (34.8), and 40 female $\mu = 98.6$ (32.3) OCD patients. Non-clinical norms are also reported, broken down according to age (between 16 and 70) and gender. The measure can discriminate between obsessional patients and neurotic controls.

Factor analysis produced a four-factor structure: impaired control over mental activities, becoming contaminated, checking behaviours, and urges and worries of losing control over motor behaviours. These results have been replicated elsewhere (Sternberger & Burns, 1990b; van Oppen, 1992). PI scores are correlated with other OCD measures, for example the LOI symptom score (0.71), the LOI trait score (0.66), and the MOCI (0.70).

A relatively wide range of symptoms are represented, but the content of the PI is by no means comprehensive. The inclusion of scaled disturbance ratings means that the PI is more likely than the MOCI to register high scores in individuals with only a few, but disabling, symptoms. However, even this increased sensitivity would not discriminate many monosymptomatics with severe OCD from normal controls. It should also be noted that there are no modifications suitable for children.

Sanavio chooses to call Factor I items 'impaired control over mental activities'. This is interesting, in that it reflects a shift of emphasis in the literature from content to process variables (cf. Wegner, 1989; Wells & Mathews, 1994). Although Sanavio maintains that items describing emotional and personality traits were omitted during the development of the PI, many Factor I items might legitimately be said to reflect personality characteristics. In addition to the ubiquitous 'doubt', indecisiveness (cf. Reed, 1985) and 'incompleteness' (cf. Janet, 1903) are also referred to. Again, a broader view of obsessional illness might embrace certain traits, and their presence in a measure of this kind need not necessarily compromise the measure's integrity. Although the PI takes a little longer to complete than the MOCI, the absence of 'double negatives' makes it an attractive alternative. Moreover, completion does not demand any unusual procedural manoeuvres, such as returning to rate previously endorsed items for resistance and interference as in the written form of the LOI (Snowden, 1980).

A problem with the PI is that its psychometric properties were determined employing a non-clinical population. In order to address this shortcoming, van Oppen, Hoekstra & Emmelkamp (in press) examined the factorial structure of the PI in a study which recruited large clinical samples (patients with OCD, patients with other anxiety disorders) and a non-clinical sample.

Simultaneous components analysis revealed a five-factor solution capturing 41 items. These factors are (I) impulses, (II) washing,

(III) checking, (IV) rumination, and (V) precision. The internal consistency (Cronbach's alpha) for the factors in the three samples used in the study was satisfactory to excellent. All of the subscales, with the exception of 'impulses', discriminated panic disorder patients, social phobics, and normal individuals, from patients with OCD. Although the impulse subscale discriminated patients with OCD from normal individuals, it did not discriminate OCD from other anxiety disorders. The 41-item Padua Inventory Revised (PI-R) is sensitive to treatment effects (van Oppen, 1994) with respect to several treatment modalities (i.e. pharmacotherapy, behaviour therapy, cognitive therapy or combination therapies). It is too early to assess whether the PI will gain general academic acceptance; however, initial interest indicates that a favourable outcome is likely.

THE NIMH-GLOBAL OBSESSIVE COMPULSIVE SCALE

The NIMH-GOCS is perhaps the most frequently used of several rating instruments developed and endorsed by the NIMH (Insel et al., 1983b; Rapoport, Elkins & Mikkelsen, 1980). It is a single item clinician rated measure with 15 gradations ranging from 1 (minimal) to 15 (very severe). Unfortunately, there is little information available on the instrument's psychometric properties. However, the HIMH-GOCS does appear to be sensitive to the effects of medication (Goodman & Price, 1992).

Clearly, the NIMH-Global OCD scale is a very different kind of measure to those described above. It does not include any reference to content and the accuracy of the scale will be largely determined by the experience and skills of the examining clinician. In essence, it provides a modest set of guidelines which facilitate the attachment of a numerical value to a clinical judgement.

YALE BROWN OBSESSIVE COMPULSIVE SCALE

The Y-Bocs (Goodman et al., 1989b; Goodman et al., 1998c) was developed to provide a measure of severity that could be calculated independent of the type and number of obsessional symptoms. The core section of the Y-Bocs is a clinician rated 10-item scale (Table 4). Severity ratings for each item are indicated on 0-4 point scales representing 'no symptoms' through to 'extreme symptoms'.

In addition to a grand total, subtotals can be calculated for obsessions (sum of items 1-5) or compulsions, (6-10). Goodman & Price (1992, p. 864) point out that 'resistance' on the Y-Bocs refers to 'how much

Table 4   The severity dimensions of the Y-Bocs; corresponding with items 1–10

1.	Time occupied by obsessive thoughts
2.	Interference due to obsessive thoughts
3.	Distress associated with obsessive thoughts
4.	Resistance against obsessions
5.	Degree of control over obsessive thoughts
6.	Time spent performing compulsive behaviours
7.	Interference due to compulsive behaviours
8.	Distress associated with compulsive behaviours
9.	Resistance against compulsions
10.	Degree of control over compulsive behaviours

effort the patient exercises in opposing obsessions and compulsions by means other than avoidance or performance of compulsions'. Therefore, greater resistance is considered an indicator of health and is given a lower score. This is quite different to the LOI and NIMH Global OC, where resistance is associated with a distressing 'inner struggle' and its presence will elevate the total. Several investigational items (Table 5) are also included on the Y-Bocs. These are for the clinician's benefit alone and are not added to the severity total. It should be noted that items 17 and 18 were adapted from the Clinical Global Impressions (CGI) Scale (Guy, 1976), and subsequently, a slightly different rating system is employed (i.e. 7 point). Goodman et al. (1989b) report Y-Bocs means and standard deviations for three groups of OCD patients just prior to participation in separate drug trials. On assessment, all patients had been unmedicated for three weeks, although a small number were permitted low doses of benzodiazepines for anxiety and insomnia. A total of 81 participants were assessed. The mean for combined groups was 25.1 (6).

Administration is performed in the following way: the patient is provided with a definition of obsessions and compulsions and illustrative examples are given. Symptoms are then identified using the Y-Bocs

Table 5   Y-Bocs investigational items (11–19)

11.	Insight and obsessions and compulsions
12.	Avoidance
13.	Degree of indecisiveness
14.	Overvalued sense of responsibility
15.	Pervasive slowness/disturbance of inertia
16.	Pathological doubting
17.	Global severity
18.	Global improvement
19.	Reliability

Table 6 Y-Bocs content areas

Aggressive obsessions
Contamination obsessions
Sexual obsessions
Hoarding/collecting obsessions
Religious obsessions
Obsessions with need for symmetry, exactness, or order
Miscellaneous obsessions
Somatic obsessions/compulsions
Cleaning/washing compulsions
Counting compulsions
Checking compulsions
Repeating rituals
Ordering/arranging compulsions
Hoarding/collecting compulsions
Miscellaneous compulsions

symptom checklist, which can be divided into 15 content areas (Table 6). In addition to all the well-recognised features of OCD, a miscellaneous category is included to capture unusual or idiosyncratic presentations. All current symptoms are recorded on the Y-Bocs Target Symptom List. Those symptoms that are to be the primary targets for ratings are indicated. If a patient has several target symptoms of different severity, then the final score is based on their combined effect. If a patient has a concurrent disorder on the OCD type spectrum (e.g. trichotillomania), then the 10 core items can be readministered with this problem in mind.

The inter-rater reliability ($r = 0.98$) and internal consistency ($\alpha = 0.89$) of the Y-Bocs are excellent (Goodman et al., 1989b). The convergent validity of the Y-Bocs is less satisfactory (Goodman et al., 1989c). The Y-Bocs was found to correlate significantly with the CGI-OCS (Guy, 1976) and the NIMH GOCS, but not with the MOCI. Moreover, the Y-Bocs does not discriminate severity of OCD from severity of depression or anxiety in OCD patients with significant secondary depression (Goodman et al., 1989b). However, the Y-Bocs is sensitive to changes brought about by medication (Goodman et al., 1989a; De Veaugh-Geiss, Landau & Katz, 1989) and both cognitive and behavioural interventions (van Oppen, 1994).

A weakness of several of the measures cited earlier is that individuals debilitated by monosymptomatic obsessions could potentially score in the normal range. The Y-Bocs would certainly yield a score that reflected the severity of their illness. Moreover, the clinician is provided with a comprehensive symptom check list as a guard against significant omissions. There is also a children's version of the Y-Bocs (Cy-Bocs) (Goodman et al., 1986), which is virtually the same as the adult version with the exception of the use of simpler language. For example, obsessions are referred to as 'thoughts' and compulsions as 'habits'. The symptom check list has also been modified slightly to increase its relevance to paediatric populations. Preliminary data on the psychometric properties of the Cy-Bocs suggest that its reliability and validity are good. Moreover, results from a drug trial suggest that the Cy-Bocs is sensitive to the therapeutic effects of clomipramine (Goodman & Price, 1990).

Like the LOI, the Y-Bocs involves a lengthy administration. However, Goodman and Price (1990) suggest that a first administration should take no more than 45 minutes. Clearly, the length of administration will also be related to the number of symptoms reported by the patient. Likewise, the accuracy of the measure will be strongly influenced by the experience of the administering clinician. Not all would agree that increases in resistance are an indication of improvement, and the discriminant validity of the measure could be improved.

Chapter 8

ASSESSMENT: SPECIFIC COGNITIVE MEASURES

MEASURES OF COGNITION AND GUILT

In this chapter, a number of specific cognitive measures are described. These comprise: the Intrusive Thoughts Questionnaire (ITQ) (Edwards & Dickerson, 1987), the Cognitive Intrusions Questionnaire (CIQ) (Freeston et al., 1991), the Obsessive Thoughts Checklist (OTC) (Bouvard et al., 1989), the Inventory of Beliefs Related to Obsessions (IBRO) (Freeston et al., 1993), and the Lucky Belief Questionnaire (LBQ) (Frost et al., 1993). In addition to the above, several measures of guilt are described: the Mosher Guilt Inventory (Mosher, 1966), the Criterion Items (Moulton et al., 1966), the Perceived Guilt Index (Otterbacher & Munz, 1973), and the Guilt Inventory (Kugler et al., 1988; Kugler & Jones, 1992).

THE INTRUSIVE THOUGHTS QUESTIONNAIRE

Edwards & Dickerson (1987) report the development of an Intrusive Thoughts Questionnaire. The ITQ was devised as a research instrument and is not exclusively relevant to OCD in clinical settings. It contains 21 items that are linked with a range of response formats; for example, open question, multiple choice, and Likert-type scale. After an introductory section, the respondent is requested to write his or her most unpleasant and frequently occurring intrusive thought. Thereafter, all questions relate to that thought. In addition to many other parameters, information is requested with respect to frequency of occurrence, duration, coping strategies, emotional impact, and ability to exercise cognitive control. The ITQ is rather impractical as a self-report questionnaire and cannot be considered a 'measure' in the usual sense; rather, it represents a framework within which to undertake a comprehensive and detailed analysis of the phenomenology of intrusive cognition. As such, it might best be deployed in clinical settings as a structured interview schedule.

THE COGNITIVE INTRUSIONS QUESTIONNAIRE

The CIQ (Freeston et al., 1991) was developed from the Distressing Thoughts Questionnaire (Clark & de Silva, 1985) and the ITQ (Edwards & Dickerson, 1987). Like the ITQ, it was devised primarily as a research instrument; however, the information it systematically elicits is clearly relevant with respect to the clinical presentation of OCD. Respondents are requested to report whether or not they have experienced thoughts, images, or impulses, over the last month, related to six content areas: health problems, an embarrassing personal experience, an unacceptable sexual experience, verbal aggression, a terminal illness affecting a significant other, and an accident involving a significant other. In addition, respondents are asked to report any anxiogenic idiosyncratic thoughts, images or impulses. The most frequent exemplar is then rated on a number of nine-point Likert Scales. The range of phenomena and contructs associated with intrusive cognition and included on the CIQ are shown in Table 7.

Psychometric data were derived after the questionnaire was administered to a large non-clinical population. Internal reliability coefficients are reported for scales consisting of the dimensions measured for each thought. These are satisfactory given the multi-dimensional nature of the contructs measured. The CIQ is considerably more practical than the ITQ as a self-report measure. Moreover, many of the critical parameters

Table 7   Constructs and phenomena relevant to intrusive cognition as measured by the CIQ

Frequency
Associated sadness
Associated worry
Difficulty experienced attempting to remove the intrusion
Associated guilt
Belief strength
Self-disapproval
Responsibility
Awareness of triggers
Extent of avoidance of triggers
Response to intrusions   (e.g. reassurance seeking)
Resistance
Efficacy of control strategies
Extent of relief
Associated shame
Associated self-blame   (if the thought 'really happened')
Severity of consequences   (if the thought 'really happened')
Likelihood of actual occurrence
Insight
Formal qualities   (e.g. image, idea, etc.)

---

measured by ITQ items are retained in the CIQ. Unfortunately, there are no clinical norms currently available. The utility of the CIQ is therefore restricted to the provision of a systematic investigation of key cognitive variables. It should be noted however, that both normative data for clinical populations and change sensitivity data with respect to therapy outcome are currently being collected.

THE INVENTORY OF BELIEFS RELATED TO OBSESSIONS

The IBRO is a 20-item measure closely associated with cognitive appraisal theories of OCD (see Chapter 9). Each item is rated on a 1–6 point scale ranging from 'I believe strongly that this statement is false' to 'I believe strongly that this statement is true'. It was originally developed employing a non-clinical sample (Freeston et al., 1993).

An initial item pool was derived from beliefs considered to be of central importance in appraisal theories (McFall & Wollershein, 1979; Salkovskis, 1985). A two-step item selection procedure employed criteria from existing work on intrusive thoughts (Freeston et al., 1991). Items that distinguished an escape/avoidance group from a minimal attention group were retained. The measure has good internal consistency (Cronbach's alpha) 0.76 and item-total correlations varied from 0.13 to 0.52. With respect to reliability, the value of coefficient alpha was 0.82 and stability (test–retest) was 0.70.

Principal component analysis revealed three factors: the first, comprising 11 items, is concerned with responsibility, guilt, blame, punishment, and loss. The second, comprising five items, is concerned with the overestimation of threat. Finally, the third factor, comprising four items, is concerned with intolerance of uncertainty. The reported mean for a small sample of OCD patients was $\mu = 75.59$ (10.82) and $\mu = 59.20$ (10.27) for non-clinical controls. This represents a significant difference. The IBRO discriminated subjects in the index sample who employed escape/avoidance strategies from those who employed minimal attention. The IBRO also distinguished the same two groups in a validation sample where the escape/avoidance group also reported more troubling intrusive thoughts and depressive and obsessive compulsive symptoms. The IBRO also distinguished clinical OCD patients from matched normal controls.

THE OBSESSIVE THOUGHTS CHECKLIST

The OTC is a measure of obsessional thinking style (Bouvard et al., 1990). It consists of 28 items and a final open item. Each item is rated on a

0 ('this thought does not trouble me at all') to 4 ('this thought troubles me continuously') point scale. Good test–retest reliability ($\rho = 0.80$) is reported for non-clinical controls. Internal consistency for the first 28 items of the questionnaire is reported for a mixed clinical and non-clinical sample ($\alpha = 0.94$). The OTC has two principal factors. The first reflects perfectionism, while the second reflects a pathological sense of responsibility. Convergent validity with the compulsive activity checklist (Steketee & Freund, 1993) and the Y-Bocs is satisfactory.

THE LUCKY BELIEFS QUESTIONNAIRE

The LBQ (Frost et al., 1993) is a 30-item instrument generated from the superstition questionnaire used by Leonard et al. (1990) and items drawn from The Encyclopedia of Superstitions (Radford & Radford, 1969). Subjects are asked to indicate their belief strength for each item on scales ranging from 1 ('do not believe') to 5 ('strongly believe'). It is complemented by the Lucky Behaviours Questionnaire (LBehQ). This also contains 30 items which 'parallel' the LBQ items and represent the actual performance of behaviours in response to superstitious beliefs. Initial development was undertaken on a non-clinical population.

The LBQ and LBehQ have good reliability (i.e. 0.95 and 0.91 respectively). Obviously the two measures are highly correlated ($r = 0.86$). Both the LBQ and the LBehQ are significantly correlated with the total score on the MOCI and the checking subscale. They are also significantly correlated with the Checking subscale of the Compulsive Activity Checklist-Revised (Steketee & Freund, 1993) and the Everyday Checking Behaviour Scale (Sher et al., 1983). Finally, the LBQ and the LBehQ were correlated with OTQ total scores, and the perfectionism and pathological responsibility subscales.

GUILT QUESTIONNAIRES

The Mosher Guilt Inventory (Mosher, 1966) assesses a cognitive predisposition to experience guilt. It contains 114 items (Mosher, 1988) arranged in pairs of endings to the same sentence stem with a seven-point Likert response format. It contains three subscales: Sex Guilt (50 items), Hostility Guilt (42 items), and Guilty Conscience (22 items). There have been numerous studies that support the construct validity of the inventory in relation to Mosher's operational definition (Mosher, 1979).

Moulton et al. (1966) devised three criterion items to assess the recency, frequency, and ease with which guilt is provoked. The items are rated using a five-point scale. Some validity data for these items has been reported by Moulton et al. (1966).

The Perceived Guilt Index (Otterbacher & Munz, 1973), was developed to measure guilt as an affective state. The measure consists of 11 adjectives that are weighted along a guilt continuum. The same items can be used to measure state or trait guilt depending on the form of the instructions provided. Good construct validity has been found, although there is some doubt as to whether the adjectives really do correspond to increasing levels of guilt.

The most recent and well-developed measure of guilt is the guilt inventory (Kugler et al., 1988; Kugler & Jones, 1992). It has 45 items that are rated on five-point scale ranging from 1 (very untrue of me or strongly disagree) to 5 (very true of me or strongly agree). Items were generated from previous research and theorising about the experience of guilt (cf. Ausubel, 1955; Lewis, 1984; Kohlberg, 1980) in order to assess three content domains: trait guilt, defined as a continuing sense of guilt beyond guilt circumstances; state guilt, defined as present guilty feelings based on current or recent transgressions; and moral standards, defined as subscription to a code of moral principles without reference either to specific behaviours or overly specific beliefs (Kugler & Jones, 1992). Although a theoretical distinction is made between state and trait guilt, Kugler & Jones (1992) conducted several analyses suggesting that a distinction could not be made between state and trait guilt. The guilt inventory scales meet acceptable standards of internal consistency (Cronbach's alpha ranging from 0.81 to 0.89), and test–retest reliabilities (for the trait and moral standards subscales) show substantial temporal stability. Finally, the Guilt Inventory shows concurrent validity when compared with other measures of guilt and related constructs.

CONCLUSION

In sum, assessment should involve a psychiatric interview and the use of an established diagnostic system. The symptom profile and the severity of the illness can be determined using a range of self-report and observer-rated measures. Those measures discussed in the previous and the present chapter have a number of strengths and weaknesses, and choice of measure will ultimately be determined by factors such as the purpose of the assessment, the time available in which to assess, patient compliance, and the personal preferences of the examining clinician.

COGNITIVE EVENTS, STRUCTURES, AND PROCESSES

Chapter 9

APPRAISALS, BELIEFS, AND DEFENCES

OBSESSIONAL IDEATION: CONTENT AND MEANING

There have been several attempts to describe the phenomenology of OCD and associated processes within the context of a well-developed theoretical formulation. They have in common an interest in the content of obsessional ideation and its meaning to the individual. The earliest of these can be attributed to Freud, the elements of which are described in his seminal '*Notes upon a case of obsessional neurosis (the rat man)*' of 1909. The development of appraisal theories of emotion (Lazarus, 1966) and the success of cognitive therapies (Ellis, 1962; Beck, 1976; cf. Emmelkamp & Beens, 1991; van Oppen et al., in press), have influenced the development of cognitive and cognitive-behavioural formulations (McFall & Wollersheim, 1979; Salkovskis, 1985; Warren & Zgourides, 1991); however, it should be noted that McFall & Wollersheim (1979) also make explicit use of psychodynamic concepts. Other theorists have also attempted a more comprehensive integration of psychodynamic and cognitive behavioural approaches (cf. Guidano & Liotti, 1983), but this has been achieved at the expense of precision.

PSYCHODYNAMIC CONCEPTS

Freud speculated on the nature of OCD throughout his career. During this time, his theoretical ideas were frequently modified, a process of refinement that continued within the context of the psychoanalytic tradition. Given the many permutations of psychoanalytic theory, a comprehensive account of the work of Freud and his disciples is beyond the scope of this chapter. Instead, selected observations pertinent to phenomenology and experience of OCD are described. Although some reference will be made to mechanisms subserving the phenomenology of OCD, little reference will be made to the broader theories in which they are conventionally embedded. This is for the simple reason that there is little, if any, evidence to support a theory of OCD in which infant sexuality and regression to a pre-oedipal stage of development have a pivotal role. To explore these concepts in greater detail would require a more thorough discussion of the foundations of psychoanalytic theory. Such an endeavour is of questionable value, given the weaknesses of psychoanalytic theory *per se* (Eysenck, 1985), and the disappointing outcome associated with the psychoanalytic treatment of OCD (Cawley, 1974). Notwithstanding these criticisms, it should be noted that many of Freud's clinical observations are as valid today as they were at the turn of the century. From the very outset, Freud's writings were greatly concerned with what have come to be known as cognitive events, processes, and appraisals. Moreover, several of the symptoms of OCD considered important by Freud are now relatively high on the contemporary research agenda (e.g. fear of causing harm to others and intrusive thoughts).

One of the key features of psychoanalytic theory is 'defence'. The defensive reaction, or process, occurs in response to a forbidden wish or impulse. In the context of OCD, this is usually of an aggressive or hostile nature. Defence mechanisms have a specific function: to keep *unacceptable* cognition out of awareness. The purpose of this is to protect the individual from painful emotions, principally anxiety and guilt. However, because defence mechanisms are imperfect, the affect associated with unacceptable thought content may still be experienced. When this happens, further defensive mechanisms may come into operation. It has been suggested that the principal defence mechanism is repression, and it is only in response to its failure that other defence mechanisms are required.

Several secondary defences have been implicated in OCD; however, 'undoing' is perhaps the one which is most closely associated with the central feature of 'neutralising'. Indeed, the two concepts are virtually synonymous. As the word suggests, undoing refers to an act that is undertaken in order to prevent, or undo, the feared consequence of an obsessional thought or impulse. For example, an individual who experiences the obsessional thought 'My father will die' when turning off a light, will then feel compelled to switch the light back on as a reparative gesture. Such superstitious behaviour is no doubt reinforced by the apparent efficacy of such measures. Given that it is unlikely that the untoward events anticipated by individuals with obsessional illness will actually happen, reparative measures are proved to be effective on a daily basis, confirming and strengthening underlying superstitious beliefs. Needless to say, discomfirmatory evidence is rarely sought.

Although the above provides a parsimonious explanation of the maintenance of superstitious or magical thinking, it does not explain why such superstitious thinking should arise in the first place. Psychoanalytic theory attempts to account for this by suggesting that the psychic apparatus has regressed to an earlier stage of development, characterised by feelings of omnipotence. For Freud (1909), the 'overestimation' of 'personal power' is 'a relic of the old megalomania of infancy' (p. 113). The connection between magical thinking and infant cognition is strengthened by the reflections of Freud's most famous obsessional case, the rat man, who suggested that his obsessional illness began in early childhood. At this time, he felt that the occurrence of unacceptable thoughts (e.g. naked girls) would cause his father's death, and that he 'must do all sorts of things to prevent it' (p. 43). As suggested above, for Freud, superstitious thinking in the adult is caused by a regression to an earlier stage of development where perhaps, such thinking is more commonplace; however, where early onset OCD persists into adulthood, magical thinking might be more parsimoniously explained by invoking the more contemporary concept of a developmental delay. Irrespective of preferred discourse, the overestimation of personal influence causes the individual to believe that by merely thinking something, it will actually happen. If a thought is associated with unacceptable consequences, the same inflated personal influence can be employed to 'undo' those consequences.

A further defence mechanism worthy of brief consideration in the context of OCD is that of reaction formation. Here, overt behaviour patterns and attitudes are formed in exact opposition to underlying impulses. Therefore, the hostile intentions considered fundamental to obsessional illness are 'contained' by the adoption of an excessively non-violent persona.

As suggested in the introduction to this section, the foundations of psychoanalytic theory are largely untenable; however, it will become apparent in due course that several of Freud's concepts and observations are acquiring a contemporary resonance. Intrusive thoughts, fear of harming others, guilt avoidance, magical thinking, inflated personal influence, and the repression of unacceptable thought content, are all, in some shape or form, the subject of renewed interest.

CONTEMPORARY APPRAISAL THEORIES

Although Freud's concepts and observations implicitly acknowledge the role of cognition and cognitive processes in OCD, the explicit recognition of these factors, framed in contemporary language, did not occur until the publication of McFall & Wollersheim's (1979) *cognitive-behavioural* formulation of obsessive compulsive neurosis. It is perhaps fitting that the cognitive behavioural formulation proposed also draws upon psychoanalytic theory, suggesting continued interest in phenomenology. McFall & Wollersheim (1979) develop their model within the framework of appraisal theory (Lazarus, 1964, 1966), which suggests that the experience of threat is mediated by cognitive processes. These processes consist of a 'primary' and 'secondary' appraisal. The former is an estimate of personal danger, while the latter is an evaluation of coping resources. Within the context of OCD, primary appraisals are distorted by abnormal risk assessments (Carr, 1974), leading to the experience of anxiety. As suggested earlier, this formulation is applicable to all the anxiety disorders. McFall & Wollersheim's original contribution was an attempt to isolate the dysfunctional assumptions or beliefs (Beck et al., 1979) that serve to potentiate abnormal risk assessment specific to OCD.

As in psychoanalytic accounts, particular emphasis is given to the unacceptability of certain types of thought, and an inflated sense of personal influence. McFall & Wollersheim suggest (p. 335) that the following beliefs underlie these features: 'Certain thoughts and feelings are unacceptable, having them could lead to catastrophe (e.g. anger will result in homicide), and one should be punished for having them', and 'One is powerful enough to initiate or prevent the occurrence of disastrous outcomes by magical rituals or obsessive ruminating'. These fundamental assumptions are more complex than those found in disorders such as depression; however, it may be that depression is a more primitive emotional state, supported by more primitive cognitive structures. In addition to the above, McFall & Wollersheim emphasise the importance of beliefs about maintaining high standards in order to avoid criticism or punishment (cf. Rachman, 1976a).

Once a primary appraisal of threat has been made, a deficient secondary appraisal results in an underestimate of coping resources. Subsequently, the individual will experience a feeling of uncertainty, loss of control, and increased levels of anxiety. McFall & Wollerheim suggest that several unreasonable beliefs influence the secondary appraisal, and the preferred coping strategies of obsessional individuals. Most significantly, these include 'It is easier and more effective to carry out a magical ritual or to obsess than it is to confront one's feelings/thoughts directly' and 'Feelings of uncertainty and loss of control are intolerable, should make one afraid, and something must be done about them'. Again, the psychoanalytic concept of extended personal influence is highly pertinent. McFall & Wollersheim suggest that the obsessional patient 'assumes an omnipotent position of power and control whereby he holds himself *responsible* for preventing the occurrence of potential disasters' (p. 337). The concept of responsibility will be given more detailed consideration in due course.

In comparing their cognitive-behavioural formulation with that of psychodynamic formulations, McFall & Wollersheim point out that both accounts recognise the central role of anxiety generated by unacceptable thoughts. They go on to suggest that the individual will attempt to block these thoughts from awareness. In psychodynamic theory, suppression, as opposed to repression, is the exercise of largely conscious effort to protect the ego from the uncomfortable affect associated with unacceptable thoughts. McFall & Wollerheim do not consider the implications of this process; however, some theorists have suggested that it may be a particularly significant factor in the etiology and maintenance of obsessional thinking.

Wegner (1989) summarises a series of studies demonstrating that attempts to suppress cognitive content can result in what is described as a 'rebound effect', that is, the increased return of previously suppressed content at a later point in time. He suggests that cycles of suppression and rebound (or expression) may combine in the manner of a positive feedback system, producing the frequent intrusions and compromised cognitive control characteristic of OCD: 'The release of suppression leads to a rebound of expression, and this then requires a greater level of suppression to eliminate. The greater suppression, in turn, may yield a still greater rebound ... to produce a thought that is alarmingly frequent and insistent ...' (p. 170). Although laboratory investigations of the paradoxical effects of thought suppression have yielded mixed results (Lavy & van den Hout, 1990; Merkclbach et al., 1991; Clark, Ball & Pape, 1991; Clark, Winton & Thynn, 1993: Salkovskis & Campbell, 1994), the notion that attempts to censor the contents of awareness may have adverse consequences is relatively sound. In attempting to stop thinking about certain events or concepts, it is logically necessary to represent them in awareness first.

A further phenomenological feature of OCD that deserves comment is the frequent report of worries about loss of, or at least compromised, cognitive control. These worries largely arise from the fundamental belief that the contents of awareness should be regulated by an act of will, and further, any small reduction in cognitive control may be the first phase of a total disintegration of personality. Against this background, the affected individual fears that unacceptable urges or impulses will be acted upon, incurring embarrassment, or at worse, causing harm to others. It is widely recognised that most cognitive events occur spontaneously, and not in response to an act of volition (cf. Rachman, 1981). For the individual who firmly believes that the contents of awareness should be regulated by an act of will, the 'stream of consciousness' that characterises everyday human experience can prompt continuous anxiety. Moreover, affected individuals may be constantly monitoring the contents of awareness and/or constantly engaging in counter-productive control strategies such as thought suppression. It is highly likely that certain beliefs will promote the exercise of inappropriate control strategies, interrupting 'thinking', to the extent that cognitive efficiency is actually impaired. Underlying fears are subsequently confirmed, encouraging the further exercise of inappropriate control strategies (see Case 1.3).

A second, and considerably more refined cognitive-behavioural account of OCD has been proposed by Salkovskis (1985). Although Salkovskis rejects many of the psychodynamic concepts espoused by McFall & Wollersheim, there are perhaps more similarities between the Salkovskis and McFall & Wollersheim models than there are differences. For example, both models recognise the importance of appraisals which are influenced by underlying dysfunctional assumptions. There are several accounts of Salkovskis' formulation in the literature (Salkovskis, 1985; Salkovskis & Warwick, 1988; Salkovskis; 1989a); however, emphasis is given here to later work.

Salkovskis' (1989b, p. 678) specific formulation is as follows: 'Clinical obsessions are intrusive cognitions, the occurrence and content of which patients interpret as an indication that they might be responsible for harm to themselves or others unless they take action to prevent it'. Salkovskis observes that obsessional thoughts are a universal phenomenon (Rachman & de Silva, 1978; Salkovskis and Harrison, 1984). Therefore, it is not their presence that determines obsessional illness, but rather, the individual's subsequent response or appraisal. The presence of underlying dysfunctional assumptions is an important determinant of whether discomfort follows the intrusive thinking.

Salkovskis suggests that intrusive thoughts are more likely to cause discomfort in a depressed individual, due to the increased accessibility of specific types of negative automatic thoughts (Beck et al., 1979). In instances where an intrusion is appraised as indicating that an individual has become responsible for harm to themselves or others, the thought becomes a source of discomfort and a signal for preventative or reparative action. The reduction in discomfort following neutralising behaviour can be attributed to a perceived reduction of responsibility. The recurrence of the obsessional cognition becomes more likely for several reasons; however, attempts to suppress or avoid the thought are given particular consideration in later studies (Salkovskis & Campbell, 1994).

Like McFall & Wollersheim, Salkovskis suggests that the significance of intrusive thoughts will be determined largely by underlying beliefs. Some of these beliefs are common to individuals suffering from OCD; however, others are more specific to the individual. Examples of under- lying dysfunctional assumptions or beliefs are: 'Having a thought about an action is like performing the action', 'Failing to prevent (or failing to try to prevent) harm to self or others is the same as having caused the harm in the first place', 'Responsibility is not attenuated by other factors (e.g. low probability of occurrence)', 'Not neutralising when an intrusion has occurred is similar or equivalent to seeking or wanting the harm involved in that intrusion to happen', 'One should (and can) exercise control over one's thoughts'.

The traditional behavioural model of OCD suggests that neutralising behaviour reduces discomfort because of rewarding non-punishment (cf. Gray, 1975). This form of reinforcement serves to increase the likelihood of further neutralising behaviour. Salkovskis suggests that the reinforcing effects of neutralising behaviour are mediated by cognitive factors, for example, 'I acted on my belief and felt better, therefore the belief must have some basis in truth', or 'The disaster I attempted to forestall has not come about, which may mean that my neutralisation was a reason- able and effective thing to do'. Moreover, Salkovskis points out that, at least in the early stages of an obsessional illness, the effort required to neutralise is slight when compared to the perceived negative conse- quences of failing to neutralise.

Recently, Salkovskis (in press) has elaborated on a component of his cognitive behavioural model; namely, the importance of beliefs relating to responsibility and inaction. He suggests that non-clinical individuals regard themselves responsible for what they actively do, rather than what they fail to do; however, clinical experience, and some pilot work, suggests that obsessional patients do not show evidence of this omission bias. Clearly, a general belief that any *influence* over an outcome incurs responsibility, will increase concerns with omissions, promoting preven- tative behaviour. Salkovskis suggests that if a negative event is foreseen, responsibility is established: 'because to do nothing the person would have to decide not to act to prevent the harmful outcome'. Deciding not to act, 'becomes an active decision, making the person a causal agent in relation to ... disastrous consequences'.

The author has observed that many individuals with OCD often exhibit enhanced awareness of potential networks of cause and effect. In some cases, this could be attributable to the specific manifestation of OCD. For example, an individual with contamination fears will readily describe how a particular contaminant might be passed from one individual to another until a pregnant woman is contaminated. The result of this might be that her child is born with some physical abnormality; however, individuals without specific contamination fears, but with concerns about harming others, will often describe extended causal chains that will potentiate the occurrence of a feared outcome. This feature of obsessional thinking places the affected individual at the epicentre of a network of potential disasters. Clearly, under such conditions, the pressure to act in order to prevent disasters will be maximised.

In addition to McFall & Wollersheim (1979) and Salkovskis (1985), two other 'cognitive' accounts of OCD have been proposed. Guidano & Liotti (1983) suggest the presence of a fundamental cognitive structure which serves to organise knowledge in OCD patients. This structure is comprised of a set of beliefs about perfectionism, the need for certainty, and the existence of an absolutely correct solution. Guidano & Liotti (1983) suggest that this structure is relatively invariant, and accounts for a range of superficially different obsessional symptoms. Although Guidano & Liotti's account is of some interest, it lacks specificity. Moreover, there is little in their account to explain parsimoniously why these particular beliefs produce OCD, rather than any other Axis I condition such as depression.

Warren & Zgourides (1991) have proposed a rational emotive therapy (RET) model of OCD. As with Guidano & Liotti (1983), a few fundamental beliefs are given central importance, namely, 'I must make the correct decision', 'I must have perfect certainty that I won't be the cause of harm to anyone', and 'I must not have bizarre or unacceptable thoughts or impulses'. Although Warren & Zgourides discuss other cognitive factors and processes that might be important with respect to the development of OCD, the beliefs they underscore do not add significantly to existing accounts.

Chapter 10

INFLATED PERSONAL INFLUENCE, RESPONSIBILITY, AND THE PSYCHOLOGICAL FUSION OF THOUGHT AND ACTION

EXAGGERATED RESPONSIBILITY

To a greater or lesser extent, most of the theories described in Chapter 9 recognise the importance of an exaggerated sense of responsibility; however, 'responsibility' has always been recognised as a concept of considerable importance (e.g. Pollitt, 1969). Rachman (1976a) suggests that 'The significance of the checkers' feeling of responsibility can be accounted for by the fact that it is only those acts for which they can be held *responsible* that are liable to produce guilt or criticism. If the checker is not responsible for the act or its consequences, then it relieves him of being criticised for the action and it also helps to avoid guilt' (p. 274). Although the concept of responsibility has been discussed with respect to OCD for many years, it is only recently that it has received more detailed consideration.

The concept of exaggerated responsibility has considerable explanatory power, especially with respect to clinical observations. Rachman & Hodgson (1980) noted that it was difficult to provoke anxiety in obsessional checkers immediately after hospitalisation. Indeed, this is one of the main difficulties in attempting to undertake exposure and response prevention work on an inpatient basis. This swift evaporation of anxiety is readily explained if responsibility is given a central place in a revised anatomy of obsessions. In the presence of a therapist, responsibility is shared, with subsequent reduction of anxiety. Rachman (1993) also notes that when compulsive checkers remain as inpatients, anxiety is more easily provoked, as the ward setting is 'claimed' as personal psychological territory. The same effect is also sometimes reported by obsessional patients when going on holiday. At first, checking remits; however, symptoms tend to reemerge with increasing time spent in the new environment.

Rachman (1993) also suggests that an exaggerated sense of responsibility may have a role to play in the generation of uncomfortable affect in the context of obsessional thinking. It has already been suggested that intrusive or unwanted thoughts are a universal experience (Rachman & de Silva, 1978; Salkovskis & Harrison, 1984). In OCD, normal intrusive cognition, particularly on aggressive, sexual, or blasphemous themes, is associated with intense guilt, on account of the individual's self-attribution of moral and psychological responsibility.

Rachman (1993) considers the specific phenomenology underlying this process. For examples, he suggests that an affected individual may experience the following self-appraisal: 'My immoral sexual thoughts reveal something important and unflattering about the kind of person that I really am' and 'I am responsible for these objectionable thoughts' (p. 151). The exaggerated sense of responsibility observed in OCD can reach a level of intensity whereby the simple occurrence of an intrusive thought can be considered equivalent to wishing it to be true. In severe cases, the occurrence of an intrusive thought may even be considered equivalent to undertaking a related act. For example, an individual who experiences intrusive cognitions relating to the sexual abuse of children might experience the degree of guilt usually associated with being *directly responsible* for sexually abusing a child. This phenomenon, described as thought-action fusion, is clearly related to some of the underlying beliefs described in cognitive accounts of OCD, particularly Salkovskis (1985).

The presence of moral thought-action fusion is described in the psycho-analytic literature, although the underlying beliefs are not made explicit. Freud (1909) notes that whenever his patient experienced a 'criminal impulse', he would seek out a friend for whom he had a particularly high opinion, in order to ask the friend whether he 'despised him as a criminal' (p. 40). His friend would assure him that he was a man of irreproachable conduct. The phenomenon of thought-action fusion is also interesting with respect to the association between religiosity and OCD (Suess & Halpern, 1989; Steketee, Quay & White, 1991). For example, in Roman Catholicism, a sinful thought *is* considered to be the moral equivalent of a sinful action.

INFLATED PERSONAL INFLUENCE

The concepts of responsibility and thought-action fusion are also clearly relevant to superstitious thinking. The moral equivalence of thought and action is a likely consequence of a perceived causal relationship between mental events and the occurrence of events in the real world. This may be mediated by the inflated sense of personal influence described in the psychoanalytic literature (see Chapter 8). Responsibility, and associated guilt, are the consequences of the above (see Figure 2).

For example, the underlying primary belief may be similar to one of those described by McFall & Wollersheim (1979), namely, 'Certain thoughts and feelings are unacceptable, having them could lead to catastrophe ...'. A consequence of this belief will be the moral equivalence of thought and action, that is, 'Having a thought about an action is like performing the action' (Salkovskis, 1985). The inevitable result of the above is an acceptance of responsibility, with associated guilt if an inner rule reflecting a desired standard of moral conduct has been violated. Reparative behaviour, in the form of undoing or neutralising, will then be necessary to reduce emotional discomfort. The apparent success of this reparative behaviour will reinforce beliefs associated with inflated personal influence.

It has already been suggested that psychoanalytic theory accounts for an inflated sense of personal influence in terms of a regression to an earlier stage of development; however, a more parsimonious account may be afforded by consideration of learning history. If an individual

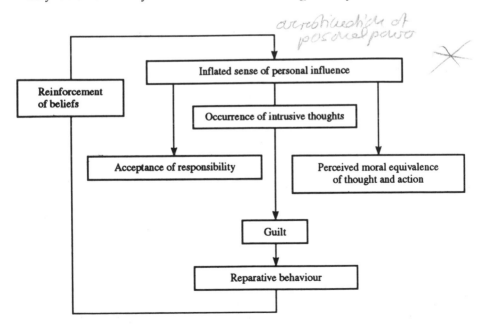

Figure 2   Causal factors in superstitious behaviour

experiences an apparent causal relationship between mental events and the occurrence of events in the real world, this might potentiate the formation of associated beliefs on the theme of inflated personal influence. Indeed, Freud (1909) describes a learning experience of this nature in his celebrated obsessional patient, the 'rat man'. When visiting a hydropathic establishment for a second time, the patient learned that his room was already taken by an old professor. Freud notes that he reacted to this news by thinking: 'I wish he may be struck dead for it!'. A fortnight later the aged professor died from a stroke.

Similar histories are described by Tallis (1994). In the first case, an obsessional patient recalled that, when approximately six years of age, she prayed that her grandfather would die. The following day her grandfather died of a heart attack. In a second case, the patient recalled that, when she was 15 years of age, she formed the intense wish that her father would 'go', or be 'taken away', and prayed to this effect. Within a week her father was involved in a rail accident and was killed instantly. The author has collected several other examples of this phenomenon since reporting the above.

Rachman (1994) underscores the clinical observation that obsessional patients have difficulty in expressing anger. If this clinical observation is correct, then one might expect it to be more apparent in individuals who have developed an exaggerated sense of personal influence. Clearly, in such individuals, the expression of aggressive urges is associated with considerable perceived risks. In one of the cases reported by Tallis (1994), the patient suggested that she had suppressed the expression of anger throughout her life for fear of causing fatalities. There are interesting similarities here between this cognitive-behavioural account and the psychodynamic account of OCD, which places particular emphasis on the role of suppressed hostility (although it should be noted that in psychodynamic theory, hostility is usually displaced, and arises in association with oedipal wishes). Moreover, perhaps the paradoxical effects of thought suppression described by Wegner and colleagues may be particularly important with respect to the maintenance of repetitive and intrusive thoughts on violent themes.

It is intriguing that intrusive thoughts are a universal experience, and further, tend to reflect blasphemous, aggressive, and sexual themes. In attempting to understand this specificity, they might be construed as cognitive alarms, arising more frequently in certain high risk situations in order to promote caution and deter inappropriate behaviour. A common example is the frequent occurrence of intrusive thoughts just prior to the arrival of a train. Many individuals report intrusive thoughts about being pushed off the platform, pushing someone else off the platform, or having the urge to jump off the platform. All of these are considered unacceptable, and serve to promote caution. Similarly, when individuals are in situations requiring high standards of moral propriety, sexual or blasphemous thoughts appear to be more frequent. The effect was noted by the seventeenth-century preacher and writer John Bunyan, who wrote: 'When I have been preaching, I have been violently assaulted with thoughts of blasphemy, and strongly tempted to speak them with my mouth before the congregation' (cited by Toates, 1990, p. 76). Alternatively, it may be that in situations demanding high levels of propriety, suppression is more likely, with subsequent increased levels of intrusion.

Chapter 11

APPRAISAL THEORIES

AN EVALUATION

Cognitive approaches provide a refined description of the key phenomenological features of OCD. By emphasising fundamental beliefs, they allow us to understand the symptoms of OCD in a meaningful way. Moreover, they suggest that specific beliefs, or systems of related beliefs, will be associated with specific symptoms. For example, an inflated sense of personal influence may be more closely associated with superstitious thinking than with contamination fears. At the same time, other constructs from this discourse go some way towards explaining the comorbidity of apparently heterogeneous symptoms. For example, washing and checking may both be mediated by an inflated sense of responsibility. Both behaviours, to a greater or lesser extent, are attempts at reducing harm to others. Although the link between responsibility and checking is more readily understood, the same link is also evident with respect to contamination fears. Again, this is clear in the early writings of Freud (1909) whose celebrated patient would iron his money: 'It was a matter of conscience for him ... for they [paper florins] harboured all sorts of dangerous bacteria that might do harm to the recipient' (p. 77).

By giving inflated responsibility a central role in a revised anatomy of OCD, a range of other clinical phenomena are explained. The most important of these is the relationship between symptom severity and environment. Checking occurs more frequently in the home and at work because these locations are associated with the greatest personal responsibility; however, the presence of another individual will ameliorate symptoms on account of the diffusion of responsibility. Moreover, the common feature of reassurance seeking often takes the form of questions that are clear attempts at sharing responsibility, for example, 'You did see me lock the door, didn't you?'.

Although the cognitive formulations described above have considerable explanatory power, they are associated with a number of contentious issues. First, and perhaps foremost, is that fact that many compulsive behaviours appear to occur in the absence of identifiable cognition reflecting appraisals and underlying beliefs. This is especially true of early onset OCD in children (cf. Rapoport, 1989a). Although it might be argued that an inability to explain behaviour is a characteristic of children *per se*, there is little evidence to suggest that affected children are unable to account for non-obsessional behaviour. In addition, there appears to be a range of obsessional behaviours that seem particularly resistant to a cognitive analysis, at least in terms of appraisal and beliefs. These include repetitive behaviours such as walking backwards and forwards through doors, or getting up and down from a chair several times. Individuals will report getting 'stuck', having to repeat an action until it 'feels right', or 'something making me do it' (cf. Rapoport, 1989a).

Although cognitive events and beliefs do not seem to play a significant role in these behaviours, other features of the processing system may be relevant. Toates (1990) suggests that the issues relating to why individuals engage in compulsive behaviour may be less important than understanding what it is that prevents them from stopping. Getting 'stuck' may be the result of a fault in the feedback systems that influence behaviour. Indeed, there are three accounts of OCD that give special significance to the role of negative feedback (Reed, 1985; Pitman, 1987b; Gray, 1982). Feedback systems are self-regulatory, and depend on the accurate comparison of a goal state and an actual state. A typical example drawn from engineering is the thermostat: when room temperature reaches a set point, the heating system is switched off. When room temperature drops below that set point, the heating system is switched on again. In OCD, it is suggested that the feedback pathway and comparison process are at fault. Differences between the actual and goals states are not registered and the system is said to have gone 'open loop'. Reed (1985) suggests that the 'cybernetic' approach offers a framework within which to understand the apparent indecision exhibited by obsessionals in relation to lower level, or 'automatic' activities. For the affected individual, a failure in the feedback system is experienced as a diffuse lack of satisfaction during the performance of routine behaviours. Repetition represents a largely futile attempt to achieve a match between actual and goal states.

Although a fundamental deficit in feedback systems offers an attractive explanation of compulsive behaviour in the absence of appraisals and beliefs, it too is associated with several problems. It seems implausible that the effects of a faulty feedback system should only be apparent in those behaviours that characterise OCD. Further, in individuals whose feedback system is severely impaired, repetitive behaviour should never stop. Getting 'stuck' would be a pervasive and *permanent* feature of their behaviour.

In addition to the repetition of routine behaviours, a number of other obsessional phenomena are likely to be reported in the absence of significant appraisals and beliefs. These include order and symmetry rituals, number rituals, and touching rituals. With respect to order rituals, phenomenology is again dominated by a desire to 'get things right', although the exact nature of that 'rightness' remains obscure. One of the author's patients would routinely fill and empty a kettle several times in order to get the water at exactly the same level as the volume marker. She would also pull and draw her house curtains, sometimes for hours, so that they would 'hang' correctly. These behaviours were not undertaken to avoid a future catastrophe and the patient readily acknowledged that a failure to undertake these behaviours would have few, if any, negative consequences.

Certain types of counting and number obsessions also appear to be beyond the remit of appraisal theories. Affected individuals describe 'safe' numbers and 'bad' numbers, without being able to explain why this should be the case (Swedo & Rapoport, 1989). Again, one of the author's patients described the frequent and spontaneous counting from 1 to 20. This behaviour was repeated until an inner sense of 'satisfaction' was felt. There was no evidence that the counting was part of a harm avoidance ritual.

Touching rituals are closely associated with counting, insofar as objects must usually be touched a certain number of times. Although this phenomenon is commonly associated with superstitious beliefs, the absence of a clearly identifiable superstitious belief system is not uncommon. There is some evidence to suggest that number rituals, and perhaps accompanying touching rituals, are more common in boys (Swedo & Rapoport, 1989). It is interesting to note that counting and touching are also common features of autism, which also predominantly affects males. This gender-linkage seems to suggest some biological causation.

The above examples are largely atypical examples of OCD; however, the absence of appraisals and beliefs can also be evident in individuals with washing and checking compulsions. In such cases, washing is undertaken in order to reduce a general feeling of discomfort or 'dirtiness', which may not be associated with fears of contamination, or harm being visited upon the self or others. These feelings of discomfort might be engendered after contact with substances that are clear non-contaminants, for example perfume or after-shave. Similarly, certain checking behaviours appear to occur in the absence of appraisals and beliefs. For example, an individual might feel compelled to retrace a journey in order to see if 'something' has been accidentally dropped. Where the article is of little value, such as a handkerchief, it is difficult to see how concepts such as guilt avoidance, inflated responsibility, and fear of harming others are central, or indeed relevant.

To underscore the different phenomenologies of OCD, a stark contrast is being made between individuals who are able to report relevant beliefs and those who are not; however, it should be noted that in the clinic, it is not uncommon to find individuals who are able to report cognition meaningfully related to some types of behaviour (e.g. checking), but are unable to report cognition related to other types of behaviour (e.g. counting). Moreover, accounts of OCD in the literature are most probably coloured by the theoretical orientation of researchers and clinicians. As such, those endorsing biological accounts may underplay the role of beliefs, to the same extent as those endorsing cognitive-behavioural approaches overplay the role of beliefs!

As suggested above, fear of harming others and an inflated sense of responsibility have been given a central position in contemporary cognitive accounts of OCD; however, these concepts can only explain certain facets or key elements of OCD. It is unlikely that they can, of themselves, account for the complete clinical syndrome, even within the context of a modulating belief system. Many guilt-prone individuals find the idea of harming others extremely unpalatable, yet do not develop OCD. In addition, it is unclear why the appraisals and beliefs described in cognitive behavioural models result in the emergence of predominantly washing and checking behaviours. Given the immensity of the human behavioural repertoire, it is remarkable that preventative and reparative behaviours take, in the main, only two forms. Moreover, some affected individuals exhibit glaring inconsistencies in their behaviour. In their efforts to avoid harm coming to others, they cause enormous distress to their own family members. This is often considered acceptable. Finally, it is unclear why individuals with OCD feel excessively responsible for negative events, but not positive events.

Section III

NEUROPSYCHOLOGY

Chapter 12

INTELLIGENCE AND HEMISPHERIC ASSYMETRIES

NEUROPSYCHOLOGY AND OCD

Increasing interest in the biological substrates of OCD has been complemented by the publication of several studies seeking to investigate its
neuropsychological correlates. In the following section, the neuropsychological test literature on OCD will be reviewed. Neuropsychological investigations can be divided into four broad areas: first, investigations of general intellectual functioning; second, investigations of
mnestic functioning; third, investigations of frontal lobe functioning; and
fourth, investigations demonstrating an underinclusive bias on category
formation tasks. These domains of investigation are supplemented by a
number of miscellaneous studies, characterised by the administration of
neuropsychological tests in the absence of any clear theoretical rationale. Unfortunately, many of the studies cited in the following section
could be described as 'psychometric tests' (rather than neuropsychological investigations) on account of work being undertaken in a theoretical
vacuum. It is hoped that future research programmes will be undertaken
within the framework provided by contemporary cognitive neuropsychology.

Investigations of mnestic functioning in obsessional patients have been
encouraged by the mnestic deficit hypothesis, which suggests that the
occurrence of obsessional doubt may be closely related to memory
impairment. The rationale for the administration of a range of frontal
lobe tests is less clear; however, the similarity between *perseverative
behaviour* in individuals with frontal lobe damage and *repetitive behaviour*
in individuals with OCD has clearly influenced the frequent selection
of set shifting tests. An underinclusive thinking style on category
formation tests might correspond with certain obsessional personality
characteristics, namely, perfectionism and attention to detail.

INTELLIGENCE AND HEMISPHERIC ASYMMETRIES

Before the widespread use of psychometric instruments to assess intellectual functioning, psychiatrists had formed the impression that OCD patients were of superior intelligence (e.g. Lewis, 1936). When systematic psychometric assessments of OCD patients were finally undertaken, clinical impressions were apparently confirmed. Several studies showed that OCD patients had a slight but consistent intellectual advantage (Eysenck, 1947; Payne, 1960; Ingram, 1961). However, more recent studies employing the Wechsler Intelligence Scales, conducted on both adults and paediatric populations (Flor-Henry et al., 1979; Coryell, 1981; Insel et al., 1983a; Keller, 1989), have found only small and insignificant differences between OCD patient and control groups. Moreover, such differences that do exist have not necessarily demonstrated an advantage in the obsessional groups.

Although the relationship between general intelligence and specific cognitive capacities can be extremely variable, associations tend to be positive. Given this relationship, recent neuropsychological investigations of cognitive functioning in clinical and non-clinical obsessionals cast considerable doubt on the 'superior intelligence' claim; indeed, several specific deficits have been noted (Head, Bolton & Hymas, 1989; Sher, Frost & Otto, 1983; Sher, Mann & Frost, 1984; Sher et al., 1989; Boone et al., 1991; Christensen et al., 1992; Zielinski, Taylor & Juzwin, 1991) suggesting inferior rather than superior levels of general functioning. Where full scale IQ measures (Wechsler, 1955; Wechsler 1981) have been taken, depressed scores in OCD patients are particularly attributable to the poor execution of Performance IQ (PIQ) subtests (Boone et al., 1991; Keller, 1989). Verbal IQ (VIQ) is relatively unaffected. These results suggest general right hemispheric impairment; however, it should be noted that PIQ tests are timed and *obsessional slowness* (Rachman & Hodgson, 1980) might interfere significantly with task performance.

Moreover, PIQ subtests are less likely to 'hold', compared with VIQ subtests, even when cortical damage is diffuse (Lezak, 1983). Therefore, inferring an underlying right hemispheric deficit from these test results alone would be unwise. Nevertheless, it is of some interest to note that other tests of general intellectual functioning that rely strongly on visuo-spatial skills also pose problems for patients with OCD. Two studies using Raven's Matrices, for example, have revealed significant differences between OCD and control subjects (Flor-Henry et al., 1979; Zielinski, Taylor & Juzwin, 1991).

It seems unlikely that the early clinical observations and psychometric assessments of obsessional patients were either mistaken or inaccurate. Perhaps these inconsistencies can be explained with respect to the heterogeneity of OCD. If obsessional neurosis represents only one end of a continuum of OCD spectrum disorders, then it may be that those patients who cluster towards the 'biological' end show greater cognitive impairment. Boone et al. (1991) reported that OCD patients with a positive, rather than negative, family history of OCD, produced significantly lower WAIS Full Scale IQ scores than non-clinical controls. Alternatively, it may be the case that certain manifestations of OCD are associated with less intellectual impairment than others. For example, Arts et al. (1993), found that individuals with both obsessions and compulsions were more intelligent than individuals with obsessions and no compulsions. In 1980, Rachman and Hodgson concluded that there was little reason to continue investigating intellectual functioning in OCD on account of the consistent findings and lack of clinical relevance. More recent and broader conceptualisations of OCD suggest that their conclusion may have been premature and the picture is far from complete.

Chapter 13

MEMORY FUNCTIONING

MEMORY AND DOUBTING

Over the past 10 years, the mnestic deficit hypothesis has stimulated a growing body of research. Early work, conducted by Sher and colleagues (Sher, Frost & Otto, 1983; Sher, Mann & Frost, 1984; Sher et al., 1989), demonstrated the presence of memory deficits in non-clinical and clinical (but not OCD) 'checkers'. Recently, more mainstream neuropsychological investigations, using OCD subjects (Christensen et al., 1992; Boone et al., 1991; Zielinski, Taylor & Juzwin, 1991; Hollander et al., 1990; Cox, Fedio & Rapoport, 1989; Martinot et al., 1990; Aranowitz et al., in press; Ecker & Engelkamp, submitted) have found similar deficits. Less direct evidence supporting the mnestic deficit hypothesis can be derived from three other sources: electroencephalographic and brain scan studies (Jenike & Brotman, 1984; McGuire et al., 1994), questionnaire work (Gordon, 1985) and doubt-reduction treatment procedures that rely on memory enhancement (Toates, 1990; Tallis, 1993).

Although results supporting the mnestic deficit hypothesis are presented here, the reader should note that many studies have yielded negative results (Flor-Henry et al., 1979), or at best, mixed results (Christensen et al., 1992; Boone et al., 1991). In an attempt to provide an easily understood review of neuropsychological investigations, an effort has been made to tease out patterns of positive findings. Conclusions are therefore tentative, rather than firm.

Before reviewing the contemporary literature on OCD and memory, a few studies conducted by Reed require acknowledgement. They are different from all of the other studies cited in this section in so far as the population under investigation is anancastic, rather than OCD. Reed (1977) conducted a number of studies which sought to examine the nature of remembering in individuals suffering from anancastic personality disorder (Schneider, 1958). Subjects included were 30 anancasts, and 30 matched psychiatric controls suffering from other personality disorders. No significant differences between groups emerged on the

Information subtest of the WAIS, a measure of long-term memory. Anancasts showed significantly superior recall on the digit span subtest, which was employed in the study as a test of immediate recall; however, the validity of this latter measure is debatable and digit span differences might be more plausibly attributed to attentional factors (Reed, 1991). More recent investigations comparing digit span performance of OCD patients and controls have revealed no significant differences between groups (Boone et al., 1991), or a difference demonstrating the superiority of controls (Flor-Henry et al., 1979).

A further study in this series conducted by Reed (1977) employed 10 anancasts and 10 matched controls. Anancasts showed superior recall for insoluble problems; however, this most probably reflects unprompted rehearsal rather than mnestic superiority. Finally, Reed undertook a small-scale phenomenological analysis of remembering. All subjects were asked to describe personal events and then to describe 'the experience of recollection itself.' (p. 181). Anancasts reported more visual imagery than controls, but 'as though from the viewpoint of a non-participant observer'. Obsessionals also ' ... expressed uneasiness, not as to what they were recalling, but about the quality of the recollection' (p. 182).

Contemporary research into memory functioning and obsessionality began with a study conducted by Sher, Frost & Otto (1983) who divided a student sample into several groups according to MOCI scores. These were subjects who both cleaned and checked ($n = 13$), subjects who checked but did not clean ($n = 13$), subjects who cleaned but did not check ($n = 13$), and subjects who neither cleaned nor checked ($n = 15$). Checking or cleaning status was determined according to whether an individual scored 5 or above on the relevant subscale. Subjects were given seven separate tasks during the course of the experiment. After completing the final task, they were asked to describe each one briefly. The total number of tasks recalled served as a 'memory for actions' measure.

Analysis of this data yielded a significant main effect, showing that checkers had poorer recall than non-checkers. Further research (Sher, Mann & Frost, 1984) confirmed a memory for actions deficit in non-clinical checkers. After being given 13 tasks, checkers were found to have poorer recall for prior action than non-checkers, although the linear association between checking status and memory for actions did not reach significance. Psychometric testing, using the Wechsler Memory Scale (WMS) (Wechsler & Stone, 1945) showed that checkers have significantly lower Memory Quotients (MQ) than non-checkers. The task most sensitive to checking status in the Wechsler battery was the logical memory subtest. However, it should be noted that all subjects scored within the normal range.

Sher, Frost & Otto (1983) did not control for affective variables. However, Sher, Mann & Frost (1984) included a state anxiety measure (Spielberger et al., 1980) and the BDI (Beck et al., 1961); analyses showed that results could not be attributable to anxiety or depression. Nevertheless, these studies by Sher and his colleagues are problematic for two reasons. First, the population are non-clinical and second, the checkers had MQs within the normal range. This latter fact is difficult to reconcile with an 'absolute' (rather than relative) mnestic deficit account.

Sher et al. (1989) selected a clinical sample from 99 consecutive community mental health centre admissions. DSM-III Axis I diagnoses were dysthymic disorder, marital problems, alcohol abuse, and adjustment disorder with depression. The most common Axis II diagnoses were anti-social and dependent personality disorder. Checking status was determined by MOCI-check subscale scores of either 0 to 1 (non-checkers), or 4 and above (checkers). Thirteen were classified as checkers and 12 were classified as non-checkers. These two groups were diagnostically equivalent and did not differ in terms of intellectual functioning, measured on the Peabody Picture Vocabulary Test (Dunn, 1959).

Consistent with the non-clinical sample of Sher, Mann & Frost (1984), checkers had significantly lower WMS MQs than non-checkers. However, none of the subtests found to be most sensitive to memory deficits by Sher, Mann & Frost (1984), namely logical memory, digits forward, and paired associate learning, differentiated checkers and non-checkers in the clinical sample. Interestingly, it was the visual memory subtest that proved to be the most discriminative using clinical subjects. More consistent confirmation of earlier work was achieved by collecting 'memory for actions' data. Outpatient checkers had inferior recall of tasks performed during the testing session than outpatient non-checkers.

Unfortunately, some of the criticisms that apply to Sher and his colleagues' earlier work also apply to their outpatient study. First, and most significantly, none of the outpatients employed carried an Axis I diagnosis of OCD, or for that matter, an Axis II diagnosis of obsessional personality disorder. Second, the outpatient checkers' WMS scores were within the normal range. Finally, the outpatient checkers scored significantly more on the SCL 90-R anxiety subscale (Derogatis & Melisaratos, 1983) than non-checkers, suggesting that the memory deficits detected might be secondary rather than primary.

Rubenstein et al. (1993) conducted a more ecologically sound investigation of the memory for actions deficit; however, once again, a non-clinical sample was employed. Checkers were determined by MOCI subscale scores greater than, or equal to 4. Non-checkers were determined by MOCI subscale scores of 2 or less (and a MOCI total of less than or equal to 8). Twenty checkers and 20 non-checkers took part in a series of experiments. In experiment 1A, subjects listened to statements describing 90 actions which could be responded to depending on allocation to one of three conditions: (1) write, (2) observe, or (3) perform (e.g. 'pace the length of the room'). Subjects were first requested to recall as many actions as they could remember, and then to identify whether recalled actions had been written, observed or performed. Checkers remembered significantly fewer actions than non-checkers and were more likely to confuse the assigned condition. Checkers were also more likely to identify actions that had not been part of the procedure. In experiment 1B, subjects watched two cartoons; a subsequent memory test showed no differences with respect to recall of the characters' actions. This finding suggests that 'agency', rather than passive observation, is the critical feature of paradigm sensitivity. The final experiment in this series was a word recognition task. Although checkers performed better than non-checkers on this task, they made significantly more errors of commission than non-checkers (as with memory for actions). This effect could not be attributed to state anxiety. The authors suggest that their data raise important issues for treatment; namely, that it may not be entirely accurate to describe some checking behaviour as 'completely irrational'.

Given that the above series of experiments were conducted on non-clinical groups, or clinical (but not OCD) patients, it could be argued that more significance should be attached to the results of mainstream neuropsychological studies which have used OCD rather than analogue subjects. Particular reference will be made to investigations conducted by Ecker & Engelkamp (submitted), Martinot et al. (1990), Boone et al. (1991), Zielinski, Taylor & Juzwin (1991), Christensen et al. (1992), and Aranowitz et al. (in press).

Ecker & Engelkamp employed three groups of subjects: frequent checkers with OCD ($n = 24$), a high checking clinical control group ($n = 24$), and a low checking clinical control group ($n = 48$). Both high checking groups were significantly more anxious and depressed than the low checking group. All OCD and non-OCD high checking patients scored 4 and above on the checking subscale of the MOCI. The mean MOCI total score for the OCD group was 18, while the mean MOCI total scores for the high and low checking clinical control groups was 14.4 and 5.5 respectively. There were no significant differences between groups with respect to age.

Subjects were told that the experimenters were interested in the effects of different learning strategies on memory performance. They were then introduced to four types of encoding instruction (1) motor encoding with imaginary objects (i.e. miming an action), (2) motor imaginal encoding (i.e. 'imagine yourself performing an action'), (3) visual imaginal encoding (i.e. 'imagine someone else performing an action') and (4) subvocal rehearsal (as a control condition). Two lists of 32 phrases were read out with changes of encoding instruction after each four-item subblock. After list presentation, subjects were requested to recall items on both lists. This was followed by a recognition task.

The OCD group did not show a general free recall deficit, but did show poorer free recall of prior actions than the low checking clinical control group. This difference could not be attributed to the effects of depression or anxiety. With respect to the recognition task, it was found that OCD subjects confused motor imaginal and motor encoding tasks more frequently than did low checking clinical controls. The motor imaginal/motor confusion score was significantly correlated with the MOCI checking subscale but not with the MOCI total. Subsequent analyses showed that OCD patients produced more type A errors (i.e. incorrectly believing that an action was imagined rather than performed) than low checkers. Interestingly, the high checking control group were more likely to produce type B errors (i.e. incorrectly believing that an action was performed rather than imagined). OCD subjects were also less confident than low checking controls with respect to their memory functioning. Confidence ratings for OCD and high checking groups did not differ significantly. The authors conclude that their results are consistent with a specific motor memory deficit in OCD checkers. Although no significant differences emerged between high clinical checkers and OCD patients, it is difficult to conclude much from this. The so-called non-OCD group scored in the clinical range on both the MOCI total and MOCI checking subscale. It is unclear why members of the high checking control group did not qualify for inclusion in the OCD group.

Martinot et al. (1990) employed 14 inpatients and 17 normal controls. The mean age of the patient groups was 44 (SD = 12) while the mean age of the control group was 29.6 (SD = 11.9). All patients met DSM-III (APA, 1980) criteria for a primary diagnosis of OCD, agreed by three psychiatrists. All patients scored greater than 10 on the Compulsive Activity Checklist (Marks et al., 1977). Exclusion criteria were a diagnosis of major depressive episode, drug or alcohol addiction, electroconvulsive therapy in the previous six months or the presence of gross pathology on CT scan. Ten patients were medicated at the time of testing, receiving clomipramine ($n = 3$), trazadone ($n = 1$), and/or benzodiazepines ($n = 6$) or neuroleptics ($n = 3$). Memory functioning was tested using the Rey–Ostereith (Rey, 1941; Ostereith, 1944) complex figure, a test originally developed to investigate perceptual organisation and visual memory in brain-damaged patients. It involves the reproduction from memory of a previously copied complex geometric figure. OCD patients performed significantly worse than controls on this test, suggesting compromised memory functioning; however, it is possible that this deficit might be attributable to medication effects. No comparison of medicated versus unmedicated patients is reported. Moreover, no correlations between neuropsychological test indices and symptom severity are reported.

Boone et al. (1991) recruited 20 non-depressed OCD patients (scoring less than 14 on the Hamilton (1960) Depression Rating Scale), and 16 non-clinical controls. Assessment was conducted according to DSM-III-R criteria and only subjects scoring above 10 on the Y-Bocs were included. All OCD subjects were medication free for at least four weeks prior to testing and none had previously required regular medication. The mean length of illness was 17.54 years. Matching was achieved according to age and years in education; however, women were overrepresented in the control group (9F 7M) and men were overrepresented in the patient group (11M 9F). Two of the patients and two of the controls had a history of learning disability; however, analyses excluding these patients did not affect results.

The experimental group scored more poorly than controls with respect to the percentage retention measure of the Rey–Ostereith Complex Figure. Moreover, ANOVA comparisons of patients with and without a family history of OCD revealed significant differences on the copy measure of the Rey–Ostereith (but not percentage retention). Performance on the WMS Visual Retention Test (percentage retention measure) was also significantly impaired with respect to the family history group. Visual spatial skills deficits were also detected according to performance on the Hooper Visual Organisation Test (HVOT) (Hooper, 1958), several items of which are thought to be particularly sensitive to right frontal lobe lesions (Lezak, 1983). OCD patients scored more poorly on the HVOT than controls, and patients with a positive family history of OCD performed more poorly on the HVOT than patients with a negative family history. Unfortunately, the relationship between symptom severity and neuropsychological indices proved to be weak. Only one significant and positive correlation was found between the Y-Bocs compulsion subscale score and performance on WMS Visual Retention Test (immediate recall measure).

Zielinski, Taylor & Juzwin, (1991) conducted an investigation employing 21 OCD patients and 21 non-clinical controls matched with respect to sex, gender, race, and education. Subjects were requested to refrain from consuming alcohol and antihistamine medication (cf. Douglas, 1980) 48 hours before testing, and to restrict caffeine intake three hours prior to testing. Clinical status was determined according to scores on the Compulsive Activity Checklist (Philpott, 1975) and the MOCI. Although nine patients were medicated, no significant differences were found after an initial analysis comparing medicated and unmedicated groups; subsequently, data were combined. An attempt was made to divide the experimental group according to symptoms (e.g. washers versus checkers); however, the sample showed predominantly mixed symptoms. No subject met criteria for major depression, though some reported depression secondary to OCD. Moreover, the number of depressive symptoms reported and state anxiety scores did not correlate with neuropsychological indices.

Visual memory was assessed with Kimura's recurring figures test (Kimura, 1963), a recognition task employing geometric and nonsense drawings. Significant differences between groups were found with respect to the number of false positives reported in immediate and delayed trials, with OCD subjects reporting more than controls. In addition, deficits were found with respect to performance on Corsi's blocks (Corsi, 1972). This consists of a wooden board on which nine blocks are randomly arranged. The subject copies the examiner's tapping pattern which becomes increasingly complex. Every third trial, a super-span sequence is repeated. This test was originally devised by Milner (1971) to test memory impairment in temporal lobe resection patients. It is particularly sensitive if resection has involved significant amounts of the hippocampus (Lezak, 1983). It is probably best considered as a measure of immediate recall of sequences and spatial memory. Zielinski, Taylor & Juzwin (1991) found significant deficits in the performance of OCD patients on the two measures of 'spatial span' and the number of correct repeated sequences. Unfortunately, correlations between symptom severity and all neuropsychological indices did not prove significant.

Christensen et al. (1992) recruited 18 patients who met DSM-III criteria for OCD and 18 non-clinical controls. Patients with depression were included only if OCD was the primary diagnosis. The mean Hamilton Depression Scale (17 item) score for the OCD sample was 7.9 (Hamilton, 1960) while the mean Y-Bocs score was 27.4. Samples were matched according to age, gender, and education. Patients were requested to stop medication two to four weeks prior to participating in the study. The mean duration of symptoms was 14.3 years. A significant group difference was identified on the WMS Visual Reproduction Test (30-minute recall), but not on the

Designs component of the Continuous Paired Associates Test (CPAT-D). Although the relationship between neuropsychological indices and symptom severity is not reported, the authors comment that multiple non-verbal measures of larger samples are required before the clinical significance of a non-verbal memory deficit can be determined.

Aranowitz et al. (in press) recruited 31 outpatients and 22 normal controls matched for age, sex, education, and occupational level. All patients met DSM-III-R criteria for OCD. The mean duration of the illness was 12.33 (SD = 9.1) years. All patients were medication free for at least four weeks and had no focal neurological disorder. Their mean Y-Bocs score was 27.07 (SD = 5.18). Memory was tested using the Benton Visual Retention Test (BVRT) (Benton, 1974), which involves the presentation of geometric figures which must be drawn after presentation. OCD patients showed significantly more errors than did normal controls, while controls showed significantly more correct responses than did patients. A significant difference with respect to performance on the Information subtest of the WAIS-R also suggested impairment in long-term memory functioning. No correlations are reported with respect to test results and symptom severity.

Cox, Fedio & Rapoport (1989) compared 42 obsessive-compulsive adolescents and 35 matched normal controls on a battery of tests. Individuals were excluded with low IQ, psychotic illness, or primary depression (but not secondary depression). It is not reported whether or not clinical participants were medicated. Significant differences were observed with respect to Rey–Ostereith Complex Figure performance; control subjects lost an average of 29% of information on delayed recall, whereas OCD patients showed a 39% loss. The authors do not report correlation analyses of the relationship between mood and neuropsychological indices; therefore, the deficit might be attributable to anxiety or depression. Moreover, as with those studies cited above, the deficit was not associated with symptom severity.

Hollander et al. (1990) studied 41 medication free patients meeting DSM-III-R criteria for OCD and 20 normal controls. There were significantly more 'soft signs' of central nervous system dysfunction in the OCD group, as shown by fine motor coordination, involuntary and mirror movements, as well as visual-spatial function. Severity of obsessions correlated significantly with the total 'soft signs' of dysfunction. These same signs did not correlate with the severity of concurrent depression. The total number of neurological soft signs was also correlated with the number of errors recorded on the Benton Visual Retention Tests (r = 0.49), a measure of visual memory (Benton, 1955).

All the evidence above suggests the presence of a visual memory deficit and/or a visual-spatial memory deficit in patients with OCD. Some studies have found verbal memory deficits; however, the overall evidence is not compelling. Martinot et al. (1990) found performance deficits in OCD patients on the Rey Auditory Verbal Learning Test (Rey, 1970); however, a large number of these patients were medicated. Cox, Fedio & Rapoport (1989) found significant differences between adolescent OCD subjects and controls on the same test (Rey 1941). Zielinski, Taylor & Juzwin (1991) found that their OCD patients performed worse than controls on the 'intrusive errors' measure of the California Verbal Learning Tests (Delis et al., 1986), a measure of 'immediate memory'. Finally, Sher, Mann & Frost (1984) found performance deficits in non-clinical checkers (compared with controls) employing the WMS logical memory subtest.

Indirect evidence for the mnestic deficit hypothesis has been derived from three sources. The first is electrophysiological and brain scan investigations suggesting abnormal functioning in regions and structures associated with mnestic performance, particularly with respect to visual-spatial skills (Jenike & Brotman, 1984; Zohar et al., 1988; McGuire et al., 1994). The second source is self-report investigations using the Cognitive Failures Questionnaire (CFQ) (Gordon, 1985; Sher, Mann & Frost, 1984), and the third intervention procedures that seek to reduce doubt by enhancing memory for past actions (Tallis, 1993). With respect to the first of these, the reader is referred to Chapter 6 for a review of brain-imaging investigations. However, in addition, it should be noted that abnormal EEG has been recorded in up to 33% of OCD patients, particularly over the temporal lobes (Jenike & Brotman, 1984). Neuropsychological evidence suggests that temporal lobe lesions are strongly associated with memory deficits (Lezak, 1983).

Gordon (1985) compared responses on the CFQ (Broadbent et al., 1982) in OCD patients ($n = 12$), phobic patients, and normal controls. The CFQ is sensitive to perceptual, action, and memory failures. Obsessionals reported significantly higher scores than either control groups. However, these differences might be attributable to general levels of anxiety. Sher, Mann & Frost (1984) found that CFQ scores were significantly related to checking status in their non-clinical sample. Unfortunately, the relationship did not remain significant when state anxiety was used as a covariate. Sher et al. (1989) report that their clinical (but not OCD) checkers scored significantly higher on the CFQ than clinical non-checkers; however, the checking group were significantly more anxious than the non-checking group, and covariate and partial correlation analyses were not employed to determine the role of anxiety.

Tallis (1993) reports the development of a doubt reduction procedure which employs distinctive artificial stimuli. Three patients suffering from severe checking compulsions were given artificial stimuli to increase the distinctiveness of behaviours that would ordinarily result in excessive checking. Increasing distinctiveness ameliorated doubt, and checking was all but completely eliminated at one-year follow up. The reader is referred to Chapter 19 for a more detailed account. Unfortunately, out of the three cases reported by Tallis (1993), only one is well controlled. The author interprets these results with due caution, suggesting that the techniques' efficacy might be mediated by increased 'confidence in memory', rather than improved mnestic functioning. Notwithstanding this criticism, these preliminary results are promising, and better controlled work might help forge the link between cognitive performance and symptom severity; a link which has been elusive with respect to conventional neuropsychological investigations.

In sum, 'memory for actions' and non-verbal memory deficits are the most commonly found in non-clinical checkers, clinical (but not OCD) checkers, and patients suffering from OCD.

Verbal memory deficits have also been detected in non-clinical and clinical samples; however, there is, as yet, insufficient evidence to suggest that verbal memory is characteristically impaired in OCD. Although most of the key findings cannot be attributed to mood effects, neuropsychological indices are not related to symptom severity. As such, it is unlikely that deficits detected by neuropsychological tests are causally related to OCD symptoms.

Chapter 14

FRONTAL LOBE FUNCTIONING

DEFICITS IN OCD

The notion that OCD and frontal lobe functioning might be in some way related has been espoused for some time (Flor-Henry, 1983; Malloy, 1987); however, speculation has been encouraged by the results of brain-scanning studies (Baxter et al., 1987, 1988; Nordhal et al., 1989; Swedo et al., 1989a) which have detected abnormally high levels of activity in frontal lobe structures and the orbital region of the frontal cortex. In this chapter, the results of several tests of frontal lobe functioning are reviewed. As in the previous chapter, an attempt has been made to underscore positive, rather than negative, findings. Therefore, any conclusions with respect to frontal lobe deficits can only be tentative at this stage. The reader should note that overall, tests have yielded inconsistent results, with some studies finding no impairment in frontal lobe functioning (Boone et al., 1991; Zielinski, Taylor & Juzwin, 1991).

Perhaps the most frequently used test of frontal lobe functioning is the Wisconsin Card Sort (Milner, 1963). The administration on this test is quite complex, and the reader is referred to the original publication for a detailed description of the test procedure. The Wisconsin, or WCST, was devised to study abstract thinking (e.g. concept formation) and the ability to shift cognitive set; however, poor performance can plausibly be attributed to a much wider range of deficits, for example, matching stimuli, or coordinating the component processes required to perform the task correctly. Poor performance is attributed particularly to left frontal damage involving the medial area (Drewe, 1974); however, the issue of laterality is far from resolved (Taylor, 1979; Robinson et al., 1980). Stuss et al. (1983) studied patients with orbitofrontal lesions; poor performance, however, was only evident on a second trial. The most distinctive feature of the performance of patients with frontal lobe damage is perseveration, that is, patients continue to sort cards according to an established rule, even after they have been informed that this rule is no longer applicable. It is postulated that perseverative behaviour reflects the patients' inability to shift cognitive set. Within a neuropsychological framework, repetitive compulsions (and to a lesser extent obsessions) can be viewed as examples of behavioural rigidity, perhaps the most established characteristic of frontal lobe patients (Stuss & Benson, 1986).

Harvey (1987) administered the WCST to 19 OCD patients diagnosed according to DSM-III criteria. Using matched normative data for Nelson's modified WCST, it was shown that OCD patients perseverated significantly more than the control group. Of greater interest was that perseveration correlated with LOI scores, suggesting a systematic and positive relationship between test deficits and symptom severity.

Head, Bolton & Hymas (1989) administered the modified WCST (Nelson, 1976) to 15 OCD patients meeting DSM-III criteria, and 15 matched (age, sex, verbal IQ, years in education, handedness) non-clinical controls. The patient group were drug free at the time of testing and had been symptomatic for at least one year. Although patients showed a broad range of symptoms, more obsessionally slow patients were included than would be routinely expected in a random sample. The patient group made significantly more errors (total) than the control group, showing that their overall proficiency with respect to task performance was low. However, the patient group also made significantly more perseverative errors, which were calculated using two methods of scoring (Nelson, 1976; Milner, 1964). No data are reported on the relationship between symptom severity and error rates.

Cox et al. (1989) administered the WCST to 42 adolescent patients and a non-clinical control group matched for age, sex, race, handedness, and IQ. Individuals with depression secondary to OCD were not excluded from the study. Correct responses, perseverative responses, perseverative errors, non-perseverative errors, and unique errors were scored as outlined by Heaton (1981). Although OCD subjects performed significantly fewer correct card sorts than control subjects, none of the other Heaton measures proved significant. Moreover, there was no systematic relationship between WCST scores and symptom severity recorded on a wide range of measures.

Christensen et al. (1992) administered the WCST (Milner, 1963) to 18 non-depressed adults with OCD and 18 matched controls (see previous chapter for further details). The number of correct responses was the measure employed. Two analyses are reported, one including and the other excluding outliers. Only the inclusive analysis proved significant. Again, no systematic relationship was found between WCST scores and symptom severity scores.

As suggested earlier, the WCST is a complex test, and poor performance might be attributed to a wide range of deficits (cf. Downes et al., 1989).

The most salient of these is visual-spatial functioning, which may be compromised in patients with OCD (Boone et al., 1991; Zielinski, Taylor & Juzwin, 1991; Head, Bolton & Hymas, 1989). In addition to interpretative problems, only one study has reported a significant relationship between WCST scores and symptom severity (Harvey, 1987). Unfortunately, in this case, the measure of symptom severity is itself vulnerable to substantive criticism (see Chapter 7). A final point should also be made with respect to the validity of inferring a frontal lesion from poor WCST performance. There is an increasing body of evidence suggesting that card sorting performance may not be as differentially sensitive to frontal lobe problems as was originally thought (van den Broek, Bradshaw & Szabadi, 1993).

In an effort to circumvent some of the problems associated with the WCST, Veale et al. (submitted), have employed the set shifting task included in the Cambridge Neuropsychological Test Automated Battery (CANTAB). In this test, the subject learns a set of discrimination tasks in which one of two stimuli is correct. Performance reflects the subject's ability to attend to a specific dimension of compound stimuli and shift attention when required. This test was designed to be a relatively pure test of set shifting ability and, unlike the WCST, does not require any matching of stimuli. In addition, Veale et al. (submitted) suggest that deficits on this task occur independent of planning impairment, which is thought to require fronto-striatal integrity.

Forty inpatients meeting DSM-III-R criteria for OCD were included in the study with 22 non-clinical controls matched for age, gender, and verbal IQ. The effects of OCPD were also controlled for. Patients suffering from contamination fears and or/ruminations were not considered for inclusion, insofar as symptoms might have interfered with test performance (e.g. hesitancy touching the computer screen because of contamination fears). OCD patients showed significant impairment on the set shifting task, with a steady increase in the number of patients failing at each stage; however, test deficits were not correlated with symptom severity.

In addition to the above, Veale et al. (submitted) administered the CANTAB version of the Tower of London, a test of planning developed by Shallice & McCarthy (Shallice, 1982), in which stimuli must be arranged from an initial position to a target position in the smallest number of moves without error. The reader is referred to the original publication for details of the test. The computerised version of the Tower of London includes other indices of task performance in addition to the number of moves required to reach the target position. These include 'initial thinking time', i.e. the interval between instruction and the first move, and 'subsequent thinking time', i.e. the time spent thinking after the first move. Veale et al. (submitted) suggest that both of these temporal indices might reflect components of bradyphrenia.

There were no significant differences between OCD patients and controls with respect to the accuracy of solutions. In addition, there were no between-group differences with respect to 'initial' and 'subsequent' thinking time when only 'perfect move' solutions were considered; however, when patients made mistakes, significantly more time was required to generate alternative solutions. Test data were not significantly correlated with symptom severity.

Veale et al. (submitted) argue that results show that patients with OCD are slower at generating alternative strategies when they make an incorrect move. It is suggested that they become more rigid, or spend longer checking that the next move will be right. This result might plausibly be related to state anxiety; a variable which was not accounted for in the study (cf. Tallis, Eysenck & Mathews, 1991; Mikulincer, Kedem & Paz, 1990). It should also be noted that employing timed tests to determine neurological impairments in patients with OCD is problematic (see Chapter 15).

A relatively robust index of frontal lobe functioning is performance on verbal fluency tests. These typically involve the generation of word exemplars from a given category in a limited time period. Frontal lesions, irrespective of laterality, tend to depress scores; however, left frontal lesions appear to result in more severe impairment than right (Miceli et al., 1981; Perret, 1974). Repetition of words is thought to reflect perseveration; however, this might be attributed to short-term memory impairment resulting in the subject being unable to keep track of words already said (Estes, 1974). 'Set' tests (e.g. Newcombe, 1969) are a variation of the standard verbal fluency test, in which the subject is requested to generate exemplars from alternate categories (e.g. colours, animals). An inability to shift categories swiftly will depress the test score.

Head, Bolton & Hymas (1989) found that OCD patients produced significantly fewer words beginning with 's', compared with non-clinical controls; however, no differences were found with respect to perseverative errors. Christensen et al. (1992) found that OCD patients were significantly inferior to non-clinical controls on a test of verbal fluency, but only when outliers were included in the analysis. Neither Head, Bolton & Hymas (1989) or Christensen et al. (1992) report a correlational analysis involving neuropsychological indices and symptom severity; however, Harvey (1987) administered an alternate category verbal fluency test to 19 DSM-III OCD patients. Set test scores were negatively correlated with LOI scores (i.e. fewer set shifts were made by patients with more severe OCD). Collectively, these results provide modest support for frontal abnormalities in OCD; however, it should be noted that verbal fluency tests are timed tests, posing problems of interpretation.

The Money Road Map Test (Money, 1976; Lezak, 1983) is a test of directional orientation. Butters, Soeldner & Fedio (1972) compared Road Map performance of patients from four localised lesion groups (right parietal and temporal, left frontal and temporal); patients with left frontal lesions showed greatest levels of impairment. Poor performance may reflect the visuo-spatial demand associated with mental rotations, however, general difficulty shifting set will also depress scores on a test requiring frequent changes of left–right orientation.

Behar et al. (1984) administered the Road Map Test to 16 adolescents with OCD and 16 non-clinical controls matched for age, sex, race, handedness, and IQ. OCD patients with secondary depression were not excluded from the study. OCD patients made significantly more errors than control subjects; however, neuropsychological test indices did not correlate with an anatomical measure, ventricular brain ratio. Cox, Fedio & Rapoport (1989) describe an extension of the Behar study. It is assumed that additional subjects were recruited to enlarge the sample size to 42 patients and 35 controls. Inclusion criteria were unchanged. More left–right errors were detected in the patient group. The largest discrepancy between OCD subjects and controls was reported when left–right judgements had to be made in an inverted direction (i.e. when subjects had to imagine travelling in a direction incongruent with body position). Finally, Head, Bolton & Hymas (1989) found that their adult OCD patients produced significantly more errors on the Road Map Test compared to non-clinical controls.

Milner (1965, 1969) was the first to demonstrate how maze learning tests could be employed to reveal the restricted ability of frontal lobe patients to carry out simple instructions in spite of verbal comprehension. As above, poor performance might be attributable to set shifting difficulties, for example, switching to an alternative response pattern after making a mistake. However, poor performance might also be attributed to other factors such as an inability to attend to rules, visuo-spatial memory impairment, or motor functioning. It is not surprising therefore, to discover that Milner also reported deficits in patients with bilateral hippocampal lesions, while others have shown deficits associated with temporal and parietal lobe disorder (Fedio et al., 1979; Milner & Teuber, 1968). The Austin Maze (Walsh, 1978) is employed to test maze learning. Using a metal-tipped pen, the subject must learn, by trial and error, an invisible pathway connecting a starting point and goal. Correct moves are signalled by a tone or changes in a light display. Horizontal moves are not accepted.

Adolescent OCD patients (Behar et al., 1984; Cox, Fedio & Rapoport, 1989) produce more route errors and rule breaks on the Maze Learning Task compared with matched non-clinical controls. Rettew et al. (1991) administered the Maze Learning Task to 21 female patients with trichotillomania (TTM), and three age and sex matched control groups, comprised of 12 OCD patients, 17 anxiety patients, and 16 non-clinical individuals. OCD patients showed significantly more rule breaks than non-clinical controls; however, this was also true of the TTM and anxiety groups. This suggests that rule breaking is associated with mood disturbance (or clinical status), rather than a frontal deficit related specifically to OCD.

In sum, there is some evidence to suggest that OCD patients are impaired on the Maze Learning Task; however, a 'set shifting' deficit is only one of several that might account for poor performance. As with the Money Road Map Task, the contribution of impaired visuo-spatial functioning must also be considered, especially in the context of results reported in the previous chapter (Zielinski, Taylor & Juzwin, 1991). Finally, the results of Rettew et al. (1991) weaken arguments favouring a deficit specific to OCD.

The Trail Making Test (War Department, 1944) is another example of a procedure thought to be sensitive to set shifting difficulties. The essential part of the test involves drawing lines connecting a letter sequence and a number sequence, while alternating between the two. Aranowitz et al. (in press) compared the performance of 31 patients with OCD and 22 normal controls on this task (see previous chapter for further details). The OCD group showed mild impairment relative to controls.

The power to think in abstract (rather than concrete) terms is considered to be a relatively recent evolutionary development. As such, conceptual thinking has been linked closely with the frontal lobes. The Halstead Category Test measures 'abstract concept formation' (Pendleton & Heaton, 1982) and the ability to maintain attention on a lengthy task. It also has a visuo-spatial component correlating most highly with Block Design and Picture Arrangement subtests of the WAIS (Lansdell & Donelly, 1977). Flor-Henry et al. (1979) employed the Halstead Category Test to examine higher level functioning in 11 obsessional syndrome patients and 11 non-clinical controls matched for age, years in education, handedness, and WAIS full scale IQ. OCD patients were significantly impaired on this test compared with controls. Christensen et al. (1992)

report similar findings, in so far as OCD subjects produced more errors on the Booklet Category Test (Section I–IV) than non-clinical controls.

The Stroop Test (Stroop, 1935) is a timed task, thought to measure the ease with which an individual can shift set to conform to changing demand (Lezak, 1983). The essential feature of the task involves reading colour words (e.g. the word 'blue') in incongruent coloured print. Performance of this task also requires the inhibition of inappropriate responding. Significant differences in test performance were found between OCD patients and normal controls (Martinot et al., 1990). Moreover, cerebral glucose metabolic rates as determined by PET scan were negatively correlated with interference scores. Thus, lower rates of metabolism were associated with more errors in the interference subtest. It should be noted, however, that many of the patients in this study were medicated. In addition, PET scan results showed that the OCD patients exhibited cortical hypometabolism. This is a rather unusual finding, in so far as most other PET scan investigations have revealed cortical hypermetabolism.

The final piece of evidence suggesting frontal involvement in OCD is derived from performance on time estimation tasks. It has been suggested that in order to estimate a fixed time period (e.g. 60 seconds), an individual must create a temporal marker, i.e. the equivalent of a cognitive alarm that is activated in due course (Shallice & Burgess, 1991). The creation and activation of temporal markers is associated with frontal lobe functioning in the context of prospective memory. The hyperfrontality account of OCD proposed by Insel & Winslow (1990) is compatible with the notion that, once created, temporal markers will be more readily activated in OCD patients. This issue is given more thorough consideration in Chapter 22. The frequent activation of temporal markers might impair performance on time estimation tasks, favouring the underestimate of time durations. Flor-Henry et al. (1979) found significant differences with respect to minute estimation deviations from 60 seconds between OCD patients and normal controls. The mean figure for patients was 36.364, compared with 46.60 for non-clinical controls. Although of some theoretical interest, this single demonstration of distorted time estimation cannot be considered strong evidence for abnormal frontal lobe functioning.

Chapter 15

NEUROPSYCHOLOGICAL INVESTIGATIONS: AN EVALUATION

OTHER NEUROPSYCHOLOGICAL TESTS

A number of other neuropsychological tests have detected relatively consistent deficits in patients with OCD. The most important of these are tests of tactual performance (Flor-Henry et al., 1979; Christensen et al., 1992; Insel et al., 1983a; Ludlow et al., 1989) and the Block Design subtest of the WAIS (Christensen et al., 1992; Head, Bolton & Hymas, 1989; Keller, 1989). With the exception of the Ludlow et al. (1989) study, all of the other tests described above were timed (i.e. required completion within a set duration). Unfortunately, interpretation of timed tests given to OCD patients is fraught with difficulties. OCD patients often exhibit 'slowness' which might be attributable to non-neurological factors (cf. Veale, 1993). For example, test performance might be interrupted or delayed by the occurrence of intrusive thoughts. On the other hand, personality characteristics reflecting either meticulousness or indecision could delay task performance significantly. To date, only one investigation using timed tests has attempted to control for either of these factors (cf. Veale et al., submitted).

Data collected by Christensen et al. (1992) strongly suggest that timed tests should only be employed under rigorously controlled conditions. In order to assess the impact of time restrictions on test scores, timed tests were selected from the Multidimensional Aptitude Battery (Jackson, 1984). These consisted of two verbal subtests (Comprehension and Similarities) and two visuo-spatial subtests (Spatial and Object Assembly). When OCD and control group performance was compared within a seven-minute condition, groups differed significantly on all subtests with the exception of Object Assembly. When OCD and control group performance was compared with respect to an extended 12-minute condition, only similarities and spatial subtests proved to be significantly different;

moreover, significance levels had dropped from the 0.005 level to the 0.05 level.

Similar findings were also found with respect to WAIS Block Design (BD) performance. Christensen et al. (1992) found that the performance of OCD patients and non-clinical controls was significantly different; however, when speed-related bonus points were omitted from the scoring procedure, this difference disappeared. Clearly, the conventional scoring of the BD subtest of the WAIS is misleading when applied to an obsessional population. Low scores are more likely to reflect the phenomenological features of OCD, rather than an underlying right parietal lobe deficit.

In view of the above, the results of numerous other timed tests purporting to reflect neuropsychological test deficits in obsessional patients must be treated with due caution. These include performance on the Purdue Pegboard (a test of manual dexterity), WAIS Digit Symbol (Flor-Henry et al., 1979), and WISC-R/WAIS-R Object Assembly (Keller et al., 1989).

MNESTIC DEFICITS AND OCD EVALUATED

With respect to clinical and non-clinical checkers, the mnestic deficit hypothesis suggests that the following conditions are necessary for the emergence of doubt. First, an action must take place. Second, the individual must question whether the action occurred (or at least whether the action occurred in a particular form), and finally the individual must experience a retrieval failure. In its strong form, the mnestic deficit hypothesis suggests that the retrieval failure is attributable to a neurological abnormality. In its weaker form, the mnestic deficit hypothesis suggests that retrieval failure occurs secondary to anxiety; however, the reader is reminded that many of the neuropsychological test indices cited above were not correlated with measures of anxiety or depression. Although further investigations employing clinically anxious controls would be desirable, there is sufficient evidence to suggest that the memory functioning of some obsessional individuals is in fact impaired.

The reader is reminded that the most consistent memory deficits detected in OCD patients are associated with visual and visuo-spatial functioning. Although such deficits might be attributed to problems in several structures and systems in the brain, most of the authors cited above suggest that their key findings are consistent with 'basal ganglia accounts' of OCD. Boone et al. (1991) point out that basal ganglia lesions are associated with prominent visuo-spatial deficits (Boller et al., 1984;

Bowen, Hoehn & Yahr, 1972; Chiu et al., 1986) while Zielinski, Taylor & Juzwin (1991) suggest that visuo-spatial deficits are also detectable in basal ganglia disorders; in particular non-demented Parkinson's disease (Pirozzolo et al., 1982) and Tourette's Syndrome (Golden, 1984). Christensen et al. (1992) conclude that their results implicate limbic and paralimbic regions of the right hemisphere. Nevertheless, they go on to state that their results are also broadly consistent with the frontal lobe-limbic-basal ganglia hypothesis as currently formulated. The basal ganglia, and the role of basal ganglia structures in the development of OCD are given full consideration in Chapters 21 and 22.

Although the mnestic deficit hypothesis is appealing, it has a number of weaknesses that compromise its significance with respect to a general theory of obsessional behaviour. As reported earlier, there is no evidence to suggest that memory impairment is correlated with symptom severity. Therefore, mnestic deficits should not be considered causal with respect to compulsive checking. In addition, much of the evidence suggesting visual and visuo-spatial memory deficits in OCD has been derived from studies using experimental groups with mixed symptom profiles. It is unclear why mnestic deficits should also be characteristic of individuals with predominantly washing compulsions. On the other hand, it is perhaps conceivable that the mere presence of checking (albeit of secondary importance to washing), will be indicative of comorbid memory impairment.

More perplexing still is the specificity of checking behaviours. If mnestic impairment were causal, then one would expect OCD patients to exhibit a broad range of checking behaviours, rather than the narrow range commonly described in the literature (e.g. light switches, front doors etc.). Such specificity strongly suggests that metacognitive factors are of greater importance. However, the specificity of checking behaviours might be explained from a mnestic deficit perspective with recourse to interference theory (McGeough & MacDonald, 1931), which suggests that 'accuracy of recollection' is inversely related to stimulus similarity. Interference theory suggests that frequently performed actions lacking distinctiveness, such as those commonly reported by checkers, would be those most likely to provoke doubts in individuals with mnestic impairment.

Although memory deficits might be detectable in checkers, these deficits may not be the cognitive substrate of doubting. It is possible that OCD is associated with general neuropsychological impairment, and memory deficits are merely one example of a potentially wide and non-specific range; however, a more penetrating criticism of the mnestic deficit hypothesis can be derived from clinical experience, namely, that doubt can be observed in obsessional patients when memory functioning is not a relevant factor. The most compelling example would be how some checkers are able to look at a switch in the 'off' position, while continuing to doubt that the switch is turned off. Under such circumstances, the quality of memory has little to do with the experience of doubt. The problem appears to be best conceptualised in terms of meta-cognitions ('I can see that it's off, but it could be a trick of the light'), or an inability to process the information properly. With respect to the latter, attentional problems and a breakdown of automatic processing functions have been implicated (Watts, submitted). This phenomenon of maintaining doubt in the presence of decisive, and usually doubt-reducing information, has been described as a defect in knowing or epistemological sense (Rapoport, 1989a; Wise & Rapoport, 1989).

As suggested above, the fact that memory deficits are detectable in checkers does not mean that such deficits are the cognitive substrate of doubting. Metacognitive factors, for example, 'confidence in memory', may be of equal or even greater importance. A further alternative account of doubting implicates a capacity of the processing system described as 'reality monitoring'; that is, the ability to distinguish mental representations of actions from genuine memories of the same. This deficit has clear parallels with concepts such as thought–action fusion (see Chapter 10). Unfortunately, attempts to demonstrate reality-monitoring deficits in 'checkers' have yielded mixed results (Sher, Frost & Otto, 1983; McNally & Kohlbeck, 1993; Ecker & Engelkamp, submitted); nevertheless, both OCD patients and non-clinical checkers have a tendency to make false positive errors on recognition tasks (Zielinski, Taylor & Juzwin, 1991; Rubenstein et al., 1993), a performance characteristic that might be attributable to poor reality-monitoring skills.

In sum, the mnestic deficit hypothesis suggests that poor memory may be the cognitive substrate of doubt relating to past actions. Neuropsychological investigations suggest that memory impairment is characteristic of non-clinical checkers and individuals with OCD. Moreover, impairment demonstrated in laboratory settings cannot be attributed to anxiety or mood effects. Although some studies have yielded negative results, the literature suggests that visual memory functioning, spatial memory functioning, and 'memory for actions' are those capacities most consistently affected. In addition, it is of some interest to note that many of the tests of frontal lobe functioning that yielded positive results were also, to a lesser extent, tests of visuo-spatial and motor functioning. As such, further modest support for the association between visuo-spatial deficits and OCD can be derived from these studies.

Although the mnestic deficit hypothesis is appealing, it has several weaknesses. There is little evidence to suggest that memory impairment causes compulsive checking; OCD may be associated with a diffuse syndrome of deficits, and memory impairment may have no special significance. In addition, obsessional doubt often occurs under conditions where memory functioning is not relevant. At this stage, therefore, it is unwise to suggest that memory impairment explains the presence of doubt in OCD; nevertheless, it is possible that memory impairment serves as a contributory factor in many cases. For example, deficits may act as a vulnerability factor, where occasional errors serve to amplify existing worries (e.g. 'I left the front door wide open two years ago, the same thing could easily happen again'). Finally, an exciting *speculative* prospect, is the identification of a subgroup for whom memory deficits are of central importance with respect to presenting symptoms (cf. Tallis, 1995; Rubenstein et al., 1993).

FRONTAL LOBE DEFECTS AND OCD EVALUATED

Before evaluating the results of neuropsychological tests of frontal lobe functioning in OCD, a few general points need to be made. The frontal lobes represent an extremely large area of the brain, and frontal lobe damage has been associated with a wide range of cognitive and behavioural deficits (Lezak, 1983). As a general statement, to suggest that OCD phenomena are related in some way to frontal lobe functioning is relatively meaningless. It would be extraordinary if this was not the case. Therefore, any speculation about the relationship between frontal lobe functioning and obsessional phenomena must be specific to be of any value at all.

When neuropsychologists refer to 'frontal tests', they are referring to a group of tests that are poorly performed by individuals with frontal lobe damage. Such damage is often associated with a general deterioration of functioning reflected in decreased levels of biological activity (cf. Upadhyaya et al., 1990). Scanning studies have demonstrated that OCD patients show the exact opposite pattern, with increased metabolic rates in the caudate nuclei and orbital gyri (see Chapter 6). Moreover, Baxter et al. (1987) suggest that patients with frontal lobe damage exhibit personality features (e.g. disinhibition, lack of appropriate concern for others) that are the exact opposite of those characteristic of individuals with OCD. It is therefore intriguing that tests sensitive to frontal lobe damage have been those most frequently chosen to test for cognitive deficits in OCD, a disorder occupying the opposite poles of both biological and phenomenological continua.

In spite of the obvious differences that exist between frontal lobe patients and individuals with OCD, both groups are similar with respect to the presence of repetitive or perseverative behaviours; however, it is unclear whether similar neuropsychological test profiles indicate a common neurological substrate or mechanism. It is possible that both hypofrontality, and hyperfrontality produce set shifting deficits, but for very different reasons.

With the exception of set shifting difficulties, neuropsychological testing of frontal lobe functioning in patients with OCD has not yielded compelling results. Flor-Henry et al. (1979) report that obsessional syndrome patients tend to underestimate the passage of time; although consistent with contemporary theories of frontal lobe functioning, the test results of 11 patients are insufficient to substantiate a 'temporal marker' theory of OCD (see Chapter 22). The poor verbal fluency performance of patients with OCD reported by Head, Bolton & Hymas (1989) might have been influenced by the large number of slow patients included in the test sample. Moreover, evidence for verbal fluency deficits derived from other sources is weak (cf. Christensen et al., 1992). Employing the Tower of London test, Veale et al. (submitted) found that obsessional patients did not exhibit any general planning deficits; moreover, those deficits that were detected could be attributable to the effects of state anxiety. Only two tasks have revealed conceptual or abstract thinking deficits in OCD (Flor-Henry et al., 1979; Christensen et al., 1992); moreover, one of these, the Halstead Category Test, makes strong demands on visuo-spatial skills. Given that OCD patients may suffer from modest visuo-spatial deficits, results cannot be confidently attributed to abstract thinking problems alone.

Evidence for set shifting difficulties in OCD patients is stronger, but by no means conclusive. Three studies have shown that OCD patients are impaired on the WCST relative to controls (Head, Bolton & Hymas, 1989; Cox, Fedio & Rapoport, 1989; Christensen et al., 1992). A further study has shown a systematic and positive relationship between symptom severity and WCST scores (Harvey, 1987). Unfortunately, the cogency of these findings is compromised by recent criticism of the Wisconsin test. Maze learning and stylus maze studies also provide support for the set shifting hypothesis, but this evidence is weaker still. Such tests are equally a test of visuo-spatial and/or motor functioning. Veale et al. (submitted) provide the strongest evidence for set shifting difficulties in OCD patients, by employing a relatively pure measure included in the CANTAB battery.

As with the mnestic deficit hypothesis, a set shifting account of OCD has obvious weaknesses. In particular, it is difficult to understand why a general 'set shifting' problem should potentiate specific behaviours such as washing and checking. If OCD patients share a deficit with frontal lobe patients, one would expect such a deficit to affect a much wider range of behaviours. Moreover, there is, as yet, insufficient evidence to suggest a causal relationship between 'frontal' cognitive deficits and symptom severity. Again, we must conclude that such deficits that have been described are, at best, contributory only.

Taken together, the results of *all* the tests cited above seem to suggest that OCD patients exhibit impaired performance on tests that are sensitive to frontal lobe damage; however, on close inspection, the results are less convincing. In spite of these general criticisms, there is modest support for a set shifting deficit in OCD; however, the exact relationship between 'rigidity of set' and the occurrence of repetitive behaviours remains unclear, especially with respect to behavioural specificity. More optimistically, this pattern of results may be consistent with biological evidence, in so far as impairment of the basal ganglia is related to perseveration (Mettler, 1955).

A final, but important, general point needs to be made with respect to all of the above neuropsychological tests. To date, there have only been two neuropsychological investigations employing traditional tests that have included a clinical control group. Cohen et al. (submitted) assessed neuropsychological test performance in 65 patients with OCD, 17 social phobics, and 32 normal controls. All participants were given an extensive battery consisting of selected WAIS-R subtests, the Matching Familiar Figures Tests, The Benton Visual Retention Test, and the Trail Making Test. Impaired functioning was demonstrated in both patient groups compared to normal controls. However, only one significant difference emerged between patients with OCD and social phobics, on the Trail Making Test. In this particular case, social phobics performed significantly worse than the OCD patients.

Clearly, the above demonstrates the importance of including a clinical control group in neuropsychological investigations of patients with OCD. It is of course possible that all of the performance deficits so far described in the literature are simply attributable to anxiety. Indeed, a precedent already exists with respect to the test anxiety literature (Flett & Blankstein, 1994). Notwithstanding this criticism, a pattern of deficits does seem to be emerging from neuropsychological investigations, and the specificity of this pattern may go some way towards supporting cognitive deficit accounts of OCD.

Chapter 16

CATEGORY FORMATION AND UNDERINCLUSION

UNDERINCLUSION

Before concluding this section, a final chapter is devoted to the literature on category formation. This has developed somewhat independently of mainstream neuropsychology, and is subsequently discussed separately.

Work relating to category definition in obsessionals has been dominated by the concept of 'underinclusion' (Reed, 1969a). The presence of this particular cognitive feature was anticipated by Reed (1968), who suggested that the formal characteristics of obsessional thinking are related to an inability to organise and integrate experience. This impairment results in compensatory overdefining of category boundaries. In this chapter, evidence for the cognitive characteristic of underinclusion is reviewed. Although early work was conducted on anancasts, rather than individuals with OCD, there has been some recent interest in investigating the phenomenon in both patients with OCD, and non-clinical individuals exhibiting some obsessional symptoms.

Reed's first empirical investigation confirmed his clinical observations (Reed, 1969a). Subjects consisted of 25 patients suffering from obsessional personality disorder, 25 psychiatric controls, and 25 normal controls. Although formal psychometric assessment of IQ was not undertaken, triads were matched for number of years in full-time education. Patients were diagnosed according to Schneider's (1958) criteria. Members of the obsessional group received a primary classification of 'anancastic personality disorder', and the psychiatric controls received various Schneiderian personality disorder diagnoses; however, 'attention-seeking psychopaths' were the predominant subgroup. A cognitive test of the 'essentials' type was developed to investigate differences between groups. A concept word, for example 'table', was presented together with five other words (e.g. cloth, vase, legs, drawer, top), and subjects were asked to decide which of the five were essential to the concept. Fourteen concept words were presented, ranging from the concrete (e.g. knife) to the abstract (e.g. sin). The obsessional patients chose significantly fewer words (mean = 25.80) than the psychiatric (30.64) and normal (29.4) controls ($p < .001$). When analysing error type, it was found that obsessionals were more likely to overdefine (i.e. select too few alternatives), compared to the non-obsessional and normal groups ($p < .001$).

The 'essentials' test described above is a task of deductive reasoning in that the subject deduces membership of a class that is already given. However, Reed (1969b) then examined performance on a task of inductive reasoning, requiring the subject to induce classes from an array of possible members. Reed predicted that when required to produce their own categorical systems, the obsessional patients would overspecify, minimising category membership and producing a greater number of classes. Subjects consisted of 10 patients suffering from obsessional personality disorder, 10 matched psychiatric controls, and 10 matched normal subjects. Again, intellectual functioning was matched according to the number of years spent in full-time education. The members of the psychiatric control group were diagnosed as 'attention-seeking psychopaths' or 'hysterics', according to Schneiderian criteria. Subjects were given the Vygotsky test of concept formation, which involves the categorisation of 22 blocks, varying according to colour, shape, and size. First, subjects were requested to group the blocks into 'families', and then they were asked to group them using the smallest number of categories possible.

The results of the first trial revealed no significant differences between normal and psychiatric control groups. However, normals and obsessionals differed significantly ($p < .02$) in the predicted direction, with the obsessionals producing more categories. Although obsessionals produced more categories than psychiatric controls, this result failed to reach significance, but showed a modest trend ($p < .09$). When asked to produce the smallest number of categories possible, no significant differences were found between normals and psychiatric controls. However, significant differences were found between obsessionals and normals ($p < .016$), and obsessionals and psychiatric controls ($p < .03$). Differences were in the predicted direction, with the obsessional group forming more categories. Reed notes that during testing, 'anancastic subjects betrayed more indecision in deciding upon categories than did the controls, and more anxiety as to the logic or aptness of those categories after they had arrived at a decision' (p. 789). Further questioning revealed that obsessionals' criteria for categories were qualitatively different from controls, in that they considered 'too many complicating features'. In effect, they were more likely to be distracted by irrelevant detail.

Reed's findings are consistent with earlier work conducted by Hamilton (1957), whose principal concern was reaction to ambiguity. Subjects included in the study were 20 obsessionals, 20 conversion hysterics, 22 anxiety state patients, and 40 normal controls. Diagnoses were established by five psychiatrists. For present purposes, the most interesting finding to emerge from this study concerned performance on a block sorting task, where 44 wooden blocks of various dimension and shape were presented to subjects. Fourteen were rectangular or triangular, five were circular, and 25 included both rectangular and circular features. Sorting categories were 'Circular', 'Rectangular', 'May be circular or rectangular, I can't decide which', and finally, 'To be sorted into separate groups afterwards'. The final category was thought to be particularly sensitive to differences between obsessional subjects and conversion hysterics. This expectation was based on clinical observations and experimental evidence suggesting that obsessionals are concerned with minute differences (Rosenberg, 1953), whereas conversion hysterics tend to gloss over differences (Davis, 1948). No differences were found between obsessionals and normal controls. Obsessionals made significantly less ($p < 0.05$) 'can't decide' responses than those with anxiety states. However, obsessionals and conversion hysterics were significantly differentiated ($p < 0.05$) by their scores on the final 'To be sorted into separate groups afterwards' category. Conversion hysterics classified by using a few, mutually exclusive categories, while obsessionals classified using a large number of small categories. Hamilton suggests that this style of categorising was also evident when obsessionals were classifying Ambiguous Drawings. Given the opportunity, the obsessional patients preferred to split a 'bad fit' group into subsidiary groups.

Although the obsessional patients produced higher scores ($\mu = 24.90$) on the final block sorting category than controls (18.80), anxiety state patients (18.73), and conversion hysterics (17.25), the reader is reminded that it is only the comparison with the latter group which yielded a significant probability value.

Foa & Steketee (1979) suggested that the obsessional excessive concern with detail would lead to overinclusion, rather than underinclusion. An example of obsessional overinclusion might be the concept of contamination. For most non-clinical individuals, the category of contaminating objects will be relatively small, while for the obsessional, the sources of contamination are perceived as many and varied, producing a broad category with ill-defined, rather than stringent boundaries. However, subsequent investigations provided the most thorough vindication of underinclusion to date (Persons & Foa, 1984). Subjects were seven patients who currently, or at some time, met DSM-III criteria for OCD, and also scored 10 or above on the MOCI. The 11 control patients had never met diagnostic criteria for OCD, and scored less than 10 on the MOCI. The OCD and clinical control groups did not differ with regard to age, Wechsler Adult Intelligence Scale (WAIS) (Wechsler, 1955) vocabulary, and state anxiety (Spielberger et al., 1980). However, they did differ significantly on the Beck Depression Inventory (BDI) (Beck, 1972) scores ($p < 0.01$). All subjects were given four decks of cards. Each card carried a written description of a particular object or situation. Each deck included a range of objects and situations, which were to be sorted according to particular category headings. Two neutral categories, 'Size' and 'Temperature', and two corresponding to the most common fears of OCD patients 'Contamination' and 'Making serious or dangerous mistakes', were included in the study. Results showed that OCD patients made more piles than clinical controls ($p < 0.05$), and took more time to accomplish the task ($p < 0.01$). OCD subjects took significantly longer to sort cards associated with fears than neutral cards ($p < 0.01$), while non-OCD subjects showed roughly equivalent times. Persons & Foa (1984) acknowledge that higher levels of depression in the obsessional group may have accounted for the extended time required in which to complete the sorting task. They also suggest that depression might account for the emergence of subsidiary groups. It is unlikely, however, that higher levels of depression can account for the greater time requirement displayed by obsessionals when sorting feared items compared to neutral items.

The Persons & Foa (1984) study has been replicated by Frost et al. (1988) using a non-clinical population. Subjects were students scoring < 5 or > 9 on the MOCI. Fifteen low compulsives and nine high compulsives were identified for inclusion. High compulsives did not sort cards into more categories than low compulsives, and results are therefore inconsistent with the original study.

Jakes (1992) has used Reed's essentials task, and the Persons and Foa card sort, to investigate underinclusion in a clinical sample. His study included five groups of 10 subjects, matched for sex, age, and intelligence, estimated on the basis of Mill-Hill vocabulary scores (Raven, 1958). His groups were as follows: obsessionals with predominantly checking compulsions, obsessionals with predominantly cleaning compulsions, a mixed obsessional patient group in remission, a mixed anxiety state psychiatric control group, and a group of non-clinical controls. Analyses have shown no significant differences between groups.

In sum, the characteristic of underinclusion has been investigated empirically by several authors. Reed has found supportive evidence on the 'essentials' (Reed, 1969a) and Vygotsky tasks (Reed, 1969b), although his samples were anancasts rather than patients with OCD. Hamilton (1957) reports similar findings, using 'obsessional' subjects. Further evidence has been collected by Persons & Foa (1984), who have shown that patients with OCD tend to create more categories in a sorting task.

Failures to derive evidence for underinclusion come from two sources. Frost et al. (1988) were unable to find underinclusion effects in a non-clinical compulsive group, whereas Jakes (1992) was unable to find support for the underinclusion hypothesis using clinical subjects.

Reed's suggestion that 'obsessionals' have a fundamental cognitive deficit with respect to the organisation and integration of perceptual experience has some contemporary resonance. Doubt-related phenomena, and the information-processing functions of the basal ganglia (see Chapters 2 and 22) might be considered consistent. Moreover, the suggestion that compensatory strategies might develop in such individuals is also plausible. However, the degree to which 'underinclusion' reflects compensation for poor integration of experience must be questioned. In addition, it is difficult to see how a tendency to define small categories might contribute with respect to the development of most of the symptoms of OCD, particularly in the absence of OCPD. Indeed, in some cases, one might expect an underinclusive thinking style to have a beneficial effect. For example, attention to detail in compulsive checkers might facilitate the recollection of past actions by increasing distinctiveness. This would presumably ameliorate doubt.

PSYCHOLOGICAL TREATMENT

Chapter 17

GENERAL CONSIDERATIONS

INTRODUCTION

This chapter is concerned with the treatment of OCD employing cognitive-behavioural methods. The behavioural treatment of OCD has been described in considerable detail by numerous practitioners, and the reader is referred to Steketee (1993) for a comprehensive and practical guide. Although the present chapter contains descriptions of behavioural techniques, an effort is made to understand their efficacy from a cognitive perspective. In addition to the above, techniques of a purely cognitive nature are given due consideration. These are closely related to the cognitive formulations described in Chapter 9. The application of cognitive techniques is subsequently evaluated. Finally, a number of suggestions are made throughout the chapter with respect to clinical practice.

ENGAGING THE PATIENT

Before providing a summary of intervention procedures employed in the treatment of OCD, it is necessary to consider the more general issue of engaging the patient. Many clinicians have noted that individuals with OCD may develop elaborate means of disguising their symptoms. In some cases, the afflicted individual's family and work colleagues may be completely unaware of their difficulties. The average time to elapse between onset and first contact with a clinician is thought to be around 7.5 years (Pollitt, 1957; Yaryura-Tobias & Neziroglu, 1983, p. 20), suggesting considerable resistance to consulting a health professional. Moreover, once clinical contact has been established, the affected individual may not disclose obsessional symptoms, but instead may prefer to report the ostensibly more 'acceptable' features of generalised anxiety or depression. Indeed, the reader is reminded that as early as 1875, Legrand de Saulle suggested that the reason for hospital admission would more likely be depression than obsessional behaviour. Resistance to seeking professional help is also evident in the prevalence estimates based on community samples (Myers et al., 1984; Robins et al., 1984), which dramatically exceed those based on the incidence observed in the clinic (e.g. Rudin, 1953).

There are a number of factors that account for the 'hidden morbidity' of OCD. First, a lack of public awareness has resulted in the failure of many sufferers to construe their behaviour as a recognisable clinical condition that may be treatable. In the absence of such a framework, there are few incentives to seek a medical consultation. This problem may also be compounded by a complementary lack of awareness in the medical profession itself. It is the author's impression that many sufferers report a history of poor primary care. The formation of charities such as the OCD Foundation in the United States, and Obsessive Action in the UK, promise to redress this situation with the provision of information for both sufferers and health professionals alike. Addresses are given in an Appendix at the back of this volume.

In addition to the above, there is perhaps a more fundamental reason to account for the obsessional patient's reluctance to seek help. OCD is unique, in that the individual can exhibit quite bizarre symptoms while retaining relatively intact insight. The result of this is considerable embarrassment. Moreover, the patient often fears that the symptoms of OCD are indicative of an immanent mental decline, possibly ending with insanity. Accompanying fears of 'breakdown' or forcible incarceration often result in extreme reticence. Finally, intrusive thoughts are only intrusive to the extent that they are unacceptable to the individual. Admitting to thoughts that are considered morally reprehensible will clearly be difficult and painful for the individual concerned.

In view of the above, the provision of education about the nature of OCD is essential. Discussion of obsessional symptoms as occupying the extreme end of a normal continuum of phenomena can serve to reassure the patient that he or she is not qualitatively 'abnormal'. Giving patients copies of Rachman & de Silva's (1978) seminal paper on normal and abnormal obsessions can be very useful to this end with respect to intrusive thoughts. In addition, stressing that OCD is distinct from conditions such as schizophrenia can serve to facilitate self-disclosure. Even so, it is often the case that sufferers will choose to disclose symptoms slowly, over a period of time, when rapport and confidence in the therapist improves. It is the author's impression that patients will more readily report behaviours than underlying cognitions. Cases 17.1 and 17.2 serve to illustrate this point.

Case 17.1

A young man in his late twenties was referred with checking compulsions and a fear of harming others. It eventually transpired that his most trouble-some symptom was intrusive thoughts about sexually abusing his girlfriend's 3-year-old child. He was reluctant to admit to this thought earlier in therapy, fearing that he might be considered a paedophile.

Case 17.2

A young man in his late teens was referred with a range of compulsive behaviours. These included the repetitive cleaning of his spectacles. At first he only reported that this behaviour reflected his high standards. Eventually, he disclosed that a mark on his spectacles would impair his visual acuity, and that this might cause him to misinterpret facial expressions. He feared that an inappropriate response on his part would cause offence. He was reluctant to admit to these thoughts on account of their 'absurdity'.

Although providing patients with information about OCD is highly recommended, even this can be fraught with problems. Many patients express concern that reading about OCD will make them more anxious, or result in the emergence of new symptoms. Again, constructive reassurance that this is unlikely to happen will be necessary. Framing this in terms of a behavioural experiment can be a useful first exercise in demonstrating the inaccuracy of appraisals and beliefs. Although reading educational material can sometimes exacerbate symptoms, it is the author's impression that this only occurs in approximately 1–2% of patients.

COGNITIVE-BEHAVIOURAL INTERVENTIONS

It was suggested in Chapter 1 that the division between cognitive and behavioural psychologies is somewhat artificial, reflecting historical and academic prejudices rather than an actual divide. This argument is particularly valid with respect to psychotherapy, where, of *necessity*, the terms 'cognitive' and 'behavioural' have been linked together. Although cognitive and behavioural interventions have evolved from separate academic traditions, they share a number of similarities.

First, both approaches are skills based, requiring the application of techniques to alleviate symptoms; however, it should also be noted that recent developments in cognitive therapy show a marked shift away from the learning of symptom control skills as an end in themselves. Rather, strategies are applied in order to test and modify existing unhelpful beliefs. Second, the 'relationship' between therapist and patient, a cornerstone of the psychoanalytic approach, is not considered essential as an agent of change in either cognitive or behavioural therapy. Nevertheless, the importance of non-specific factors is recognised in the behavioural literature and many would argue that a defining feature of cognitive therapy is a type of relationship characterised by guided discovery and the 'Socratic method' (Wells, personal communication). Third, both behavioural and cognitive therapy tend to give special importance to proximal antecedents of behaviour and maintaining factors. Distal antecedents may be discussed, but do not necessarily influence the intervention procedure. Finally, both cognitive and behavioural approaches reject the notion of a 'dynamic unconscious', as formulated within the psychoanalytic tradition. As such, 'insight', in the psychoanalytic sense, is not viewed as a necessary condition for therapeutic change.

Before discussing intervention procedures, it will be judicious to provide a brief account of the behavioural, or learning, theory of OCD. Although learning theory has provided several models that account for 'stereotypical' behaviour, the following has become the dominant model. It has been suggested that obsessions serve as anxiety-evoking stimuli, and that compulsions are undertaken in order to reduce anxiety (Rachman & Hodgson, 1980). Anxiety reduction is reinforcing and therefore increases the likelihood of further compulsive behaviour. This account is largely based on Mowrer's (1947) two-factor theory, which suggested that, via classical conditioning (Pavlov, 1928), a phobic individual might learn to fear a neutral (or 'conditioned') stimulus (CS) if it is paired with an intrinsically aversive (or 'unconditioned') stimulus (UCS); however, conditioned fear can be reduced by escaping from, or avoiding, the CS. Avoidance behaviour is maintained because of its reinforcing consequences. As such, avoidance behaviour obeys the principles of operant conditioning (Skinner, 1953). With respect to OCD, compulsive 'avoidance' behaviour may become fixed according to a 'learned' pattern.

In its pure form, the behavioural account has two fundamental problems. First, the process whereby obsessions become anxiety-evoking stimuli is thought to be classical conditioning; however, few patients report a conditioning experience in which obsessional thoughts become associated with an aversive event. Second, many patients report that their compulsive behaviours increase anxiety, rather than reduce it. This is particularly true of checkers and ruminators. In view of these criticisms, attempts have been made to elaborate the behavioural model in order to incorporate cognitive elements.

In spite of the above criticisms of the traditional behavioural account, there can be little doubt that behavioural therapy is an effective means of treating OCD. O'Sullivan & Marks (1991) discuss the outcome of 10 follow-up studies after exposure and response prevention treatment (Marks, Hodgson & Rachman, 1975; Mawson et al., 1982; O'Sullivan et al., 1991; Kasvikis & Marks, 1988; Roberston, 1979; Foa & Goldstein, 1978; Visset, Hoekstra & Emmelkamp, in press; Boulougouris, 1977; Meyer, Levy & Schnurer, 1974; Catts & McConaghy, 1975). Follow-up duration was one to six years, with a mean of three years. It should be noted that two cohorts, (O'Sullivan et al., 1991; Kasvikis & Marks, 1988), received exposure plus either medication or placebo, although no 'drug' effect was detectable at follow-up. Overall, 79% of patients were improved or much improved with respect to OCD symptoms.

Predictors of Poor Outcome

There are a number of factors that may limit the efficacy of behaviour therapy. Patients who are severely depressed do not seem to habituate to feared situations, even when subjected to prolonged exposure sessions (Foa, 1979); however, depression may also have the effect of decreasing motivation leading to non-compliance. Poor outcome is also associated with what Foa (1979) describes as overvalued ideas. These are strong beliefs that fears are realistic and that ritualistic behaviour actually prevents the occurrence of disastrous consequences. Foa's patients did not manifest thought disturbance characteristic of psychotic patients, but Foa notes that their overvalued ideation 'seemed to border on a delusional system' (p. 170). Concomitant Axis II diagnoses may also compromise the efficacy of behaviour therapy (cf. Rachman & Hodgson, 1980). Minichiello, Baer & Jenike (1987) suggest that schizotypal personality disorder (SPD) is a particularly significant indicator of poor prognosis. It is interesting to note that, like Foa's patients, individuals with SPD strongly believed that their rituals were necessary to prevent the occurrence of catastrophes.

Chapter 18

BEHAVIOURAL THERAPY

BEHAVIOURAL TREATMENT OF OCD

Behavioural treatment almost invariably involves the two components of exposure and response prevention. The individual is encouraged to enter feared situations, or undertake activities that evoke anxiety, while refraining from the compulsive activities that are usually employed as a means of reducing anxiety. In the absence of anxiety-reduction rituals, the individual is forced to experience (and tolerate) discomfort, which characteristically follows a course of increasing and decreasing intensity. Repetition of this procedure results in habituation of the anxiety response (cf. Lader & Wing, 1966; Rachman, 1968). Habituation is a property of the nervous system, associated with the gradual loss of a reflexive behaviour after repeated presentations of an evoking stimulus (Peeke & Petrinovich, 1984). After anxiety has 'habituated', anxiety reduction rituals become redundant. Moreover, any subsequent performance of compulsive behaviour will not be negatively reinforced, leading to extinction of the compulsive behaviour.

Initial attempts at treating OCD using behavioural techniques employed systematic desensitisation (Wolpe, 1958). This had already been successfully applied to a range of phobias. The procedure involves constructing a graded hierarchy of anxiogenic activities or situations. The individual is asked to relax while imagining the least anxiogenic activity. Rapid relaxation is usually achieved after a course of progressive muscular relaxation (cf. Jacobson, 1929). When anxiety is reduced, the next step of the hierarchy is addressed, and so on. The patient may be encouraged to undertake desensitisation exercises *in vivo*, between sessions.

Attempts at deconstructing systematic desensitisation have shown that the *sine qua non* of therapeutic change is exposure (Marks, 1990). In the treatment of OCD this element of traditional systematic desensitisation has been retained, as indeed has the graded hierarchy. However, relaxation is less commonly employed during exposure exercises. There is some evidence to suggest that relaxation may in fact impair the efficacy of exposure. Foa & Kozak (1986), for example, have suggested that some anxiety must be experienced if 'emotional processing' (cf. Rachman, 1980) is to occur. Perhaps this goes some way towards explaining why systematic desensitisation has, on the whole, produced unpredictable and unstable results when applied to OCD. At a more fundamental level, the early application of desensitisation procedures may have produced disappointing results due to a strong emphasis on imagined scenarios. Advocates of 'flooding' on the other hand, favoured *in vivo* exposure (Rachman & Hodgson, 1980, p. 354–355). In its traditional form, flooding consisted of the imagined or real life toleration of the most anxiogenic stimuli for extended periods of time.

Response prevention, or 'apotrepic therapy' as it was originally termed, was developed by Meyer in 1966, although it is of some interest to note that Janet suggested a similar approach in 1903 (cf. Pitman, 1987a). The word 'apotrepic' is derived from Greek, meaning to turn away, deter, or dissuade. Response prevention has several antecedents in the experimental literature. Perhaps the most important of these is an animal study conducted by Solomon, Kamin & Wynne (1953), who noted that avoidance behaviour could continue long after removal of an unconditioned aversive stimulus; however, prevention or punishment of avoidance will result in the swift cessation of this redundant avoidance behaviour. The traditional behavioural model of OCD suggests that compulsive behaviours can be construed as avoidance behaviours, in so far as washing or checking will allow the individual to 'avoid' the experience of anxiety (Rachman & Hodgson, 1980).

The first substantive outcome evaluation of response prevention (Meyer, Levy & Schnurer, 1974) provided encouraging results. Fifteen inpatients with OCD were prevented from engaging in their rituals. After treatment, 10 were described as asymptomatic or markedly improved, while the remaining five were judged to be 'improved'. Of 12 patients followed up over a period of six months to six years, only four patients had experienced periods of relapse.

Although there is now sufficient evidence to suggest that response prevention *per se* is a powerful therapeutic intervention, it should be noted that Meyer's original inpatient programme did involve other elements, for example, therapist modelling and social reinforcement (cf. Bandura, 1977). Participant modelling, in which the patient copies the therapist, is still recommended as an adjunct to the core elements of behaviour therapy, particularly with patients who exhibit contamination fears (cf. Roper, Rachman & Marks, 1975); however, it should be noted that modelling is not always considered essential (de Silva, 1987).

THE ROLE OF COGNITION IN BEHAVIOUR THERAPY

It has long been recognised that the efficacy of behaviour therapy must, at least in part, be attributable to changes at the cognitive level. Contemporary theories of emotion (and in particular anxiety), stress the presence of at least three loosely linked systems, relating to subjective, behavioural, and psychophysiological components (Lang, 1970, 1977, 1979). Rachman & Hodgson (1980) note that: 'Sometimes during the conduct of a flooding session the patient readily acquires the ability to engage in previously avoided activities, but the change is accompanied by persistent feelings of subjective discomfort' (p. 402). Indeed, a 'cognitive lag' is a widely recognised feature of exposure therapy. Patients will often say, for example, 'Yes, I can now touch this door handle, but I still feel dirty and still want to wash'. Explicit recognition of desynchrony in exposure sessions can be a source of constructive reassurance when patients fail to experience immediate cognitive change. Moreover, the very existence of desynchrony implies that strategies which attempt to modify cognitive appraisals directly are a legitimate means of producing therapeutic change. Of greater importance is the fact that failure to address the cognitive substrates of OCD after behavioural change has occurred may leave the individual particularly vulnerable with respect to relapse.

Foa & Kozak (1986) have suggested that exposure may be effective because relevant memories are activated, and modified by the incorporation of incompatible or 'corrective' information. Activation is inferred on the basis of physiological reactions. Therefore, a major source of incompatible information is provided by the process of habituation itself. However, another important element is that exposure alters representations of the severity and probability of harm associated with the fear-evoking stimulus. As such, the abnormal risk assessment (see Chapter 2), at the very core of all anxiety states, is modified. More recent accounts of this process have suggested that corrective information may result in the formation of new representations, which supersede the earlier dysfunctional representations in terms of accessibility and importance.

It is interesting to note that Foa & Kozak's (1986) account of the cognitive substrate of therapeutic change has some striking similarities when compared with the early writings of Breuer & Freud (1893), who suggest that 'Our observations have taught us that a [traumatic] memory ... which has hitherto provoked [hysterical] attacks, ceases to be able to do so after the process of reaction and associative correction have been applied to it under hypnosis' (p. 66). For Breuer & Freud, abnormal risk assessments are modulated when a traumatic memory 'comes alongside other experiences, which may contradict it' (p. 59).

In cognitive therapy, behavioural experiments are often employed, not as an end in themselves, but rather, as a means of testing predictions (Beck et al., 1979). The critical change is considered to be cognitive, in so far as corrective information has the effect of altering risk assessments and unhelpful beliefs. It is interesting to note that Meyer (1966) chose to attribute the success of response prevention to cognitive change: '... if the obsessional is persuaded or forced to remain in feared situations and prevented from carrying out the rituals, he may discover that the feared consequences no longer take place. Such modifications of *expectations* should result in the cessation of ritualistic behaviour' (p. 275).

It should also be noted that after Rachman & Hodgson's (1980) pioneering outcome evaluations of behaviour therapy, the authors concluded that 'therapeutic information is transmitted implicitly ... and helps modify the abnormal cognitive aspects of the person's problems' (p. 366); however, Rachman & Hodgson (1980) also suggest that Meyer's 'expectation' account is implausible, in so far as most patients with OCD do not *rationally* expect 'dreaded consequences' to occur. They do, on the other hand, expect that failure to escape a noxious situation will result in the experience of anxiety and discomfort. As such, response prevention may work by 'exposing the person's expectations of anxiety/discomfort to repeated disconfirmations' (p. 357). Although Rachman & Hodgson (1980) are correct in suggesting that patients with OCD recognise that their concerns are irrational, this effect is most probably state-dependent. Under conditions in which high levels of anxiety have been evoked, many obsessional patients do indeed expect 'dreaded consequences' to occur.

In addition to providing ideal conditions for the acquisition of corrective information, exposure and response prevention exercises will inevitably influence an individual's self-concept. By facing feared situations, and coping, the individual is perhaps forced to modify negative representations of the self. Patients often suggest that the successful accomplishment of exposure exercises is associated with increased self-esteem and self-confidence. Such changes will clearly facilitate further engagement in exposure exercises, potentiating both specific and non-specific therapeutic gains.

HETEROGENEITY AND THE APPLICABILITY OF BEHAVIOUR THERAPY

Although there are many arguments favouring the suggestion that OCD is a homogenous disorder, the predominance of particular features in particular individuals is an undeniable clinical reality. Moreover, it may be the case that exposure and response prevention should be given differential priority given a particular symptom profile. Rachman & Hodgson (1980) suggest that in cases characterised by a strong phobic element, namely individuals with contamination fears and washing compulsions, 'repeated exposures can be expected to achieve a good deal, regardless of the role of response prevention. In checking compulsions, failure to institute response prevention is likely to end in therapeutic failure' (p. 350).

The marked success of exposure with individuals who suffer from contamination fears and washing compulsions might be attributable to the predominance of physiological disturbance among the 'three systems'. Habituation to feared stimuli will therefore address a more fundamental aspect of the patient's experience of anxiety. Individuals with washing compulsions also appear to conform to the 'behavioural model' more than checkers. In the same way that a simple phobic will experience swift relief after escaping feared stimuli, so it is that washers obtain more reliable anxiety reduction when performing their rituals. This is consistent with the clinical observation that, on the whole, washers tend to ritualise for shorter durations (cf. Rachman & Hodgson, 1980, p. 128). Once habituation has occurred, escape behaviour (i.e. washing) will become automatically redundant, serving no anxiety-reducing function.

Checking, on the other hand, appears to be an altogether more complex phenomenon. Associated features such as doubting, inflated responsibility, excessive guilt, fear of criticism, and impaired memory, suggest that cognitive events and processes are of greater significance (see Chapters 2, 10, & 15). Moreover, for checkers, exposure appears to be of less relevance than response prevention. This might be attributable to the 'technical' difficulties involved when defining suitable exposure targets. For individuals with checking compulsions, discomfort is associated with the negative consequences of failing to check, rather than a discrete fear stimulus (such as a toilet seat or dustbin). This has necessitated certain modifications of the exposure procedure.

Foa et al. (1980) and Foa, Steketee & Grayson (1985), note that it is important to match the content of exposure to the patient's 'internal fear model'. Those who fear disastrous consequences, which cannot be contrived during therapy sessions, should experience accelerated improvement with the addition of imaginal exposure. Initial results showed that the addition of imaginal exposure to *in vivo* exposure procedures did not affect short-term gains; however, the addition of imaginal exposure did improve outcome with respect to the maintenance of gains.

In the above discussion, particular emphasis has been given to washing and checking compulsions; however, OCD is characterised by a range of phenomena, and the propriety of employing the standard exposure and response prevention package must be questioned in some cases. Individuals who suffer from ruminations, obsessions without compulsions, compulsive hoarding, or primary obsessional slowness, for example, will require modified procedures. The treatment of ruminations and obsessions will be given further consideration in due course; however, brief consideration will be given here to primary obsessional slowness and hoarding.

Primary Obsessional Slowness

Primary obsessional slowness (POS) was first described by Rachman (1974). The term 'primary' is something of a misnomer, in so far as the slowness described was mostly secondary to a meticulous concern for orderliness. As such, this patient group share many features with individuals exhibiting symmetry and order rituals; however, Rachman noted that individuals with POS had relatively few obsessional thoughts and did not experience anxiety reduction before or after the careful execution of routine behaviours. Although the concept of POS has been accepted by the academic community (cf. Gelder, Gath & Mayoy, 1983), its status as a separate syndrome has been questioned. In a recent review of the literature, Veale (1993) argues that POS does not require classification as a separate syndrome 'because it can be found to be secondary to recognised phenomena of obsessive compulsive disorder or anancastic personality disorder' (p. 198). This is consistent with Rasmussen & Eisen (1992), who suggest that compulsive precision can be found in 28% of OCD patients on admission.

The behavioural treatment programme devised for patients suffering from POS involved prompting, pacing, and shaping with regular reminders of the passage of time (Rachman & Hodgson, 1980). Veale (1993) suggests that although this treatment programme may initially help by preventing the patient from maintaining desired order or exactness, such strategies are too difficult to preserve in the absence of a therapist. He goes on to suggest that, 'in theory, the main strategy for patients with orderliness, exactness, or meticulousness would be repeated exposure to disorder, inexactness or unmeticulousness' (p. 202). Clearly, Veale's exposure targets are also relevant for individuals with traditional order and symmetry rituals.

Hoarding

Hoarding compulsions are relatively rare, although some research suggests that as many as 18% of patients with OCD suffer from this problem (Rasmussen & Eisen, 1992). This particular manifestation of OCD remains controversial, and some commentators have suggested that hoarders should be differentiated from other types of OCD (Greenberg, 1987). Behavioural intervention can involve urging the patient to throw away unnecessary possessions that are ranked with respect to a graded hierarchy (Tallis, 1992), although there is, as yet, no established behavioural treatment strategy. If a patient finds throwing away some items too difficult, the therapist might consider safeguarding these possessions as an intermediate step. This may be more acceptable to patients who experience extreme distress when irreversibly parting with objects (cf. Shafran & Tallis, submitted).

Recent research suggests that hoarding is an attempt to avoid the decision to throw something away, and the subsequent worry that a mistake has been made (Frost & Gross, 1993). If this account proves to be accurate, then there may be scope for additional cognitive procedures. It may also be the case that hoarding has some functional significance to the patient founded on idiosyncratic beliefs (Case 18.1).

Case 18.1

Edith was a 51-year-old woman with severe hoarding problems. She was unable to throw anything away. Her house became so full that there was little room available in which to move without difficulty. Although she had attempted in the past to sell some of her possessions, when prospective buyers came to the house she was unable to complete transactions. In accounting for her symptoms, she described an early life characterised by frequent travel and change. This continued, to a lesser extent, in adulthood. In her own mind, the acquisition of an enormous number of possessions made moving an impossibility. The fact that she couldn't move engendered feelings of stability and permanence which she described as comforting.

ISSUES IN THE APPLICATION OF BEHAVIOURAL TECHNIQUES

There are a number of issues that require consideration in the application of behavioural treatment strategies. It was suggested above that relaxation may interfere with habituation and subsequently retard therapeutic progress; however, notwithstanding this possibility, some patients do seem to find applied relaxation helpful. If applied relaxation enables the patient to tolerate somatic discomfort during exposure, future compliance with exposure exercises is more likely. Although applied relaxation can be useful as an adjunct to exposure, relaxation without exposure instructions is of little value (Marks, Hodgson & Rachman, 1975; Marks, 1990). De Silva (1987) raises the issue of whether exposure should be graded (as in systematic desensitisation), or rapid (as in flooding). Although some practitioners recommend graded exposure (Foa & Tillmanns, 1980), others suggest that it is expedient to focus on the more anxiogenic items of a graded hierarchy (Hodgson, Rachman & Marks, 1972) and that less anxiogenic items should be addressed only as part of generalisation training. Clearly, the choice of procedure will very much depend on the patient's willingness or ability to tolerate extreme anxiety. Although, behaviour therapy is not usually associated with 'bad outcome', the author has interviewed numerous patients who, treated insensitively during 'flooding' sessions, claim that the procedure made their symptoms worse. If the cost of attempting to achieve rapid progress carries the risk of a high dropout rate or the provocation of very high levels of distress, then a graded exposure programme should be considered the more appropriate course of action.

In spite of the above caveat, it should be noted that some patients with OCD are extremely avoidant and intensive exposure may be necessary if treatment is to be effective. For example, many individuals with contamination fears will ostensibly touch a contaminated item, while mentally delineating a 'safe corner' (de Silva, 1987). Alternatively, they may only touch a contaminated area with a particular part of the hand. As such, therapists must monitor patient behaviour carefully during exposure sessions, and encourage full contact. Using exaggerated exposure (e.g. rubbing the hands vigorously on a seat) may be necessary to ensure that full contact occurs.

Recently, there has been an increasing shift in behavioural therapy from therapist-assisted procedures to self-treatment (Marks, 1990; Tallis, 1992). Self-imposed delay (Welch, 1979; Vingoe, 1980; Junginger & Turner, 1987; Junginger & Head, 1991) is particularly useful as a treatment strategy for patients wishing to undertake a self-help programme. Patients are responsible for progressively delaying the execution of compulsive behaviour and/or progressively decreasing the extent of their compulsive behaviour. Once delayed execution has extended to an hour or so, the urge to execute the compulsion may have diminished to the extent that the patient feels the behaviour is no longer necessary. The advantage of self-imposed delay procedures, compared with strict response prevention, is that the patient does not have to abandon anxiety-reducing rituals altogether. This may be more acceptable to some patients, who prefer to relinquish their compulsions gradually. A liberal programme of this kind can increase the likelihood of continued compliance in patients who complain of extreme anxiety.

Reassurance seeking is a well-attested feature of OCD. If an inflated sense of responsibility is given special importance with respect to the phenomenology of OCD, then diffusion of responsibility may be functionally equivalent to avoidance behaviour. As such, anxiety might not be evoked during an exposure exercise. This could conceivably interfere with the efficacy of the procedure. Salkovskis & Warwick (1988) suggest that patients should be asked to carry out homework assignments without disclosure to significant others. Indeed, taking full responsibility for the construction of exposure and response prevention exercises could be an important factor in maximising therapeutic gains. A common misconception is that patients with OCD should not be reassured at all. A distinction should be made between constructive reassurance and unconstructive reassurance and this should be made explicit to the patient. Reassuring patients that exposure and response prevention are effective strategies that are likely to result in long-term improvement is indeed permissible. Moreover, a blanket failure to reassure will inevitably interfere with the therapeutic relationship. Such an approach might lead a patient to feel unsupported, which in turn may lead to poor compliance.

A final footnote on behavioural self-treatment is the creative use of novel technological developments. Baer, Minichiello & Jenike (1987) have provided OCD patients with exposure and response prevention instructions stored on portable computer programs. Initial results are promising and it is likely that appropriate interactive computer modules will continue to be developed, thus facilitating the refinement of self-help approaches. Moreover, computer-based interventions facilitate the process of accepting and tolerating responsibility.

BEHAVIOURAL THERAPY FOR OBSESSIONS

A range of techniques based on behavioural principles have been developed for the treatment of covert obsessional phenomena. The most established of these is 'thought stopping', a procedure whereby unwanted cognition is terminated by a command. Taylor (1963) reported the treatment of a patient with trichotillomania, who was instructed to say 'no, stay where you are', as soon as she felt the urge to pluck her eyebrows. Cautela (1969) elaborated this procedure by requesting patients to retrieve distressing thoughts, and to indicate their entry into awareness by lifting a finger. The therapist responds by shouting 'Stop!' (which can be accompanied by another auditory stimulus such as a loud handclap). Characteristically, the patient's mind clears. The procedure can be repeated, and eventually patients may be asked to deliver the stop command themselves. After further repetitions, the command is delivered subvocally, and may be reinforced by the use of an elastic band, pulled and released against the wrist (Bass 1973; Mahoney, 1971). Although the use of mildly aversive stimuli is recommended, the procedure has been taken to an excessive and rather impractical extreme in the form of 'faradic disruption' with respect to the treatment of obsessional thoughts (Kenny, Mowbray & Lalam, 1978; Kenny, Solyom & Solyom, 1973).

Numerous articles on thought stopping have been reported in the literature; however, results are mixed (Stern, 1970; Stern, Lipsedge & Marks, 1973; Tryon, 1979). This relative inconsistency might be attributable to the application of the technique to the 'wrong' targets. Kirk (1983) reports the highly successful treatment of ruminations; however, patients were instructed to apply thought stopping to anxiety-reducing thoughts (or covert rituals), rather than the anxiety-evoking obsessional thoughts. In this way, exposure to anxiogenic thoughts is maximised and thought stopping becomes the functional equivalent of response prevention.

Clearly, attempting to maximise exposure to covert obsessional phenomena is fraught with difficulties. Individuals may complain that the thoughts keep 'slipping away', or suggest that their contrived obsessions lack the tenacity of spontaneous exemplars. In satiation or habituation training, patients are encouraged to keep anxiogenic thoughts in awareness for prolonged periods of time (Broadhurst, 1976; Rachman, 1976b; Emmelkamp & Kwee, 1977). Verbal prompts, exposure to triggering stimuli, or written repetition of the disturbing thought, can all help focus attention on the desired target (Beech & Vaughn, 1978; Farkas & Beck, 1981).

A further method of maximising exposure to covert phenomena is the use of 'tape' media. For example, Milby, Meredith & Rice (1981) employed videotaped verbalisations of obsessive thoughts. Each training tape was shown to the patient while the therapist encouraged the maintenance of full concentration. In addition, avoidance responses were prevented. A similar, and perhaps more ecologically valid, procedure has been developed by Salkovskis (1983). Loop audio cassette tapes were used to record verbalisations of obsessive thoughts, which were then played back over headphones. Salkovskis & Westbrook (1989) suggest that if the voluntary prevention of covert neutralising is a problem, then tapes can be modified so that thoughts occur at a rate which makes neutralising difficult to achieve. Short intervals between thoughts or the recording of different thoughts on each stereo channel may be useful to this end. The use of a personal stereo system (e.g. a Walkman) maximises mobility, so that exposure sessions can be undertaken in a variety of situations.

It is generally held that patients with obsessions alone, rather than obsessions and compulsions, are more difficult to treat using conventional behavioural procedures (Emmelkamp, 1982; Foa, Steketee & Ozorow, 1985; Rachman, 1985); however, recent research is inconsistent with this view (Arts et al., 1993).

Ruminations

Although a relatively clear distinction can be made between obsessions and worry (Turner, Beidel & Stanley, 1992), it is nevertheless the case that certain variants of OCD are characterised by cognition bearing a close resemblance to pathological worry (cf. Barlow, 1988). This is very much the case with respect to 'ruminators'. A full discussion of the topic of worry is beyond the scope of the present volume; however, the reader is referred to Davey & Tallis (1994) for a complete review of the literature.

A stimulus control treatment plan for worriers has been devised by Borkovec and colleagues (Borkovec et al., 1983). As worry can occur contiguous with a diverse range of cues, the authors suggest that poor discriminative control is established. Conversely, the restriction of temporal and environmental cues for the occurrence of worry will result in reduced frequency. With this rationale in mind, worriers are urged to refocus on 'present moment experience' when worrying occurs and to postpone worrying until a prescribed 30-minute worry period later in the day. During this allocated time period, the individual is advised to engage in formal problem solving. Although this procedure has proved successful with non-clinical worriers, it has not been tested with respect to an obsessional population. Nevertheless, it seems plausible that these instructions might be useful as a containment exercise for patients with OCD whose ruminations focus, at least in part, on 'real-life' problems.

Chapter 19

COGNITIVE THERAPY

COGNITIVE THERAPY IN OCD

It has already been suggested that behaviour therapy may influence cognition indirectly, by providing ideal conditions for the discomfirmation of beliefs associated with obsessional illness. In cognitive therapy, an attempt is made to change thinking and beliefs directly. The immediate antecedent of contemporary cognitive therapy is rational emotive therapy (RET), which was developed by Albert Ellis (1956); however, concepts such as the 'behavioural experiment' and 'collaborative empiricism' are part of a tradition that owes much to George Kelly's personal construct psychology and therapy (Kelly, 1955).

Ellis has freely acknowledged his debt to many philosophical sources, including the Stoic, Epictetus, who wrote: 'Men are disturbed not by things, but by the views which they take of them' (Ellis, 1962). RET concepts such as the primacy of cognition, the close relationship between cognition and affect, thinking errors, and 'disputing' or challenging unhelpful beliefs, have all been retained within the framework of contemporary cognitive therapy.

The term 'cognitive therapy' was coined by Aaron T. Beck, who was largely responsible for developing and refining many of the procedures that characterise the approach today (Beck, 1967; Beck & Greenberg, 1974; Beck 1976; Beck et al., 1979). Treatment usually involves the identification of inaccurate thoughts (or a particular 'thinking style'), and the demonstration of links between thinking, affect, and/or behaviour. Patients are encouraged to challenge their inaccurate thoughts, and replace them with more accurate examples. Behavioural experiments are usually employed to test the validity of potentially unhelpful thoughts. In addition, it may be possible to discover fundamental beliefs (or dysfunctional assumptions), which influence distorted thinking. These too may be modified through a discipline of self-questioning and behavioural experimentation. The procedures that characterise cognitive therapy have been described in considerable detail elsewhere (Hawton et al., 1989). In the following, discussion will be limited to cognitive therapy strategies as applied to OCD.

Cognitive therapy strategies can be used in two ways. First, as a means of facilitating traditional behavioural therapy in the form of exposure and response prevention, and second as a means of modifying appraisals and beliefs that may be central to the maintenance of an obsessional problem. In Chapters 2 and 10, it was suggested that abnormal risk assessment was a core (though not unique) feature of OCD, and that the concept of inflated responsibility was given particular emphasis in contemporary 'cognitive' theories (Carr, 1974; McFall & Wollersheim, 1979; Salkovskis, 1985). It is not surprising, therefore, that the modification of abnormal risk assessment and exaggerated responsibility have proven to be prominent targets for therapists working within a cognitive framework. Cognitive techniques employed to enhance motivation and facilitate engagement in exposure and response prevention exercises have been discussed extensively elsewhere with respect to OCD (Salkovskis & Warwick, 1988; Tallis, 1992). The reader is referred to these texts.

COGNITIVE THERAPY STRATEGIES FOR OCD

To date, there have been few clear descriptions of specific cognitive techniques aimed at modifying the appraisals and beliefs that subserve obsessional behaviour; however, recently, van Oppen & Arntz (1994) have provided a concise account of how cognitive therapy might be practised with individuals suffering from OCD.

Van Oppen & Arntz (1994) suggest that a principal focus of cognitive therapy should be the modification of abnormal risk assessment. This is undertaken by first assessing the degree to which the *probability* of 'danger' is overestimated, and second, the degree to which the *consequences* of 'danger' are overestimated. An example of a statement reflecting the first appraisal might be 'If I come into contact with a contaminant I might get a disease'. An example of the second appraisal might be 'If I contract a disease I might infect my pregnant friend and her child will be born deformed'.

Van Oppen & Arntz (1994) recommend a technique described by Hoekstra (1989) for the modification of abnormal risk assessments. This involves comparing probability estimates of feared catastrophes with probability estimates based on the analysis of event sequences leading to feared catastrophes. Initially, the patient is asked to estimate the probability of a feared catastrophe occurring. The patient is then asked to describe the sequence of events necessary for the feared catastrophe

Table 8 A cumulative probability table for the modification of an abnormal 'contamination' risk assessment

Feared catastrophe: *That I will contaminate my therapist and this will lead to the death of a hospital patient.*

Probability of occurrence: 1/10

	Sequence of events	Chance	Cumulative Chance
1.	I will tread on glass.	1/10	1/10
2.	The glass will get stuck to my shoe.	1/10	1/100
3.	A fragment will drop on the carpet.	1/10	1/1000
4.	The fragment will be transferred to my therapist's clothing.	1/100	1/10 000
5.	My therapist will go to a hospital and the glass will be transferred to a medical ward.	1/10	1/1 000 000
6.	Eventually the glass will be transferred to a life support machine.	1/100	1/100 000 000
7.	The machine will break.	1/10	1/1000 000 000
8.	A patient will die.	1/10	1/10 000 000 000

to occur. The probability of each 'event' is then estimated separately. Finally, a cumulative probability is estimated taking each separate event into account, and the product is compared with the original estimate. Inevitably, the disparity is both striking and instructive. An example of a work sheet is given in Table 8.

The first event in the sequence, treading on glass, is thought to have a 1/10 chance of occurring. The second event, a fragment of glass getting stuck to the patient's shoe, is also thought to have a 1/10 chance of occurring. The cumulative probability of both events occurring is, however, 1/100. This figure is calculated by multiplying the first chance estimate by the second. When the procedure is repeated through to event 8, a medical patient dying, the cumulative probability estimate of the total event sequence is found to be 1/10 000 000 000. The sufferer's initial probability estimate of causing a medical patient's death by contaminating the therapist was 1/10. Although only eight events are included in the above sequence, many more could have been included. It should be noted that many patients' feared catastrophes necessitate extended sequences of up to 20 or so separate events. In such cases, the feared event is found to be a highly improbable occurrence. The overestimation of the consequences of danger can be modified through standard exposure and response prevention exercises presented in the form of behavioural experiments. The provision of disconfirmatory experience serves to facilitate belief change.

The efficacy of Hoekstra's technique is most probably subserved by providing patients with a 'corrective' framework within which to examine the validity of their risk assessments. Indeed, when the technique is effective, patients will often spontaneously exclaim, 'You know, I never thought about it like this before'. A realisation of this nature is usually accompanied by a concomitant reduction in anxiety. In addition to the above, it may be possible to modify abnormal risk assessment in a more direct way, by manipulating the availability of information employed to estimate risk.

There is a considerable amount of evidence suggesting that probability estimates are influenced by the construction of mental models of the future (cf. Kahneman & Tversky, 1982). An important factor to be considered in model construction is the set of causal explanations that lead to the event's occurrence (Levi & Pryor, 1987). Therefore, individuals who find it easier to think of reasons why an event might happen, compared to why it might not, will think the event more probable (Campbell & Fairey, 1985; Sherman et al., 1981).

Explanation-based pessimism is thought to subserve the abnormal risk assessments found in high worriers (MacLeod, Williams & Bekerian, 1991). In other words, worriers are more able to access reasons favouring the occurrence of a prospective negative event than those reasons that would prevent the event from happening. MacLeod, Williams & Bekerian (1991) found that asking worriers to generate examples of the latter lowered subjective probability estimates of expected negative outcomes. Reason generation, or 'counter-explanation' (MacLeod, 1994), is therefore a potentially useful technique that can be used to modify abnormal risk assessment. Unlike many other cognitive strategies, it targets the fundamental processes that subserve risk estimation. Given that these processes are universal, counter-explanation is clearly applicable to individuals suffering from OCD as well as other anxiety-related disorders.

Steketee (1993, p. 76) describes a procedure for the assessment of insight into obsessional fears; however, this simple procedure may, in itself, result in revised assessment of risk. An example is given of a patient who feared causing the death of her family or friends at dinner by not cleaning a can carefully and spreading botulism. After the patient rated her belief in the fear at the 20% level on a 100-point scale, Steketee commented: 'OK 20 out of 100. So you are convinced that 2 out of every 10 people who eat at your home will become seriously ill and die if you stop washing each can 10 times ... That would also mean that if I came to eat at your house five times, I'd probably be dead before I could come the sixth time. Is that right ?'. Steketee suggests that 'clothing' belief estimates with everyday examples often has the effect of synchronising beliefs with reality.

Van Oppen & Arntz (1994) suggest that although OCD patients may recognise that the probability of a feared event is low, they may still wish to perform neutralising rituals. For many patients with OCD, the fact that an event can happen is sufficient to engender anxiety, irrespective of its low probability. It is therefore necessary for the therapist to focus not only on abnormal risk estimates, but also on what makes the consequences of feared events so unacceptable to the patient. For van Oppen & Arntz, the issue of perceived responsibility is of central importance.

As with abnormal risk assessment, van Oppen & Arntz (1994) suggest that two aspects of responsibility should be considered: first, the extent to which the patient overestimates responsibility, and second, the extent to which the patient overestimates the perceived consequences of having been responsible. An example of a statement reflecting the first aspect might be 'If there is a road accident it will be my fault'. An example of a statement reflecting the second aspect might be 'I will be blamed and criticised by everyone'. Van Oppen & Arntz (1994) suggest using the 'pie technique' for modifying the overestimation of responsibility. All of the factors contributing to a potential feared outcome are listed, and the patient is requested to divide a circle (or pie) into segments of differing size, where each reflects the relative importance of each factor. The patient's contribution should be represented in the final division. Percentage values can be assigned to each segment as the exercise is being undertaken. Usually, once all other factors have been accounted for, the patient's own contribution is seen to be, at most, modest. Again, the efficacy of this technique is most probably subserved by providing patients with a 'corrective' framework within which to examine the validity of their appraisals. An essential part of this process is the realistic reattribution of responsibility to a range of factors other than 'the self'. The overestimation of the perceived consequences of having been responsible can be modified through standard exposure and response prevention exercises presented in the form of behavioural experiments. As with inflated probability estimates, disconfirmatory experience will serve to facilitate belief change.

Elevated levels of anxiety can be associated with poor tolerance of uncertainty. The fact that a particular negative event might happen, however improbable, is sufficient to cause anxiety. In such cases, pointing out inconsistencies can help facilitate belief change. In some cases, it can be useful to underscore the usually much higher risks associated with routine behaviours such as 'crossing the road', compared with the usually modest risk associated with obsessional fears (such as contracting HIV from a discarded object). Many individuals with OCD are quite happy to engage in very risky behaviour that they do not perceive as such. Pointing out the discrepancy can promote a therapeutic reappraisal of risk.

METACOGNITION AND THE APPLICATION OF INAPPROPRIATE CONTROL STRATEGIES

'Metacognition' is the term used to describe self-knowledge about cognitive processes (Brown, 1978). It might, therefore, also be described as 'thinking about thinking'. Wells (1994) suggests that there are several ways in which dysfunctional self-knowledge can contribute to the distress associated with intrusive thoughts. First, individuals might believe that their thoughts are *completely* uncontrollable, when this is not the case. Second, some individuals may have unhelpful beliefs about the significance of their thoughts. In addition to these suggestions, doubt-related phenomena could also be included under the heading of metacognition, for example, beliefs about poor memory functioning (Tallis, 1993). This later case will be given further consideration in due course.

It is now widely recognised that intrusive thoughts are a universal phenomenon (Rachman & De Silva, 1978). Therefore, an underlying assumption that 'one should and can exercise control over one's thoughts' will inevitably conflict with everyday experience. The experience of being unable to exercise total control appears to have two consequences with respect to obsessional patients. First, they might conclude that the absence of total mental control increases the likelihood of loss of behavioural control. When such a conclusion is reached against a background of fears of causing harm to others the development of an anxiety state is almost inevitable. Second, efforts to reduce anxiety may take the form of excessive monitoring of mental phenomena and the application of counter-productive control strategies, for example thought suppression (see Chapter 9).

A more permissive attitude to the occurrence of intrusive thoughts can be encouraged through education. Discussion of intrusive thoughts as a universal phenomenon can help to 'normalise' the patient's experience and challenge beliefs about his or her own 'abnormality'. An examination of the content of Rachman & de Silva's 1978 paper on 'normal' obsessions within a session can be highly therapeutic to this end. Clearly, recognition of intrusive thoughts as part of everyday experience can serve to challenge beliefs concerning their unacceptability.

When a patient has reached the conclusion that they have little or no control over mental events and processes, thought control, thought switching, and attentional strategies can be employed in the form of experiments. Thought control involves the repeated retrieval and dismissal of intrusive thoughts, while thought switching involves the repeated retrieval of intrusive thoughts, followed by substitution with another pre-prepared thought (Daniels, 1976; Sturgis & Meyer, 1981). Attentional training involves instructing the patient to shift from an internal to an external focus. This can be achieved by asking the patient to describe an object in the room, or focus on specific sounds. In the latter case, attentional demands can be increased as the exercise progresses; for example, first focusing on one sound and then working towards focusing on as many sounds as possible (cf. Wells, 1990). An active demonstration that some mental control is possible can serve to challenge the notion that mental control has been severely compromised. Beliefs about a putative strong link between mental phenomena and behaviour can be challenged by asking the patient to form intrusive thoughts or inappropriate impulses within sessions. The presence of such phenomena in awareness does not typically produce congruent or inappropriate behaviours.

Persistent monitoring or 'checking' of mental functioning can in itself interfere with the automatic processes necessary for the occurrence of 'fluent' cognition. An impaired ability to 'think straight' often strengthens fears of loss of mental control. Thought stopping, aimed at reducing the occurrence of metacognitive phenomena can be a useful means of correcting dysfunctional thinking patterns.

It has already been suggested that attempts to suppress intrusive thoughts might only serve to increase their salience and frequency. Encouraging patients to refrain from thought suppression can therefore be helpful. It is interesting to note that this technique has been described in a Buddhist text called the *Satipatthana Sutta*, in which the aspirant is advised simply to concentrate on intrusive thoughts while making no effort to get rid of them. Thoughts are then said to lose their potency and disappear (de Silva, 1990).

MNESTIC FUNCTIONING AND BELIEFS ABOUT MEMORY

A special class of metacognition concerns beliefs about mnestic functioning. It has been suggested that doubt-related phenomena, particularly checking, might be associated with a primary memory deficit, a memory deficit secondary to anxiety, or poor confidence in memory (Chapters 13

& 15). Although there is growing neuropsychological evidence that individuals with OCD have a specific visuo-spatial memory deficit, the above are by no means mutually exclusive. From a cognitive perspective, increasing confidence in mnestic functioning should lead to reduced doubting, and a subsequent reduction in the need to check.

Improved mnestic functioning can be accomplished by employing distinctive imagery (cf. Morris & Reid, 1970; Morris, Jones & Hampton, 1978). Indeed, anecdotal evidence suggests that forming a distinctive image while performing a behaviour that usually results in checking can make that same behaviour 'stand out' in memory (Toates, 1990; Tallis, 1995). Clear recollection of the behaviour reduces doubt and negates the necessity to check. A problem with these techniques, if applied to compulsive checking, is that no provision is made for the effective withdrawal of intervention strategies, a necessary requirement if treatment gains are to be maintained.

Tallis (1993) reports three cases of compulsive checking treated using a doubt reduction procedure which employs distinctive artificial stimuli. Patients were given sets of coloured cardboard geometric figures. Although each particular shape was the same colour (e.g. green circles), all exemplars differed in respect of size, forming a graded continuum (see Figure 3 for an example set). Patients were instructed to associate target behaviours (e.g. closing a door) with large figures first, and then to work through to the smallest figures. Any subsequent doubt was reduced by forming a mental image of the distinctive figure employed at the time. Inclusion of a 'fading' component (i.e. graded reduction of stimulus size), improved the likelihood of treatment gains being maintained after the programme was completed. In all three cases, checking was eliminated at one-year follow-up; however, it should be noted that only one of the cases was well controlled. The author suggests that the technique's efficacy might be attributed to increased 'confidence in memory' mediated by image formation. The formation of images is associated with greater confidence in memory, irrespective of whether recall is correct or incorrect (Morris, 1992).

If obsessional doubt can be attributable, at least in part, to poor confidence in memory, then this suggests other potentially useful therapeutic procedures. Tallis (1995) suggests that psychometric tests might be employed to demonstrate to patients that their memory functioning falls within the normal range. Consistent with the tradition of cognitive therapy, psychometric tests could be introduced as a behavioural experiment, the result of which might validate or refute existing beliefs.

☆	XL	L	M	S	VS	(Blue)
▢	XL	L	M	S	VS	(Green)
△	XL	L	M	S	VS	(Red)
○	XL	L	M	S	VS	(Yellow)
▢	XL	L	M	S	VS	(Orange)

Figure 3 Geometric figures used in the doubt reduction procedure described by Tallis (1993) *Key:* XL = extra large; L = large; M = medium; s = small; VS = very small

Watts (submitted) underscores the observation that the quality of information processing involved in checking deteriorates as checking is repeated. This may be partly due to a deterioration in mood, but is more plausibly attributable to proactive interference. Proactive interference occurs when earlier learning disrupts later learning (cf. Underwood, 1957). Watts suggests the use of cognitive strategies that maximise the effectiveness of the first check in order to reduce the need for repetition. An example of such a strategy is Gendlin's (1981) 'first moment' focusing technique. Before checking, the patient is encouraged to set aside other preoccupations so that his or her attention can be 'focused'. The patient is then allowed to carry out the check as carefully as possible, using multiple sources of sensory input where they are available. Clearly, such a strategy will enhance the distinctiveness of the checking behaviour.

In addition to the above, Watts suggests a further technique which can be employed to improve the patient's confidence in mnestic functioning. He suggests introducing incidental stimuli during a checking task and testing the patient's recall of these. Initially, such stimuli would not be strongly associated with the checking problem; however, at a later stage memory could be tested for stimuli relevant to the checking problem processed only at an 'automatic' level.

Prompting swift checking, or asking the patient to undertake a secondary task, will ensure that checking is not accomplished in 'full consciousness'. Watts suggests that patients are surprised and impressed by their own ability to process information without full concentration. Again, good recollection of target stimuli in the absence of complete 'concentration' will serve to challenge appraisals of poor memory functioning where these are exaggerated or inaccurate.

A further method of increasing the distinctiveness of past actions has been described by Ecker & Engelkamp (submitted). They suggest that neuropsychological evidence indicates that compulsive checkers fail to register motor or kinesthetic feedback. Thus, checkers might be 'successfully trained to regain access to, focus on and profit from motor/kinesthetic information derived from their own motor actions in order to facilitate response prevention'. This 'regained access' might be achieved by asking patients to check only once with 'closed eyes', which would serve the purpose of blocking the visual feedback channel 'routinely used to compensate for the motor memory deficit'. Ecker and Engelkamp have used this technique with some success in their clinical practice, although its usefulness requires empirical testing.

THE ROLE OF FUNDAMENTAL AND IDIOSYNCRATIC BELIEFS

In Chapter 9, it was suggested that a number of fundamental beliefs or dysfunctional assumptions may maintain obsessional problems. Although it is possible to describe common themes, practitioners should always recognise that these evolve against the background of an individual's learning history. As such, other more idiosyncratic beliefs may also be of profound importance.

In Case 19.1, in order to access the patient's beliefs, the 'vertical' or 'downward arrow' technique (Burns, 1980) was employed. Vertical arrow requires the patient to volunteer thoughts associated with specific feelings or situations; however, instead of challenging these thoughts the therapist might ask, 'Supposing this was true, what would that mean?' or 'What is so bad about that?' It transpired that the occurrence of the word 'devil' produced anxiety because of a range of underlying appraisals and beliefs. First, the patient felt that he should be able to exercise total control over the contents of his own consciousness. Second, he believed that the absence of total control meant that he might develop a psychotic illness. Finally, loss of control was perceived as being a sign of weakness; a characteristic which was unacceptable on account of his learning history and occupation. All of these beliefs were challenged and modified within a cognitive framework.

Case 19.1

A 34-year-old man was referred for treatment suffering from a repeated intrusive thought, namely, the word 'devil'. It was usually accompanied by the physiological concomitants of anxiety. The patient was not religious, and the word 'devil' had no obvious significance. Although the patient sought to suppress the thought when it occurred, he did not engage in any anxiety-reducing rituals. He had received a range of treatments including thought stopping, habituation training, relaxation, and biofeedback. All of these were associated with only temporary relief. He presented as articulate and insightful and he did not meet criteria for an Axis II diagnosis.

This example serves to demonstrate that even a 'nonsense' obsession may have a deeper meaning. Although behavioural approaches served to reduce anxiety temporarily, the underlying beliefs remained unmodified and acted as a vulnerability factor with respect to relapse. If cognitive therapy is to be successful, then semantic issues must be addressed.

Although the symptoms of OCD may be similar between individuals, the appraisals and beliefs that maintain those symptoms may be quite different. As such, the individual's unique learning history should always be taken into account.

Consider, for example, the case of a middle-aged woman with contamination fears and washing compulsions, where fear of contamination was restricted to objects touched by her father. A background of childhood sexual abuse will cast an entirely different light on symptoms, making the exploration of associated themes mandatory if any significant therapeutic progress is to be made. It is unlikely that exposure and response prevention *per se* would result in gains that could be maintained in the long term, without considering the meaning of these symptoms and their learning context.

Chapter 20

COGNITIVE THERAPY: A PRELIMINARY EVALUATION

Although there is a considerable amount of clinical evidence suggesting that cognitive therapy can be a useful treatment with respect to OCD, it should be noted that there are, as yet, only a few outcome evaluation studies. As such, the efficacy of cognitive therapy and cognitive strategies can only be judged according to the clinical impressions of the relatively small group of practitioners who advocate this approach. In the following, a number of 'cognitive' outcome evaluation studies are reviewed; however, it should be noted that only one of these studies employs contemporary cognitive techniques (van Oppen, 1994; Van Oppen, Hoekstra & Emmelkamp, in press). Much of the work described involves the use of 'self-instruction', or simply 'disputing' irrational beliefs.

Emmelkamp et al. (1980) examined the effect of combining self-instructional training with exposure and response prevention. Inclusion of SIT did not bestow any advantage with respect to behavioural treatment. Bleijenberg (1981, cited in Emmelkamp, 1982) employed exposure and cognitive therapy in a crossover design using 10 non-clinical obsessional volunteers. The cognitive treatment involved challenging irrational beliefs and examining from a 'rational' perspective the fears associated with specific situations. Neither approaches altered cognitions or improved OCD symptoms. Needless to say, it is difficult to conclude very much from a treatment trial conducted on non-clinical subjects.

In a more promising study, Emmelkamp, Visser & Hoekstra (1988) assigned 18 patients with OCD to either RET or self-controlled exposure and response prevention conditions. Attempts were made in the RET condition to target beliefs central to McFall & Wollersheim's (1979) cognitive behavioural formulation of OCD. Both approaches produced significant improvement. Subjective ratings of anxiety and depression also improved with both methods, although RET was associated with a superior outcome on the depression measure. It should be noted, however, that the authors were dissatisfied with the composition of the patient sample, in so far as the patients who received cognitive therapy were young, well educated, and did not have chronic complaints.

In order to correct for sampling bias, the above study was replicated by Emmelkamp & Beens (1991). All 21 subjects met DSM-III criteria for a diagnosis of OCD. Moreover, symptoms were required to be present for at least six months and to be of sufficient severity to warrant intensive treatment. After a four-week waiting period, patients were allocated to either RET or self-controlled exposure and response prevention conditions. After six sessions and another four-week waiting period *all* patients received six sessions of exposure and response prevention, that is, behavioural treatment was added to the cognitive condition. Both treatments resulted in significant improvement with respect to anxiety and discomfort, and symptoms were reduced as measured by the MOCI and the Dutch Obsessional Compulsive Questionnaire (Kraaimaat & van Dam-Baggen, 1976). Scores were also reduced on the Irrational Belief Test (Jones, 1966). Improvement was maintained at six-month follow-up and no significant differences were found between the two conditions. Given that all patients received behavioural treatment, it could be argued that follow-up improvement in the cognitive group could be attributed to the effects of behavioural therapy. On the other hand, it would appear that belief change was at least a contributory factor with respect to improvement. Moreover, it is of considerable interest that belief change occurred in both groups.

To date there has only been one well-controlled outcome evaluation of cognitive therapy for OCD (van Oppen, 1994; van Oppen, Hoekstra & Emmelkamp, in press). The cognitive therapy employed was closely associated with appraisal theories (Carr, 1974; McFall & Wollersheim, 1979; Salkovskis, 1985), some elements of which were described earlier in the previous chapter (van Oppen & Arntz, 1994).

Both cognitive ($n = 28$) and behaviour therapy ($n = 29$) conditions were employed. The behaviour therapy condition involved self-controlled exposure *in vivo* with response prevention. Subjects were well matched on a number of variables: namely, sex, age, marital status, education, and duration of illness. The mean duration of illness was over 10 years in both conditions. Inclusion criteria were (1) a primary DSM-III-R (APA, 1987) diagnosis of OCD; (2) not only obsessions; (3) age between 18–65; (4) a duration of OCD for at least one year; (5) absence of an organic mental disorder, mental retardation or a psychotic disorder; (6) no cognitive treatment or behavioural treatment in the preceding six months; (7) no use of anti-depressants. Both treatments consisted of 16 sessions of approximately 45 minutes, and all sessions were audiotaped and monitored by the authors.

Data were collected at three points: pretest, after six sessions, and after 16 sessions (16 weeks). Measures included in the study were the PI-R, the Y-Bocs, The Anxiety Discomfort Scale (ADS) (Watson & Marks, 1971), the revised version of the Symptom Checklist (SCL-90-R) (Derogatis, 1977), the BDI, and the Irrational Beliefs Inventory (Koopman et al., in press). At pretest only the ADS proved to be significantly higher in the behaviour therapy group.

Statistical analyses showed that both conditions improved significantly on almost all variables. Only the SCL-90-R and the Irrational Beliefs Inventory did not show significant change in the exposure condition. MANOVA analyses revealed a significant multivariate interaction effect on the obsessive compulsive measures $(F(6, 50) = 2.7$, $p < 0.03)$ and on the generalized measures $(F(4, 51) = 3.1$, $p < 0.03)$. These results suggested that cognitive therapy was more effective than behaviour therapy. However, when significant interactions were examined with the pretest score as a covariate, no differential treatment effects emerged. In other words, differences between groups were not significant when initial differences between groups were accounted for. Notwithstanding this latter result, the effect sizes (Cohen, 1988) for improvement on the OCD measures were slightly higher in the cognitive therapy condition. In addition, the percentage of patients who fulfilled the reliable change index and the recovered index (Jacobson, Follette & Ravensdorf, 1984; Jacobson & Truax, 1991) on the ADS, Y-Bocs & PI-R was higher in the cognitive therapy condition. Subsequent *post hoc* analyses did not show differential effects of therapy with respect to symptom profile.

Cognitive therapy has several problems associated with its practice in the context of OCD. First, there are many patients with OCD who are unable to report the appraisals and beliefs that form the main target for a cognitive intervention. Although advocates of cognitive therapy suggest that underlying thoughts and beliefs can be detected with persistent and skilled questioning (van Oppen & Arntz, 1994), there are a small group of obsessional patients who seem to ritualise in the absence of significant discomfort and accompanying phenomenology. These patients may suffer from a predominantly neurological form of OCD (cf. Fox & Tallis, 1994). Similarly, the author has heard some individuals with contamination fears describe being unable to touch certain 'dirty' objects, because it is as though they are 'surrounded by a force field'. The difficulty is almost at the 'instinctual' level and can exist in the absence of appraisal. The presence of the dirt is 'felt' rather than evaluated. Notwithstanding this criticism, a cognitive therapist might still argue that under such circumstances appraisals are not absent, but merely inaccessible. The emphasis then becomes the retrieval of submerged constructs.

Cognitive therapy tends to be most successful in patients who are intellectually able and have well-developed abstract thinking skills. Although the onus is on the therapist to translate particular ideas into the readily understood language of everyday life, there are inevitably limitations. Even the most creative use of metaphor will be inadequate in some circumstances. Notions such as 'abnormal risk estimate' and 'cumulative probability' demand a certain level of mathematical sophistication in the patient; a level which may be impractical in certain clinical environments. In addition, patients who are either extremely anxious or depressed are frequently unable to concentrate on, and follow, the arguments that can eventually result in belief change. A safeguard against slipping into tortuous intellectual debate is a strong focus, wherever possible, on the behavioural experiment; however, within the context of OCD, even the design of a behavioural experiment can be problematic.

The 'behavioural experiment' can be a powerful means of disconfirming beliefs; however, some beliefs are simply not amenable to this kind of testing. For example, a patient might believe that a particular action will result in an adverse outcome at a distant point in the future. He or she may fear the evidence may not detectable in the present (e.g. minimal brain damage through exposure to toxins). Therefore, no current evidence can be recruited to challenge this belief. Moreover, the patient will suggest that such damage might only become apparent when affected individuals become more frail with age.

In addition, individuals with ruminations can often 'hijack' the Socratic questioning procedure. Indeed, for many ruminators the symptoms of OCD are nothing more than a string of evaluative questions. They are constantly considering the evidence for and against certain ideas, and may have even undertaken limited behavioural experiments themselves. Finally, Socratic questioning can be easily misappropriated for the purpose of eliciting unhelpful reassurance.

In spite of the above reservations, cognitive therapy offers a relatively new approach to OCD. Although 'pure' behavioural therapy has an impressive record with respect to treatment, approximately 20% of patients do not respond. A still larger number of patients do not respond to pharmacotherapy (Steketee, 1993). As such, there is room for improvement, and cognitive approaches may offer some hope to those who have, as yet, been unable to benefit from existing interventions.

COGNITION AND BRAIN STATE: AN INTEGRATIVE APPROACH

Chapter 21

NEUROBIOLOGICAL THEORIES OF OCD

INTRODUCTION

Although this book has been largely concerned with cognitive aspects of OCD, it is necessary to consider these aspects within a broader context. Cognition and cognitive processes are intimately related to behaviour. Moreover, cognition and behaviour appear to arise from biological systems within the brain. Given recent advances in the understanding of the biological processes that may subserve obsessional phenomena, it is appropriate to consider how cognitive aspects might relate to new information. The evidence for the biological account of OCD was briefly reviewed at the end of Chapter 6. In this chapter, several theories generated by this new data are summarised. In addition, special consideration is given to Gray's (1982) 'behavioural inhibition' model of anxiety which emphasises the role of activity in the septo-hippocampal region of the brain.

THE SEROTONERGIC SYSTEM

Insel & Winslow (1990) have proposed a 'simple' neurochemical model of OCD. They suggest the presence of a *hypersensitive* subset of serotonin receptors. It is this subset that accounts for the exacerbation of symptoms in OCD patients following administration of the serotonin agonist mCPPP (Chapter 6).

Cerebrospinal fluid (CSF) concentrations of 5-H1AA, the primary serotonin metabolite, have been used as a measure of central serotonin turnover. Sociopaths and criminals with a history of violence have decreased CSF 5-H1AA concentrations (Linnnoilla et al., 1983). This is the exact opposite of OCD, which is characterised by high levels of CSF-H1AA. Insel & Winslow point out that sociopaths seem to occupy the opposite end of a putative behavioural and phenomenological continuum. Sociopaths are actively aggressive and experience little guilt, whereas patients with OCD are hardly ever aggressive and experience excessive guilt in response to violent thoughts.

Chronic reuptake blockade, following use of clomipramine, will result in increased levels of synaptic serotonin. The presence of increased levels of serotonin will result in the downregulation of receptor cells leading to a normalisation of functioning (Chapter 6).

THE SEPTO-HIPPOCAMPAL SYSTEM

Gray (1982) has proposed a neuropsychological theory of anxiety implicating what he describes as the behavioural inhibition system (BIS). This conceptual system corresponds with the activity and function of structures in the septo-hippocampal region of the brain. According to Gray, anxiety is the product of BIS activation. The BIS is activated by threat or potential threat; namely: signals of punishment, signals of non-reward, novel stimuli and innate fear stimuli. Once the BIS is active, ongoing behaviour is inhibited, while arousal and attention are increased. These consequences of BIS activation constitute the principal components of anxiety.

In Gray's account, the hippocampus has a special role with respect to information processing. It is considered the biological substrate of the 'comparator' (cf. Vinogradova, 1975), receiving information about the current state of the world as well as predicted regularities. Two modes of operation are described: 'just checking' and 'control' (p. 262). The former represents a continuous monitoring function and ongoing behaviour is not influenced. The latter mode comes into operation when a normal routine or plan is interrupted by the threat stimuli described above. The task is then to assess the situation so that existing plans can be applied again or new ones substituted. When a 'mismatch' between an actual and expected event occurs, the consequences of BIS activation are readily apparent: 'the system stops ongoing behaviour, it takes in new information, and it prepares for rapid and vigorous action to circumvent whatever threat or unexpected circumstance the comparator has just detected' (Gray, 1985, p. 110).

Gray (1982, p. 442) suggests that the repetitiveness of compulsions and obsessions requires a common explanation, which can be provided by his analysis. If the BIS is hyperactive, then certain stimuli (e.g. dirt, sharp objects) might be tagged as important and searched for with particular care. Much of this scanning may be carried out overtly in the form of checking. Hand washing might also be considered an effective means of searching for dirt as well as a way of removing it (Gray 1982, p. 442).

Anxiety will also arise when the search for potential threats repeatedly detects unwanted internal events, such as impulses.

In view of the above, Gray suggests that the principle of ideo-motor action (James 1890) may have some explanatory significance (Gray, 1982, p. 443). This principle suggests that the thought of a particular action will, of itself, prime the system that produces it. Therefore, checking whether one has a dangerous impulse will increase the likelihood of actually experiencing such an impulse. Gray suggests that the intrusive and repetitive nature of obsessional impulses could in this way arise from the very checking process which attempts to ensure that they are absent. It is interesting to note that Gray's suggestions have taken on a more contemporary resonance with respect to the cognitive literatures on the paradoxical effects of thought suppression and thought-action fusion (see Chapters 9 and 10).

In essence, Gray suggests that most obsessional phenomena can be explained in terms of abnormalities in the septo-hippocampal system. Most symptoms, both cognitive and behavioural, are the product of a persistent search for potentially dangerous stimuli. Although Gray's account is appealing, it is rather at odds with more recent brain scanning evidence suggesting specific abnormalities in the fronto-striatal brain systems (see Chapter 6). Moreover, Gray appears to be describing a neuroanatomical system that is fundamental to the general experience of anxiety, rather than the specific experience of OCD. Although Gray argues that his description is so close to the phenomenon of OCD that it hardly counts as an explanation at all (Gray, 1982, p. 42), this is not strictly true. Monitoring the environment for threat in the form of checking is common to all anxiety disorders. For example, individuals suffering from panic often 'check' their pulse in the same way that individuals suffering from generalised anxiety disorder attempt to 'check' the future through worry (Tallis & de Silva, 1992). This aspect of Gray's theory may not be a weakness, as OCD is considered to be an anxiety disorder; however, the claim that Gray's account is particularly well equipped to explain the symptoms of OCD *per se* is probably misconceived.

THE FRONTO-STRIATAL HYPOTHESIS

Before considering the specific fronto-striatal hypotheses with respect to OCD, a brief description of the neuroanatomical features of the basal ganglia is provided. The basal ganglia feature significantly in contemporary biological accounts of OCD and provision of an overall framework may be helpful to those unfamiliar with neuroanatomy.

The Basal Ganglia

Traditionally, the basal ganglia were considered to be motor control structures. Receiving input from several regions of cortex, the basal ganglia were thought to channel output through the thalamus (a limbic structure), to the primary motor cortex. This account is now regarded as simplistic, and has subsequently been revised. Rather than focusing output to the primary motor cortex, the basal ganglia are now known to project efferent fibres to the frontal lobe, rostral to the motor cortex. Although a portion of this area contributes to the planning of movement, most of this area is prefrontal association cortex; functions associated with this region include the organisation of goal-directed behaviours, complex thought, and reasoning.

Employing connections as a means of categorising the basal ganglia, it is possible to determine three sets of nuclei.

1. *The input nuclei* — which receive afferent connections from brain regions other than the basal ganglia.

2. *The output nuclei* — which have efferent projections that leave the basal ganglia.

3. *Intrinsic Nuclei* — which receive input from, and project to, the input and output nuclei.

The individual structures that comprise these groups are shown in Table 9.

The reader will recall from Chapter 6, that neuroimaging studies suggest that the caudate nucleus (a component of the basal ganglia) has special significance with respect to OCD. The location of the caudate nucleus relative to the rest of the brain is shown in Figure 4.

The four lobes of the cerebral cortex are the main sources of input to the basal ganglia; however, only the frontal lobe is the recipient of

Table 9   The nuclei of the basal ganglia

Input nuclei (striatum)	Caudate nucleus
	Putamen
	Nucleus Accumbens
Output nuclei	Substantia nigra pars reticula
	Globus pallidus — internal segment
	Ventral pallidum
Intrinsic nuclei	Globus pallidus — external segment
	Subthalamic nucleus
	Substantia nigra pars compacta
	Ventral tegmental area

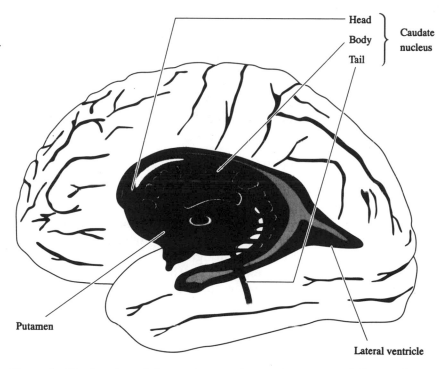

Figure 4 The location of the caudate nucleus and putamen relative to the rest of the brain. After Martin (1989), by permission

output, which is relayed via the thalamus. These organisational features are represented in Figure 5.

To a greater or lesser extent, contemporary neuroanatomical theories of OCD stress the importance of excitatory and inhibitory pathways to, through, and out of basal ganglia. These pathways are as follows:

- From the cortex to the striatum (excitatory)

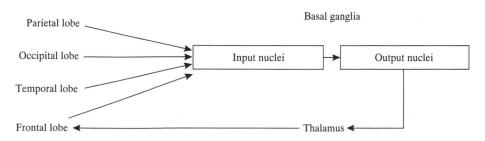

Figure 5 The input and output loops of the basal ganglia

- From the striatum to the globus pallidus (inhibitory)

- From the globus pallidus to the thalamus (inhibitory)

- From the thalamus to the cortex (excitatory)

It should be noted that this scheme is, of course, a simplification. Indeed, neuroanatomical theorists freely acknowledge the omission of important structures and related pathways (Rapoport, 1991).

Specific Fronto-Striatal Theories

Baxter and colleagues (Baxter et al., 1990; Baxter et al., 1992) have proposed two rather different fronto-striatal theories of OCD. The first of these implicates impairment in the gating and screening functions of the striatum. Baxter suggests that impulses concerning aggression, danger, hygiene and sex 'leak through' to consciousness, creating the subjective experience of obsessions. The relatively fixed content of obsessions is thought to reflect themes relevant to fundamental drives. Fixed action patterns, in the form of compulsions, may also occur as part of the individual's response to non-inhibited material. Efforts to combat impulses are essentially cortical, and may result in superstitious thinking, consciously executed rituals, or avoidance behaviour. The locus of this cortical response is the orbital region of the frontal lobe, which is unaffected by pathology, but excessively active due to compensatory demands. Baxter's account is remarkably similar to psychoanalytic account of OCD, which suggest that unacceptable urges (particularly hostile urges) are admitted into awareness because of incomplete repression, necessitating defensive responses to reduce guilt and anxiety (see Chapter 9).

A second neuroanatomical theory was proposed by Baxter and colleagues (Baxter et al., 1992) shortly after that described above. In this second account, key concepts such as caudate 'repression' and orbital 'compensation' are omitted, in favour of a more basic reverberating loop model. According to the revised theory, it is 'worry' outputs from the orbital region that drive OCD-relevant circuits in the caudate nucleus. This increases inhibitory output to regions of the globus pallidus. Inhibition of the globus pallidus reduces, in turn, inhibition of the thalamus, making this structure vulnerable to orbital activation. The excitatory connections between the thalamus and orbital region of the frontal lobe make this a potentially self-sustaining circuit and thus difficult to break.

Baxter's revised theory has much in common with an earlier model proposed by Insel & Winslow (1990), who suggest that OCD is an example of *hyperfrontality*. As such, it represents the exact opposite of the frontal lobe syndrome. Again, inhibitory and excitatory connections linking the cortex, caudate nucleus, globus pallidus, and thalamus are implicated in the formation of overactive cortical-striatal loops. According to Insel & Winslow, hyperfrontality will be associated with increased worry and guilt (especially with involvement of the orbital cortex), hyperjudgemental rigidity, and intense affect. The concurrent increase in striatal activity is thought to be associated with the emergence of repetitive 'subroutines' (cf. MacLean, 1978), or habit patterns such as grooming or checking.

In the accounts described above, fixed action patterns and subroutines feature significantly. The first clear articulation of a neuroethological model of OCD can be attributed to Rapoport and colleagues (Wise & Rapoport, 1989; Rapoport, 1991); however, the relationship between fundamental animal behaviour patterns and OCD has been considered before. For example, Gray (1982) discusses the possibility of an evolutionary continuum between the human use of soap and water and more ancient forms of grooming observed in fearful animals (Willingham, 1956). He also invokes the notion of 'response preparedness', that is, a predisposition to exhibit certain behaviours in a given situation.

Rapoport suggests that OCD represents the inappropriate activation or release of fixed action patterns. In her model, she describes a detection mechanism for recognising specific aspects of stimuli (key or sign stimuli) and a releasing mechanism for the species-typical behavioural response.

Two conceptions of basal ganglia functioning are central to Rapoport's model. First, the basal ganglia are considered to be the repository of innate motor programmes (Greenberg, MacLean & Ferguson, 1979; MacLean 1978; Murphy, MacLean & Hamilton, 1981), and second, the basal ganglia function, at least in part, as a gating mechanism for sensory input (Caligiuri & Abbs, 1987; Schneider, 1984). The reader is reminded that the basal ganglia receive efferent fibres from all of the cortical lobes.

An important feature of Rapoport's model is the convergence of two sets of inputs to the striatum, particularly the ventromedial aspect of the caudate nucleus and the nucleus accumbens (Figure 6). One of these is from the cortical association areas and is thought to be involved in the recognition of objects and sounds (i.e. the superior and inferior temporal areas). The other is from the anterior cingulate cortex and the orbital frontal cortex. Rapoport suggests that the striatum includes cell groups that act as stimulus detectors. She also postulates another striatal cell

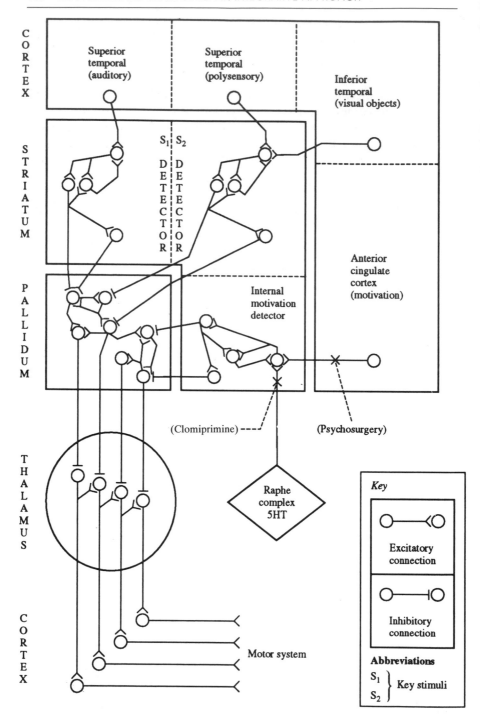

assembly, which constitutes an 'internal motivation detector'. It is activation of the cingulate-internal motivation detector circuit that is responsible for compulsive behaviour. These assemblies play an important role in the functioning of the now familiar fronto-striatal loop.

According to Rapoport, the sensory apparatus relays information to the cortex and then to the striatum. If the stimulus matches stored representations in the striatum, then the striatal cells begin discharging, thus inhibiting the pallidal cells projecting to the thalamus. An example of this is the recognition of dirtiness. If sensory information to the striatum indicates that the hands are dirty, an innately programmed striatal cell group recognises this input as dirtiness. 'That cell group then discharges vigorously and stops the tonic discharging of the appropriate pallidal cell. Removal of the inhibitory inputs to the thalamus releases the thalamocortical circuits that lead to the normal behavioural response to dirty hands, hand washing' (Rapoport, 1991, p. 87).

The second converging circuit originates from the anterior cingulate cortex and relays to the same pallidal cell group via a different set of striatal neurons. This circuit provides a signal when an individual is to perform an act due to an exclusively 'internal' motivation. When signals from the cingulate cortex to the striatum converge on the pallidal cell group, then behaviour can be released in the absence of sensory stimulation. Thus, hand washing might be triggered by the 'internal motivation detector' even though a 'dirtiness' signal is absent. Excessive activity in the cingulate cortex or striatum will potentiate this circuit. Rapoport suggests a similar set of arguments could be made for the cognitive functions of the basal ganglia in relation to obsessional thoughts.

It should be noted that fronto-striatal theories are broadly consistent with the serotonin hypothesis, and the results of psychosurgery. Animal studies suggest that concentrations of serotonin and its 5 HT-2 receptors are high in the caudate nucleus and nucleus accumbens (Pazos & Palacios, 1985). It should also be noted that the striatum receives dense serotonergic projections from the dorsal raphe (Molliver, 1987).

Anterior cingulotomy (Whitty et al., 1952) involves the bilateral excision of the anterior portion of the cingulate gyrus. In subcaudate tractotomy (Knight, 1964), lesions are placed bilaterally in the orbital cortex, ventral

Figure 6 Rapoport's 'neural' model of obsessive compulsive disorder. Note that the therapeutic effects of clomipramine and psychosurgery are accounted for with reference to links between the raphe complex, striatum (internal motivation detector), and anterior cingulate cortex. Reproduced by permission from Rapoport, 1991

to the head of the caudate nucleus. Limbic leucotomy (Kelly, 1980) combines bilateral lesions in the orbito-frontal areas, with bilateral lesions placed in the anterior cingulate, whereas anterior capsulotomy (Nauta, 1973) requires sterotactic lesions in the anterior portion of the internal capsule. It is believed that the efficacy of capsulotomy is mediated by interruption of pathways through the anterior portion of the internal capsule connecting the orbito-frontal cortex with midline thalamic nuclei (Modell et al., 1989). Clearly, all of the above procedures break the circuits considered to be of central importance in OCD by neuroanatomical theorists.

EVALUATION

The above theories have been largely inspired by brain scanning investigations. In sum, a common conclusion of these investigations is that OCD is characterised by increased rates of metabolism in the frontal lobe and the basal ganglia. There can be little doubt that these results represent a significant advance in the understanding of the neuroanatomical substrates of OCD; however, several of the models cited above ascribe highly specific functions to particular structures. Rapoport (1991) locates the 'internal motivation detector' in the striatum, whereas Baxter et al. (1990) are sufficiently bold to locate repression in the caudate. At this stage, it is most probably premature to ascribe such specific functions. The complexity of interacting excitatory and inhibitory circuits in the caudate nucleus is of an order that makes interpretation of brain scan investigations extremely difficult; a fact not overlooked by key contributors in the field (Baxter et al., 1992). At this stage, it would seem judicious to conclude that fronto-striatal circuits may play a significant role in the aetiology and maintenance of OCD; however, the exact nature of this role remains speculative. The concept of 'hyperfrontality' seems intuitively plausible. Given that the frontal lobe is particularly associated with higher cognitive functions, excessive biological activity might well correspond with the 'ruminative' features of OCD. Also, it is of some interest to note that damage to the orbital cortex is associated with violent tendencies, socially inappropriate sexual behaviour, and a lack of concern with hygiene (Stuss & Benson, 1986). Such damage is thought to result in decreased levels of activity in the frontal lobe. It is possible that the excessive caution and overconscientiousness evident in OCD is in some way related to the hyperfrontality underscored by Insel & Winslow (1990); however, the notion that a continuum of complex personality characteristics can be reduced to either increased or decreased rates of metabolism in a particular area of the brain might be construed as somewhat simplistic.

As with hyperfrontality, the notion of innate motor programmes stored in the basal ganglia also has intuitive appeal. Washing and hoarding in OCD, for example, may correspond with primitive motor programmes selected and preserved because of their importance for species survival. Abnormalities in associated brain systems could result in their inappropriate activation. A problem with this account is that many behaviours characteristic of OCD seem to have little, or no evolutionary significance: preoccupation with order and symmetry, number rituals, restarting, retracing (especially through doorways), and superstitious thinking, to name but a few. Checking, on the other hand, may have evolutionary significance, but the biological basis of such behaviour might be better accounted for within the septo-hippocampal framework provided by Gray (1982). Of course, it is possible that no single neuroanatomical system can account for all the features of OCD, and a 'hyperactive' behavioural inhibition system may work in concert with a hyperactive fronto-striatal system.

A further problem with fronto-striatal theories is the significance given to a 'reverberating' fronto-striatal loop. If such a circuit is difficult to break, then the factors that lead to the cessation of obsessional behaviour need to be specified. As yet, neuroanatomical theories have little to say about why compulsive washing or checking ultimately stops. It is possible that activity is reduced because of the system's self-limiting properties; however, again, such an explanation seems simplistic. The fronto-striatal system might be compared to a tuning fork that stops vibrating because of the diffusion of energy.

In addition to the above, fronto-striatal theories (as currently described), contribute little to our understanding of perhaps the most ubiquitous obsessional phenomenon: doubting. Although Rapoport claims that her theory suggests a biological system underlying an 'epistemological sense', she does not elaborate further than implicating the information-processing function of the basal ganglia. This involves the 'rejection or acceptance of sensory input, ideas, explanations, and thoughts' (Rapoport 1991, p. 90).

Chapter 22

AN INTEGRATED FRAMEWORK: COGNITIVE NEUROPSYCHOLOGY

AN INTEGRATED FRAMEWORK

In spite of the weaknesses of the neuroanatomical theories described above, it is impossible to ignore the impact of this growing literature. Unfortunately, there have been few attempts to integrate this literature with preexisting work. It would appear that theoretical accounts of OCD exist at three levels: first, those that attribute the symptoms of OCD to a biological abnormality (e.g. fronto-striatal theories); second, those that attribute the symptoms of OCD to the presence of fundamental cognitive deficits (e.g. the mnestic deficit hypothesis); and third, those that place particular emphasis on the evaluations and beliefs of the individual (e.g. appraisal theories).

Each of these research traditions has produced stimulating accounts of OCD; however, it is unclear how they fit together. Indeed, the discourses seem so disparate at times that it is difficult to envisage how any meaningful consolidation of approaches can be achieved. Moreover, the problem is compounded by a tendency for advocates of particular theoretical positions to defend their corner at the expense of alternative accounts.

OCD is a complex phenomenon. It is unlikely that any one theory will provide an entirely comprehensive account of the problem. It is perhaps more useful to conceptualise OCD as: *the common end with respect to several different pathways and factors*. Moreover, each pathway and factor may be of differential significance in any given individual.

A fundamental divide in the literature appears to be between those who consider OCD to be a neurological problem, and those who consider it to be a psychological problem. Support in favour of the former position is provided by those patients who exhibit biologically meaningful compulsions in the absence of significant cognition. Support in favour of the latter position is provided by those patients whose compulsive behaviour appears to be strongly associated with learning experiences and idiosyncratic beliefs and appraisals. It seems plausible to suggest that these groups represent the opposite ends of a continuum. As such, one might expect the majority of patients with OCD to occupy the middle ground. That is, their symptoms are the product of both biological and experiential factors in equal or differing measures. Although this is hardly an original or compelling idea, it is remarkable how few commentators seriously acknowledge the value of conceptualising OCD in this way. There is a strong trend in the literature to think of OCD in terms of mutually exclusive discourses. Such thinking can only limit and impoverish our understanding of such a complex disorder.

This book, as its title suggests, is primarily about cognitive aspects of OCD. How can cognition, in the broadest possible sense, be reconciled with the biological theories cited above within a single conceptual framework? Fortunately, cognitive neuropsychology already has a framework that has this potential, namely, the model of the control of thought and action proposed by Norman & Shallice (1980).

It is widely recognised that the symptoms of OCD represent exaggerated forms of normal behaviour. For example, most, if not all individuals experience intrusive thoughts, prefer to avoid contaminants, wash, and engage in some checking. Norman & Shallice devised their model to explain universal features of human behaviour. As such, it lends itself readily to explaining OCD as a disturbance in the everyday functioning of a fundamental information-processing system. In addition, it has several features that correspond closely with the biological theories cited above.

Before describing the Norman & Shallice model it is worth underscoring a particularly salient point: they provide a framework for the understanding of control processes in human behaviour, rather than a specific theory. This recommends it, in so far as it provides a superordinate system within which to embed, and therefore link, a number of specific theoretical ideas about OCD drawn from different discourses. Although the Norman and Shallice model has recently been employed by Frith (1992) to account for the symptoms of schizophrenia, in the context of psychotic illness the model requires considerable elaboration. In the following section, the Norman & Shallice model is employed to explain the symptoms of OCD; however, few, if any modifications are necessary.

THE CONTROL OF THOUGHT AND ACTION: NORMAN & SHALLICE (1980)

Norman and Shallice have adopted the position that cognition and action depend on the operation of highly specialised programmes (or schemas), each of which produces specific output for a range of inputs. A basic unit, or schema, will control a specific overlearned action. It can be triggered by perceptual information and from the output of other schemas.

Potentially, many schemas could be activated at the same time. The process of schema selection involves two qualitatively distinct processes. Routine, and to a lesser extent non-routine, selection is undertaken as part of *contention scheduling*. Exclusively non-routine selection occurs when ongoing behaviour is interrupted by the *supervisory attentional system* (SAS). A simplified version of the Norman & Shallice model (1980) representing the flow of control information is shown in Figure 7.

Contention scheduling ensures the efficient use of limited effector and cognitive resources under routine conditions. This selection procedure is necessary, given that competition to use resources for several different purposes may exist. Contention scheduling will ensure that a restricted number of compatible schemas are selected, so that they can control such resources as they require until a specific goal is achieved, unless a higher

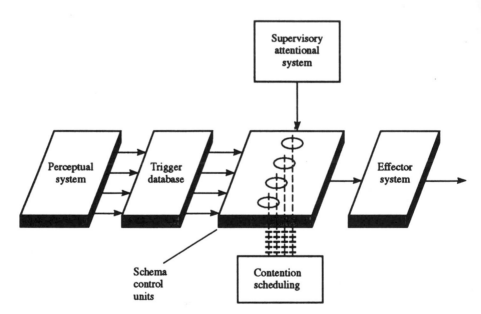

Figure 7   The model of the control of thought and action proposed by Norman & Shallice (1980). Lines with arrows represent activating input, the crossed lines represent the primarily mutually inhibitory function of contention scheduling. The term 'effector system' refers to specific purpose processing units involved in schema operation for both action and thought schemas. In the latter case schema operation involves placing information in short-term stores that can activate the trigger database. Reproduced by permission

priority schema is triggered. A schema will operate when activation in a schema control unit reaches threshold; selection is accomplished by mutual inhibition between units. The amount of inhibition will be determined by the level of incompatibility between units. After a schema has been selected, inhibition must be maintained if it is to continue controlling behaviour.

The non-routine selection of behaviours involves the biasing of the operation of contention scheduling by the additional activation of appropriate schemas. This is undertaken by the SAS, which contains general programming and planning systems. When the SAS interrupts ongoing behaviour, selection become slow and flexible, instead of fast, routine and unchanging. The SAS interrupts ongoing behaviour for several reasons, the most notable of these being the perception of threat.

In the following, this fundamental framework will be employed to explain the various forms of OCD. In addition, efforts will be made to show how this framework can embrace and link several theoretical accounts of OCD.

OBSESSIONS AND COMPULSIONS: COGNITION AND COGNITIVE NEUROPSYCHOLOGY

Perceptual information (internal or external) may trigger the entry into awareness of an intrusive thought. This becomes the subject of a negative appraisal, most probably influenced by an underlying dysfunctional belief system. A negative appraisal of danger results in the interruption of ongoing behaviour by the SAS. Once active, the SAS biases contention scheduling with respect to reparative or preventative behaviour in the form of other thought or action schemas. In the context of OCD, these will take the form of overt or covert rituals. Such behaviours may result in a failure to gather disconfirmatory evidence that might challenge underlying beliefs.

The salience of intrusive thoughts will be determined by appraisals and beliefs. The content of these appraisals and beliefs will be strongly influenced by learning history. Increased salience may lead to a lowering of the activation threshold necessary for intrusions to enter awareness. It is also possible that certain self-regulatory strategies, such as suppression, will increase the salience of intrusive thoughts (see Chapter 9). The role of generic self-regulatory plans in OCD has been elaborated elsewhere by Wells & Mathews (1994).

Over time, the occurrence of intrusive thoughts, and the conjoint operation of appraisals and underlying beliefs, might result in the development of highly integrated and complex cognitive schemas. These will necessarily inhibit other competing schemas, and will be given processing priority. Mood congruency effects may facilitate the activation of danger schemas, while inhibiting the availability of incongruent information (Lloyd & Lishman, 1975; Clark & Teasdale, 1982).

The biasing of contention scheduling by the SAS will favour the activation of reparative and preventative behaviours. These may be selected on the basis of their logical consistency with respect to the nature of the threat; for example, washing will be selected after contact with a perceived dangerous contaminant. Alternatively, it may be that in some individuals contention scheduling is already biased due to biological factors. Thus, fundamental action schemas (perhaps the equivalent of fixed action patterns) are more readily activated than others. These action schemas may correspond closely with those posited by Rapoport and colleagues and are thought to be stored in the basal ganglia. There are clear similarities between the function of the SAS and Gray's BIS. Therefore, interruption of ongoing behaviour might involve engagement of the septo-hippocampal system, resulting in anxiety and checking behaviour. The SAS, however, may have the power to override fundamental biological schemas, and under the influence of a modulating belief system, select higher order responses that have little logical relationship to the perceived threat. Under such circumstances, schemas may be selected that involve the performance of a superstitious or idiosyncratic reparative or preventative behaviour.

The excessive repetition of compulsive behaviours may be attributable to a number of factors. First, it is possible that the complex appraisal schemas remain active. Therefore, execution of anxiety-reducing compulsions may have, at least initially, little effect. Second, it may be that the reparative and preventative schemas remain active. Thus, an individual may 'know' that the behaviour is unnecessary but feel a strong urge to perform a compulsion 'anyway'. Finally, it may be that both appraisal and response schemas remain active. This scenario may have its biological basis in the fronto-striatal self-maintaining circuit described by neuroanatomical theorists (see above). In Norman & Shallice's framework, the persistence of obsessional thoughts and compulsive behaviour might also be attributable to a failure of other schemas to inhibit the schemas that are already active. Although this account is of some interest, it has already been suggested that the reverberating circuit account of OCD can be accused of oversimplifying brain functioning. Therefore, an alternative view may be necessary.

Doubt-related phenomena may provide some clue. As has been suggested, all forms of OCD are associated with doubt-related phenomena (see Chapter 2). Perhaps there is some fundamental processing deficit, whereby there is a failure to verify the successful accomplishment of reparative or preventative behaviours. A verification failure might require several repetitions of a particular behaviour before appropriate information processing is successfully accomplished. However, it should be noted that patients with OCD do not doubt everything. It is therefore highly likely that verification failures are potentiated by anxiety (cf. Zohar et al., 1989).

There are four principle input–output loops through the basal ganglia: the sensory motor loop, the occulo-motor loop, the association loop, and the limbic loop (Figure 8). Impaired functioning in any, or all, of the first three of these might account for the fundamental processing deficits arising in doubt. The presence of the limbic loop may be significant with respect to the potentiation of verification errors during acute episodes of anxiety. It is also of some interest to note that impaired functioning in these loops would be consistent with the non-verbal and action memory deficits described in the neuropsychological literature (see Chapter 13).

Recent research suggests that the functioning of the SAS may have a significant role to play in the performance of prospective memory tasks (Burgess & Tallis, in preparation). The mechanisms that subserve prospective memory might also be implicated with respect to doubt-related phenomena in OCD. Shallice & Burgess (1991) have suggested that prospective memory functioning requires the creation of what are described as 'temporal markers'. These act as triggers, the purpose of which is to interrupt ongoing behaviour. Temporal markers remain dormant until 'tagged' stimuli alert the individual that behaviour should not be treated as routine, but rather, relevant for action. Thus, closing a door might be associated with the necessity to check that it is securely closed. This can be considered a feature of normal behaviour. In OCD, repetitive 'checking' might occur when temporal markers are activated inappropriately, or when there is a failure to delete a temporal marker (cf. Burgess & Tallis, in preparation). The urge to perform a compulsive action will remain, potentiating associated action schemas. Although the example of checking is used here, the same factors may be important in a range of other obsessional behaviours.

It is interesting to note that temporal markers go some way towards explaining the more extreme doubt-related phenomena observed in OCD. If a temporal marker remains active, an obsessional individual might be fully aware that a door is closed, but still experience the motivational state that is usually 'felt' just prior to checking. This 'knowing yet not knowing' is described by many patients, and is extremely difficult to account for within a cognitive appraisal framework. The physiological

1. Sensory–motor loop

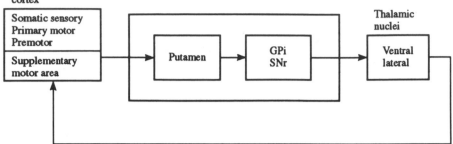

2. Oculomotor loop

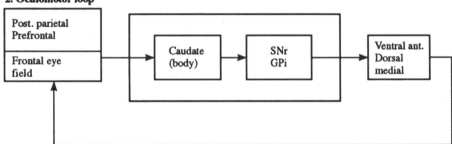

3. Association loop

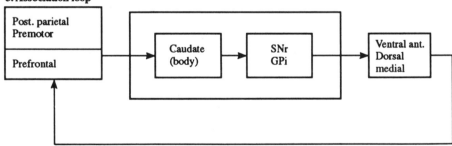

4. Limbic loop

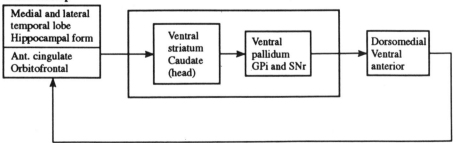

substrate associated with the creation and activation of temporal markers is thought to be the orbital area of the frontal lobe. As such, a temporal marker theory of doubt would be consistent with 'hyperfrontality' theories of OCD.

The preservation of repetitive behaviours might also be explained by a more fundamental aspect of the Norman & Shallice model, that is, contention scheduling itself. The reader is reminded that routine, or over-practised behaviours of any kind, will eventually be selected 'automatically', and the execution of such behaviours will require little cognitive effort. Many chronic OCD patients describe a steady reduction of anxiety associated with ritualising that occurs over time (Rachman & Hodgson, 1980; Stern & Cobb, 1978). It is as though the sequence of events leading to the execution of compulsive behaviours occurs as a fixed response to internal and/or external stimuli. Indeed clinicians describe the abbreviation of complex rituals in chronic cases. For example, wiping or even using a mental image or word (e.g. 'Palmolive') to replace washing with soap and water (Steketee, 1993). This automaticity is also accompanied by a loss of awareness. Again, Steketee observes that 'Some client's routines have become so habitual that they are unaware of actions that seem repetitive, unnecessary, or unreasonable to others' (p. 83). Rachman & Hodgson (1980) also describe this phenomenon: 'We also found a correlation between senselessness and duration of the disorder. That is, patients with a long history of obsessional problems were more likely to describe their rituals as senseless. (The rituals also seem to become more mechanical over time.)' (p. 20). As the elements of a practised sequence become more and more under the control of contention scheduling, the SAS becomes less likely to interrupt ongoing behaviour. The individual feels less anxiety, and the behaviours become more like habits than OCD *per se*.

Obsessions might occur in the absence of compulsions, where complex cognitive schemas are activated, but the existing belief system does not recommend reparative or preventative behaviour. The SAS may interrupt ongoing behaviour, but contention scheduling is not biased favouring the emergence of typical compulsions. This might be, at least in part, attributable to the absence of biological vulnerability factors. In attempting to locate the biological substrate of obsessional rumination, it seems likely that the orbital region of the frontal lobe might be implicated.

Figure 8   The general organisation of the four main loops through the basal ganglia (Abbreviations: GPi, globus pallidus internal segment; SNr, substantia nigra pars reticula) After Martin (1989), by permission

Where compulsions occur in the absence of obsessions there is a direct correspondence between biological theories and the Norman & Shallice model. Such patients tend to report few, if any, cognitions, and urges rather than anxiety. Although it is possible that any set of action schemas might be inappropriately activated, the biologically significant fixed action patterns described by Rapoport and colleagues may be those that are most likely to emerge. As suggested above, these may be located in the basal ganglia.

Repetition of compulsive behaviours in such cases might be attributable to impaired SAS functioning. External stimuli will elicit 'set' responses, and the SAS will fail to interrupt and bias contention scheduling with respect to further planned behaviour. This class of compulsions might be compared with the repetitive 'utilisation' behaviours described in the neurological literature (Lhermitte, 1983).

REFERENCES

Abel, J.I.. (1993). Exposure with response prevention and serotoergic anti-depressants in the treatment of obsessive compulsive disorder: A review and implications for interdisiplinary treatment. *Behaviour Research and Therapy*, **31**, 463–478.

Adams, P. (1973). *Obsessive Children*. New York: Brunner/Mazel.

Akhtar, S., Wig, N.H., Verma, V.K., Pershod, D. & Verma, S.K. (1975). A phenomenological analysis of the symptoms of obsessive-compulsive neuroses. *British Journal of Psychiatry*, **127**, 342–48.

Alanen, Y.O., Rekola, J.K., Stewen, A., Takala, K. & Tuovinen, M. (1966). The family in the pathogenesis of schizophrenic and neurotic disorders. *Acta Psychiatrica Scandinavica*, **42** (suppl. 189).

Allen, J.J. & Rack, P.H. (1975). Changes in obsessive compulsive patients measured by the Leyton inventory before and after treatment with clomipramine. *Scottish Medical Journal*, **20**, 41–45.

Allen, J.J. & Tune, G.S. (1975). The Lynfield Obsessional-Compulsive Questionnaire. *Scottish Medical Journal*, **20**, 21–26.

American Psychiatric Association (1980). *Diagnostic and Statistical Manual of Mental Disorders, 3rd edn (DSM-III)*. Washington, DC: American Psychiatric Association.

American Psychiatric Association (1987). *Diagnostic and Statistical Manual of Mental Disorders, 3rd edn revised (DSM-III-R)*. Washington, DC: American Psychiatric Association.

American Psychiatric Association (1994). *Diagnostic and Statistical Manual of Mental Disorders, 4th edn (DSM-IV)*. Washington, DC: American Psychiatric Association.

Ananth, J., Solyom, L., Bryntwick, S. et al. (1979). Chlomipramine therapy for obsessive compulsive neurosis. *American Journal of Psychiatry*, **136**, 700–701.

Aranowitz, B.R., Hollander, E., DeCaria, C., Cohen, L., Saoud, J., Stein, D., Liebowitz, M.R. & Rosen, W.G. (in press). Neuropsychology of obsessive-compulsive disorder: preliminary findings. *Neuropsychiatry, Neuropsychology, and Behavioural Neurology*.

Arts, W., Hoogduin, K., Schap, C. & de Haan, E. (1993). Do patients suffering from obsessions alone differ from other obsessive-compulsives? *Behaviour Research and Therapy*, **31**, 119–123.

Austin, L.S., Lydiard, R.B., Ballenger, J.C., Cohen, B.M. et al. (1991) Dopamine blocking activity of clomipramine in patients with obsessive compulsive disorder. *Biological Psychiatry*, **30**, 225–232.

Ausubel, D.B. (1955). Relationships between shame and guilt in the socializing process. *Psychological Review*, **62**, 378–390.

Baer, L. & Jenike, M. (1992). Personality disorders in obsessive compulsive disorder. *Psychiatric Clinics of North America*, **15**, 803–812.

Baer, L., Minichiello, W.E. & Jenike, M.A. (1987). Use of a portable-computer program in behavioral treatment of obsessive-compulsive disorder. *American Journal of Psychiatry*, **144**, 1101.

Ballerini, A. & Stanghellini, G. (1989). Phenomenological questions about obsession and delusion. *Psychopathology*, **22**, 315–319.

Bandura, A. (1977). *Social Learning Theory*. Englewood Cliffs, N.J: Prentice-Hall.

Barlow, D. (1988). *Anxiety and its Disorders*. New York: The Guilford Press.

Baron-Cohen, S. (1989). Do autistic children have obsessions and compulsions? *British Journal of Clinical Psychology*, **28**, 193–199.

Barsky, A.J. (1992). Hypochondriasis and obsessive compulsive disorder. *The Psychiatric Clinics of North America*, **15**, 791–802.

Barton, R. (1965). Diabetes insipidus and obsessional neurosis: a syndrome. *Lancet*, **1**, 133–135.

Bass, B.A. (1973). An unusual behavioural technique for healing obsessional ruminations. *Psychotherapy: Theory, Research and Practice*, **10**, 191–192.

Baxter, L.R., Phelps, M.E., Mazziotta, J.C. et al. (1987). Local cerebral glucose metabolic rates in obsessive-compulsive disorder: a comparison with rates in unipolar depression and in normal controls. *Archives of General Psychiatry*, **44**, 211–218.

Baxter, L.R., Schwartz, J.M., Guze, B.H., Bergman, K. & Szuba, M.P. (1990). Neuroimaging in obsessive-compulsive disorder: seeking the mediating neuroanatomy. In Michael A. Jenike, Lee Baer, & William E. Minichiello (eds), *Obsessive-Compulsive Disorders: Theory and Management*, Second edition. London: Mosby Year Book.

Baxter, L.R., Schwartz, J.M., Bergam, K.S., Szuba, M.P., Guze, B.H., Mazziotta, J.C., Alazraki, A., Selin, C.E., Ferng, H., Munford, P., Phelps, M. (1992) Caudate glucose metabolic rate changes with both drug and behavior therapy for obsessive-compulsive disorder. *Archives of General Psychiatry*, **49**, 681–689.

Baxter, L.R., Schwartz, J.M., Mazziotta, J.C. et al. (1988). Cerebral glucose metabolic rates in non-depressed obsessive-compulsives. *American Journal of Psychiatry*, **145**, 1560–1563.

Beck, A.T. (1967). *Depression: Clinical, Experimental and Theoretical Aspects*. New York: Harper & Row.

Beck, A.T. (1972). *Depression: Causes and Treatment*. Philadelphia, PA: University of Pennsylvania Press.

Beck, A.T. (1976). *Cognitive Therapy and the Emotional Disorders*. New York: International University Press.

Beck, A.T. & Greenberg, R.L. (1974). *Coping with Depression*. Available from: The Center for Cognitive Therapy, Room 602, 133 South 36th Street, Philadelphia, PA 19104.

Beck, A.T., Rush, A., Shaw, B. & Emery, G. (1979). *Cognitive Therapy of Depression*. New York: Guilford Press.

Beck, A.T. & Steer, R.A. (1987). *Beck Anxiety Inventory Manual*. New York: The Psychological Corporation.

Beck, A.T., Ward C.H., Mendelson, M., Mock, J. & Erbaugh, J. (1961). An inventory for measuring depression. *Archives of General Psychiatry*, **4**, 561–571.

Beech, H.R., Ceiseilski, K.T. & Gordon, P.K. (1983). Further observations of evoked potentials in obsessional patients. *British Journal of Psychiatry*, **142**, 605–609.

Beech, H. & Vaughn, M. (1978). *The Behavioural Treatment of Obsessional States*. Chichester: Wiley.

Behar, D., Rapoport, J.L., Berg, C.J. et al. (1984) Computerised tomography and neuropsychological test measures in adolescents with obsessive-compulsive disorder. *American Journal of Psychiatry*, **141**, 363-369.

Benkelfat, C., Murphy, D.L., Zohar, J. et al. (1989). Clomipramine in obsessive compulsive disorder: further evidence for a serotonergic mechanism of action. *Archives of General Psychiatry*, **46**, 23-28.

Benkelfat, C., Nordhal, T.E., Semple, W. et al. (1990). Local cerebral glucose metabolic rates in obsessive-compulsive disorder. *Archives of General Psychiatry*, **47**, 840-848.

Benton, A.L. (1955) *The Revised Visual Retention Test: Clinical and Experimental Applications*. New York: The Psychological Corporation.

Benton, A.L. (1974) *The Revised Visual Retention Test (4th edn)*. New York: The Psychological Corporation.

Berg, B. (1989). Behavioural assessment techniques for childhood obsessive-compulsive disorder. In J. Rapoport (ed.), *Obsessive-Compulsive Disorder in Children and Adolescents*. Washington DC: American Psychiatric Press Inc.

Berg, C.Z., Rapoport, J.L., Whitaker, A. et al. (1989). Childhood obsessive compulsive disorder: A two year prospective follow up of a community sample. *Journal of American Academic Child and Adolescent Psychiatry*, **28**, 528-533.

Berrios, G. (1989). Obsessive-compulsive disorder: its conceptual history in France during the 19th century. *Comprehensive Psychiatry*, **30**, 283-295.

Black, A. (1974). The natural history of obsessional neurosis. In H.R. Beech (ed.), *Obsessional States*. London: Methuen.

Black, D.W., Yates, W.R., Noyes, R., Pfoll, B. et al. (1989). DSM-III personality disorder in obsessive compulsive study volunteers: a controlled study. *Journal of Personality Disorders*, **3**, 58-62.

Bland, R.C., Newman, S.C., Orn, H. et al. (1988). Lifetime prevalence of psychiatric disorders in Edmonton. *Acta Psychiatrica Scandinavica*, **77** (suppl. 338), 24-32.

Boller, F., Passafiume, D., Keefe. N.C., Rogers, K., Morrow, L. & Kim, Y. (1984). Visuospatial impairment in Parkinson's disease: role of perceptual and motor factors. *Archives of Neurology*, **41**, 485-490.

Boone, K., Ananth, J., Philpott, L., Kaur, A. & Djenderedjian, A. (1991). Neuropsychological characteristics of nondepressed adults with obsessive compulsive disorder. *Neuropsychiatry, Neuropsychology, and Behavioural Neurology*, **4**, 96-109.

Borkovec, T.D., Wilkinson, L., Folensbee, R. & Lerman, C. (1983). Stimulus control applications to the treatment of worry. *Behaviour Research and Therapy*, **21**, 247-251.

Boulougouris, J.C. (1977). Variables affecting outcome in obsessive-compulsive patients treated by flooding. In J.L. Boulougouris, A.D. Rabavilas (eds), *Treatment of Phobic and Obsessive-Compulsive Disorders*. Oxford: Pergamon.

Bouvard, M., Mollard, E., Cottraux, J. & Guerin, J. (1989). Etude preliminaire d'une liste de pensées obsédantes. *L'Encephale*, **15**, 351-354.

Bowen, F.P., Hoehn, M.M. & Yahr, M.D. (1972). Parkinsonism: alterations in spatial orientation as determined by a route-walking test. *Neuropsychologia*, **10**, 355-361.

Brady, K.T., Austin, L. & Lydiard, R.B. (1990). Body dysmorphic disorder: the relationship to obsessive-compulsive disorder. *Journal of Nervous and Mental Disease*, **178**, 538-539.

Breuer, J. & Freud, S. (1893). On the physical mechanism of hysterical phenomena: preliminary communication. In *Studies on Hysteria*, London: The Pelican Freud Library.

Brickner, R.M., Rosner, A.A. & Munroes, R. (1940). Physiological aspects of the obsessive state. *Psychosomatic Medicine*, **2**, 369–383.

Bridges, P., Goktepe, E. & Maratos, R. (1973). A comparative review of patients with obsessional neurosis and with depression treated by psychosurgery. *British Journal of Psychiatry*, **123**, 663–674.

Broadbent, D.E., Cooper, P.J., Fitzgerald, P.F. & Parkes, K.R. (1982). The cognitive failures questionnaire (CFQ) and its correlates. *British Journal of Clinical Psychology*, **21**, 1–16.

Broadhurst, A. (1976). It's never too late to learn — an application of conditioned inhibition to obsessional ruminations in an elderly patient. In H.J. Eysenck (ed.), *Case Studies in Behavioural Therapy*. London: Routledge and Kegan Paul.

Brown, A. (1978). Knowing when, where and how to remember: a problem of metacognition. In R. Glaser (ed.), *Advances in Instructional Psychology*. Hillsdale, NJ: Erlbaum.

Brown, F.W. (1942). Heredity in the psychoneuroses. *Proceedings of the Royal Society of Medicine*, **35**, 785–790.

Burgess, P. & Tallis, F. (in preparation). Temporal markers and OCD.

Burns, D. (1980). *Feeling Good: The New Mood Therapy*. New York: Penguin (signet); First printing August 1981.

Butler, G. & Mathews, A. (1983). Cognitive processes in anxiety. *Advances in Behavior, Research, and Therapy*, **11**, 551–565.

Butler, G. & Mathews, A (1987). Anticipatory anxiety and risk perception. *Cognitive Therapy and Research*, **11**, 551–565.

Butters, N., Soeldner, C. & Fedio, P. (1972). Comparison of parietal and frontal lobe spatial deficits in man: extrapersonal vs personal (egocentric) space. *Perceptual and Motor Skills*, **34**, 27–34.

Buttolph, L. & Holland, A. (1990). Obsessive compulsive disorders in pregnancy and childbirth. In M.A. Jenike, L. Baer, & W. Minichiello (eds), *Obsessive-Compulsive Disorders: Theory and Management*. Massachusetts: Year Book Medical Publishers, Inc.

Caine, T.M. & Hawkins, L.G. (1963). Questionnaire measure of the hysteroid obsessoid component of personality: the HOQ. *Journal of Consulting Psychology*, **27**, 206–209.

Caligiuri, M.P. & Abbs, J.H. (1987). Response properties of the perioral reflex in Parkinson's disease. *Experimental Neurology*, **98**, 563–572.

Cambier, J., Masson, C., Benammous, S. & Robine, B. (1988). La graphomanie. Activité graphique compulsive manifestation d'un gliome fronto-calleux. *Revue Neurologic*, **144**, 158–164.

Campbell, J.D. & Fairey, P.J. (1985). Effects on self-esteem, hypothetical explanations and verbalization of expectancies on future performance. *Journal of Personality and Social Psychology*, **48**, 1097–1111.

Carey, G. (1978). A clinical genetic twin study of obsessive and phobic states. Ph.D. thesis, University of Minnesota.

Carey, G. & Gottesman, I.I. (1981). Twin and family studies of anxiety, phobic, and obsessive disorders. In D.F. Klein & J. Rabkin (eds.), *Anxiety: New Research and Changing Concepts*. New York: Raven Press.

Carr, A.T.A. (1970). Psychophysiological study of ritual behaviours and decision processes in compulsive neurosis. Unpublished doctoral dissertation. University of Birmingham.

Carr, A. (1974). Compulsive neurosis: a review of the literature. *Psychological Bulletin*, **81**, 311–318.

Carrol, B.J., Feinberg, M., Greden, J.F., Toriska, J., Albal, A.A., Hachet, R.F., James, M., Kronfal, Z., Lohr, N., Steiner, M., de Vigine, J.P. & Young, E. (1981). A specific laboratory test for the diagnosis of melancholia: standardization, validation and clinical utility. *Archives of General Psychiatry*, **38**, 15–22.

Catts, S. & McConaghy, N. (1975). Ritual prevention in the treatment of obsessive-compulsives. *Australian and New Zealand Psychiatry*, **9**, 37–41.

Cautela, J.R. (1969). Behaviour therapy and self control: technique and implications. In C.M. Franks (ed.), *Behaviour Therapy: Appraisal and Status*. New York: McGraw Hill.

Cawley, R. (1974). Psychotherapy and obsessional disorders. In H.R. Beech (ed.), *Obsessional States*. London: Methuen.

Ceiseilski, K.T., Beech, R.H. & Gordon, P.K. (1981). Some electrophysiological observations in obsessional states. *British Journal of Psychiatry*, **138**, 479–484.

Chiocca, E.A. & Martuza, R.L. (1990). Neurosurgical therapy of obsessive-compulsive disorder. In M.A. Jenike, L. Baer & W.E. Minichiello (eds), *Obsessive-Compulsive Disorders: Theory and Management*, 2nd edn. London: Mosby Year Book.

Chiu, H.C., Mortimer, J.A., Slager, U., Zarow, C., Bondareff, W. & Webster, D.D. (1986). Pathologic correlates of dementia in Parkinson's disease. *Archives of Neurology*, **43**, 991–995.

Chouinard, G., Goodman, W., Greist, J. et al. (1991). Results of a double blind placebo controlled trial using a new serotonin uptake inhibitor, setraline, in obsessive-compulsive disorder. *Psychopharmacol Bull*, **26**, 279–284.

Christensen, K., Kim, S.W., Dyksen, M.W. & Hoover, K.M. (1992) Neuropsychological performance in obsessive compulsive disorder. *Biological Psychiatry*, **31**, 4–18.

Clarizio, H.F. (1991). Obsessive Compulsive Diorder: The secretive syndrome. *Psychology in the Schools*, **28**, 106–115.

Clark, D.A. & Bolton, D. (1985). An investigation of two self report measures of obsessional phenomenon in obsessive-compulsive adolescents: research note. *Journal of Child Psychology and Psychiatry*, **26**, 429–437.

Clark, D.A. & de Silva, P. (1985). The nature of depressive and anxious intrusive thoughts: Distinct or uniform phenomena? *Behaviour Research and Therapy*, **23**, 383–393.

Clark, D.M., Ball, S. & Pape, D. (1991). An experimental investigation of thought suppression. *Behaviour Research and Therapy*, **29**, 253–257.

Clark, D.M., Salkovskis, P.M., Hackmann, A., Middleton, H., Anastasiades, P. & Gelder, M. (1994). A comparison of cognitive therapy, applied relaxation, and imipramine in the treatment of panic disorder. *British Journal of Psychiatry*, **164**, 759–769.

Clark, D.M. & Teasdale, J.D. (1982). Diurnal variations in clinical depression and accessibility of memories of positive and negative experiences. *Journal of Abnormal Psychology*, **91**, 87–95.

Clark, D.M., Winton, E. & Thynn, L. (1993). A further experimental investigation of thought suppression. *Behaviour Research and Therapy*, **31**, 207–210.

Clomipramine Collaborative Study Group (1991). Efficacy of clomipramine in OCD: results of a multicenter double-blind trial. *Archives of General Psychiatry*, **37**, 1281–1285.

Cohen, J. (1988). *Statistical Power Analysis for the Behavioural Sciences*. Hillsdale, NJ: Lawrence Erlbaum Associates.

Cohen, L., Hollander, E., DeCaria, C.M., Stein, D., Simeon, D., Leibowitz, M.R. & Aranowitz, B. (submitted). *Specificity of Neuropsychological Impairment in Obsessive-Compulsive Disorder: A Comparison with Social Phobic and Normal Controls.*

Cooper, J. (1970). The Leyton Obsessional Inventory. *Psychological Medicine*, **1**, 48–64.

Cooper, J.E. & Kelleher, M. (1973). The Leyton Obsessional Inventory: A principal components analysis on normal subjects. *Psychological Medicine*, **3**, 204–208.

Corsi, P. (1972) Human memory and the medial temporal region of the brain. Ph.D. thesis, McGill University.

Coryell, W. (1981). Obsessive compulsive disorder and primary unipolar depression: Comparisons of background, family history, course and mortality. *Journal of Nervous Mental Diseases*, **169**, 220–224.

Costa Molinari, J.M., Eguillor, M., Romeu, J. & Tizon, J. (1971). Semiologia Clinica. In S. Monserrat-Esteve, J.M. Costa Molinari & C. Ballus (eds), *Patologia Obsesiva*. Malaga: Graficasa.

Cox, C.S., Fedio, P. & Rapoport, J. (1989). Neuropsychological testing of obsessive-compulsive adolescents. In J. Rapoport (ed.), *Obsessive-Compulsive Disorder in Childhood and Adolescents*. Washington DC: American Psychiatric Press.

Daniels, L.K. (1976). An extension of thought-stopping in the treatment of obsessional thinking. *Behavior Therapy*, **7**, 131.

Davey, G.C.L. & Tallis, F. (1994). *Worrying: Perspectives on Theory, Assessment and Treatment*. Chichester: Wiley.

Davis, R.D. (1948). *Pilot Error*, Air publications 3139a. London: HMSO.

Delis, D., Kramer, J., Ober B. & Kaplan, E. (1986). *The California Verbal Learning Test*. San Antonio, TX: The Psychological Corporation.

Dent, H.R. & Salkovskis, P.M. (1986). Clinical measures of depression, anxiety and obsessionality in non-clinical populations. *Behavior Research and Therapy*, **24**, 689–691.

Derogatis, L.R. (1977). SCL-90: Administration, scoring and procedures manual-I for the revised version. Baltimore, MD: Johns Hopkins University School of Medicine, Clinical Psychometrics Research Unit.

Derogatis, L. & Melisaratos, N. (1983). The brief symptom inventory: an introductory report. *Psychological Medicine*, **13**, 595–605.

de Silva, P. (1987) Obsessions and compulsions: treatment. In S.J.E. Lindsay & G.E. Powell (eds), *A Handbook of Clinical Adult Psychology*. Aldershot: Gower.

de Silva, P. (1990). Self-management strategies in early Buddhism: a behavioural perspective. In J. Crook and D. Fontana (eds), *Space in Mind*. Shaftesbury, Dorset: Element Books.

de Silva, P. & Rachman, S. (1992). *Obsessive Compulsive Disorder: The Facts*. Oxford: Oxford University Press.

De Veaugh-Geiss, J., Landau, P. & Katz, R. (1989). Treatment of obsessive-compulsive disorder with clomipramine. *Psychiatric Annals*, **19**, 97–101.

Dickinson, A. (1980). *Contemporary Animal Learning Theory*. Cambridge: Cambridge University Press.

Donath, J. (1897). Zur Kenntnis des Anankasmus (Psychichesswangzustade). *Archiv für Psychologie und Nervenkrankh*, 29–39.

Douglas, W. (1980). Histamine and 5-Hyroxytryptamine (serotonin) and their antagonists. In A. Goodman, L. Goodman, & A. Gilma (eds), *The Pharmacological Basis of Therapeutics*. New York: Macmillan Publishing Company.

Downes, J.D., Roberts, A.C., Sahakian, B.J., Evenden, J.L. & Robbins, T.W. (1989). Impaired extra-dimensional shift performance in medicated and unmedicated Parkinson's disease: evidence for a specific attentional dysfunction. *Neuropsychologia*, **27**, 1329–1343.

Drewe, E.A. (1974). The effect of type and area of brain lesion on Wisconsin Card Sorting Test performance. *Cortex*, **10**, 159–170.

Dunn, L. (1959). *Peabody Picture Vocabulary Test*. Circle Pines, MN: American Guidance Service.

Ecker, W. & Engelkamp, J. (submitted). *Memory for Actions in Obsessive-Compulsive Disorder*.

Edwards, S. & Dickerson, M. (1987). Intrusive unwanted thoughts: a two-stage model of control. *British Journal of Medical Psychology*, **60**, 317–328.

Ellis, A. (1956). The basic clinical theory of rational emotive therapy. In A. Ellis & R. Grieger (eds), *Handbook of Rational Emotive Therapy* (1977). New York: Springer Publishing Co.

Ellis, A. (1962). *Reason and Emotion in Psychotherapy*. New York: Lyle Stuart.

Emmelkamp, P.M.G. (1982). *Phobic and Obsessive-Compulsive Disorders*. New York: Plenum Press.

Emmelkamp, P.M.G. & Beens, H. (1991). Cognitive therapy with obsessive-compulsive disorder: a comparative evaluation. *Behaviour Research and Therapy*, **29**, 293–300.

Emmelkamp, P. & Kwee, K. (1977). Obsessional ruminations: a comparison between thought-stopping and prolonged exposure in imagination. *Behaviour Research and Therapy*, **15**, 441–444.

Emmelkamp, P.M.G., van der Helm, M., van Zanten, B.L. & Plochg, I. (1980). Contributions of self-instructional training to the effectiveness of exposure in vivo: A comparison with obsessive compulsive patients. *Behaviour Research and Therapy*, **18**, 61–66.

Emmelkamp, P.M.G., Visser, S. & Hoekstra, R.J. (1988). Cognitive therapy vs. exposure in vivo in the treatment of obsessive-compulsives. *Cognitive Therapy and Research*, **12**, 103–114.

Enright, S.J. & Beech, A.R. (1990). Obsessional states: anxiety disorders or schizotypes? An information processing and personality assessment. *Psychological Medicine*, **20**, 621–627.

Esquirol, J. (1838). Des maladies mentales considerees sous les rapports medical, *Hygienique et Medico-legal* (2 vols). Paris: Bailliere.

Estes, W.K. (1974). Learning theory and intelligence. *American Psychologist*, **29**, 740–749.

Eysenck, H.J. (1947). *Dimensions of Personality*. New York: Praeger.

Eysenck, H.J. (1985). *Decline and Fall of the Freudian Empire*. Harmondsworth: Viking Penguin.

Eysenck, M.W. (1992). *Anxiety: The Cognitive Perspective*. Hove: Lawrence Erlbaum Associates.

Farkas, G.M. & Beck, S. (1981). Exposure and response prevention of morbid ruminations and compulsive avoidance. *Behaviour Research and Therapy*, **19**, 257–261.

Fedio, P., Cox, C.S., Neophytides, G. et al. (1979). Neuropsychological profile of Huntington's disease: patients and those at risk. In T.N. Chase, N.S. Wexler & A. Barbeau (eds), *Advances in Neurology, Vol 23: Huntington's Disease*. New York: Raven Press.

Fitz, A. (1990). Religious and familial factors in the etiology of obsessive-compulsive disorder: A review. *Journal of Psychology and Theology*, **18**, 141–147.

Flament, M.F., Rapoport, J.L., Murphy, D.L., Berg, C.J. & Lake, R. (1987). Biochemical changes during clomipramine treatment of childhood obsessive compulsive disorder. *Archives of General Psychiatry*, **44**, 219–225.

Flett, G.L. & Blankstein, K.R. (1994). Worry as a component of test anxiety: a multidimensional analysis. In G.C.L. Davey & F. Tallis (eds), *Worrying: Perspectives on Theory, Assessment and Treatment*. Chichester: Wiley.

Flor-Henry, P. (1983). *Cerebral Basis of Psychopathology*. Boston, MA: John Wright.

Flor-Henry, P., Yeudell, L.T., Koles, Z.J. & Howarth, B.G. (1979). Neuropsychological and power spectral EEG investigations of the obsessive-compulsive syndrome. *Biological Psychiatry*, **14**, 119–130.

Foa, E. (1979). Failure in treating obsessive-compulsives. *Behaviour Research and Therapy*, **17**, 169–176.

Foa, E.B. & Goldstein, A. (1978). Continuous exposure and complete response prevention on obsessive-compulsive neurosis. *Behavior Therapy*, **9**, 821–829.

Foa, E.B. & Kozak, M.H. (1986). Emotional processing of fear: exposure to corrective information. *Psychological Bulletin*, **99**, 20–35.

Foa, E.B. & Steketee, G.S. (1979). Obsessive-compulsives: Conceptual issues and treatment interventions. In M. Hersen, R.M. Eisler, & P.M. Miller (eds), *Progress in Behavior Modification*, Vol. 8. New York: Academic Press.

Foa, E.B., Steketee, G.S. & Grayson, J.B. (1985). Imaginal and in vivo exposure: a comparison with obsessive-compulsive checkers. *Behavior Therapy*, **16**, 292–302.

Foa, E.B., Steketee, G.S. & Ozorow, B.J. (1985). Behavior therapy with obsessive compulsives: from theory to treatment. In M. Mavissakalian, S.M. Turner, & L. Michelson (eds), *Obsessive-Compulsive Disorder; Psychological and Pharmacological Treatment*. New York: Plenum Press.

Foa, E.B., Steketee, G.S., Turner, R.M. & Fischer, S.C. (1980). Effects of imaginal exposure to feared disasters in obsessive compulsive checkers. *Behaviour Research and Therapy*, **18**, 449–455.

Foa, E.B. & Tillmanns, A. (1980). The treatment of obsessive-compulsive neurosis. In A. Goldstein and E.B. Foa (eds), *Handbook of Behavioural Interventions: A Clinical Guide*. New York: Wiley.

Fox, N. & Tallis, F. (1994). Utilization behaviour in adults with autism: a preliminary investigation. *Clinical Psychology and Psychotherapy*, **1**, 210–218.

Freeston, M.H., Ladoucer, R., Thibodeau, N. & Gagnon, F. (1991). Cognitive intrusions in a non-clinical population 1: response style, subjective experience and appraisal. *Behaviour Research and Therapy*, **29**, 585–597.

Freeston, M.H., Ladouceur, R., Gagnon, F. & Thibodeau, N. (1993). Beliefs about obsessional thoughts. *Journal of Psychopathology and Behavioural Assessment*, **15**, 1–21.

Freud, S. (1908). Character and anal eroticism. In *Collected Papers*, Vol 2. London: Hogarth Press.

Freud, S. (1909). Notes upon a case of obsessional neurosis (the 'rat man'). In Angela Richards (ed.), The Penguin Freud Library: *Case Histories II*. Harmindsworth: Penguin.

Freud, S. (1913a) The predisposition to obsessional neurosis. In *Collected Papers*, Vol 2. London: Hogarth Press.

Freud, S. (1913b). Totem and Taboo. In *The Origins of Religion*. London: The Penguin Freud Library.

Frith, C.D. (1992). *The Cognitive Neuropsychology of Schizophrenia*. Hove: Erlbaum.

Frost, R. & Gross, R. (1993). The hoarding of possessions. *Behaviour Research and Therapy*, **31**, 367–381.

Frost, R.O., Krause, M.S., McMahon, M.J., Peppe, J., Evans, M., McPhee, A.E. & Holden, M. (1993). Compulsivity and superstitiousness. *Behaviour Research and Therapy*, **31**, 423–425.

Frost, R., Lahart, C., Dugas, K. & Sher, K. (1988). Information processing among non-clinical compulsives. *Behaviour Research and Therapy*, **26**, 275–277.

Frost, R.O., Steketee, G., Cohn, L. & Griess, K. (1994). Personality traits in subclinical and non-clinical obsessive-compulsive volunteers and their parents. *Behaviour Research and Therapy*, **32**, 47–56.

Gaitonde, M.R. (1958). Cross-cultural study of the psychiatric syndromes in outpatient clinics in Bombay, India and Topeka, Kansas. *International Journal of Psychiatry*, **3**, 98–104.

Gelder, S., Gath, D. & Mayoy, R. (1983). *Oxford Textbook of Psychiatry*. Oxford: Oxford Medical.

Gendlin, E.T. (1981). *Focusing*. New York: Bantum Books.

George, M.S., Kellner, C.H. & Fossey, M.D. (1989). Obsessive-compulsive symptoms in a patient with multiple sclerosis. *Journal of Nervous and Mental Diseases*, **177**, 304–305.

Gittleson, N. (1966). The fate of obsessions in depressive psychosis. *British Journal of Psychiatry*, **112**, 705–708.

Gojer, J., Khannu, S. & Channabasavanna, S.M. (1987). Obsessive Compulsive Disorder, anxiety and depression. *Indian Journal of Psychological Medicine*, **10**, 25–30.

Golden, P. (1984). Psychologic and neuropsychologic aspects of Tourette's Syndrome. *Neurol. Clin.*, **21**, 91–102.

Goodman, W.K. & Price, L.H. (1990). Rating scales for obsessive-compulsive disorder. In M.A. Jenike, L. Baer & W. Minichiello (eds), *Obsessive-Compulsive Disorders: Theory and Management*. Massachusetts: Year Book Medical Publishers, Inc.

Goodman, W.K. & Price, L.H. (1992). Assessment of severity and change in obsessive compulsive disorder. *Psychiatric Clinics of North America*, **15**, 861–869.

Goodman, W.K., Price, L.H., Rasmussen, S.A. et al. (1989a). Efficacy of fluvoxamine in obsessive-compulsive disorder: A double-blind comparison with placebo. *Archives of General Psychiatry*, **46**, 36–44.

Goodman, W.K., Price, L.H., Rassmussen, S.A. et al. (1989b). The Yale–Brown Obsessive Compulsive Scale (Y-Bocs): Part I. Development, use, and reliability. *Archives of General Psychiatry*, **46**, 1006–1011.

Goodman, W.K. , Price, L.H. Rassmussen, S.A. et al. (1989c). The Yale–Brown Obsessive Compulsive Scale (Y-Bocs): Part II. Validity. *Archives of General Psychiatry*, **46**, 1012–1016.

Goodman, W.K., Rasmussen, S.A., Price, L.H. et al. (1986). *Children's Yale-Brown Obsessive Compulsive Scale (CY-Bocs), edn 1*. Bethesda, M.D: Department of Psychiatry of Yale and Brown Universities, and Child Psychiatry Branch, National Institute of Mental Health.

Goodwin, D., Guze, S. & Robins, E. (1969). Follow-up studies in obsessional neurosis. *Archives of General Psychiatry*, **20**, 182–187.

Gordon, P. (1985). Allocation of attention in obsessional disorder. *British Journal of Psychology*, **24**, 101–107.

Gorman, J.M., Liebowitz, M.R., Fyer, A.J., Davies, S.O. & Klein, D.F. (1985). Lactate infusions in obsessive compulsive disorder. *American Journal of Psychiatry*, **142**, 864–866.

Gray, J.A. (1975). *Elements of a Two-Process Theory of Learning*. London: Academic Press.

Gray, J.A. (1982). *The Neuropsychology of Anxiety: An Enquiry into the Functions of the Septo-hippocampal System*. Oxford: Oxford University Press.

Gray, J.A. (1985). A whole and its parts: behaviour, the brain, cognition and emotion. *Bulletin of the British Psychological Society*, **38**, 99–112.

Greenberg, D. (1984). Are religious compulsions religious or compulsive? A Phenomenological study. *American Journal of Psychotherapy*, **38**, 524–532.

Greenberg, D. (1987). Compulsive hoarding. *American Journal of Pychotherapy*, **41**, 409–416.

Greenberg, N. MacLean, P.D. & Ferguson, J.L. (1979). Role of the paleostriatum in species-typical display behaviour of the lizard. *Brain Research*, **172**, 229–241.

Griez, E., de Loof, C., Ols, H., Zandbergen, J. et al. (1990). Specific sensitivity of patients with panic attacks to carbon dioxide. *Psychiatry Research*, **31**, 193–199.

Guidano, V.L. & Liotti, G. (1983). *Cognitive Processes and Emotional Disorders*. New York: Guilford Press.

Guy, W. (1976). *ECDEU. Assessment Manual for Psychopharmacology*, Washington, DC: US Dept of Health Education and Welfare, publ. no. 76–338.

Hamilton, M. (1960). A rating scale for depression. *Journal of Neurology, Neurosurgery, and Psychiatry*, **23**, 56–62.

Hamilton, V. (1957). Perception and personality dynamics in reactions to ambiguity. *British Journal of Psychology*, **48**, 200–215.

Harvey, N.S. (1987). Neurological factors in obsessive-compulsive disorder. *British Journal of Pychiatry*, **150**, 567–568.

Hawton, K., Salkovskis, P.M., Kirk, J. & Clark, D. (1989). *Cognitive Behaviour Therapy for Psychiatric Problems: A Practical Guide*. Oxford: Oxford Medical Publications.

Head, D., Bolton, D. & Hymas, N. (1989). Deficit in cognitive shifting ability in patients with obsessive-compulsive disorder. *Biological Psychiatry*, **25**, 929–937.

Heaton, R.K. (1981). *Wisconsin Card Sorting Test Manual*. Odessa, FL: Psychological Assessment Resources.

Hewitt, P.L., Flett, G.L. & Blamkstein, K.R. (1991). Perfectionism and neuroticism in psychiatric patients and college students. *Personality and Individual Differences*, **12**, 273–279.

Hillbom, E. (1960). After effect of brain injuries. *Acta Psychiatrica Neurologica Scandinavia*, **35**, (Suppl.), 42.

Hodgson, R.J. & Rachman, S. (1977). Obsessional compulsive complaints. *Behaviour Research and Therapy*, **15**, 389–395.

Hodgson, R.J., Rachman, S. & Marks, I.M. (1972). The treatment of chronic obsessive compulsive neurosis: follow-up and further findings. *Behaviour Research and Therapy*, **10**, 181–189.

Hoehn-Saric, R., Pearlson, G., Harris, G.J. et al. (1991). Effects of fluoxetine on regional cerebral blood flow in obsessive-compulsive patients. *American Journal of Psychiatry*, **49**, 690–694.

Hoekstra, R. (1989). Treatment of obsessive-compulsive disorder with rational emotive therapy. Paper presented at the First World Congress of Cognitive Therapy, Oxford, 28 June–2 July, 1989.

Hoffnung, R.A., Aizenberg, D.V., Hermesh, H. & Muntz, H. (1989). Religious compulsions and the spectrum concept of psychopathology. *Psychopathology*, **22**, 141–144.

Hollander, E., Liebowitz, M.R., Winchel, R., Klumer, A. & Klein, D.F. (1989). Treatment of body-dysmorphic disorder. *American Journal of Psychiatry*, **146**, 768–770.

Hollander, E., Schiffman, E., Cohen, B., Rivera-Stein, M., Rosen, W., Gorman, J., Fyer, A., Papp, L. & Leibowitz, M. (1990). Signs of central nervous system dysfunction in obsessive compulsive disorder. *Archives of General Psychiatry*, **47**, 27–32.

Hollingsworth, C., Tanguay, P., Grossman, L. et al. (1980). Long-term outcome of obsessive compulsive disorder in childhood. *Journal of American Academic Child Psychiatry*, **9**, 134–144.

Hooper, H.E. (1958). *The Hooper Visual Organization Test Manual*. Los Angeles: Western Psychological Services.

Hunter R. & Macalpine, I (1963). *Three Hundred Years of Psychiatry*. London: London University Press.

Hwuh, Y.E., Chang, L., et al. (1989). Prevalence of psychiatric disorders in Taiwan. *Acta Psychiatrica*, Scandinavia, **79**, 136.

Hyler, S.E. & Rieder, R.O. (1987). *PDQ-R: Personality Diagnostic Questionnaire-Revised*. New York: New York State Psychiatric Institute.

Hyler, S.E., Skodol, A.E., Oldham, J.M., Kellman, H.D. & Norman, D. (1992). Validity of the personality diagnostic questionnaire-revised: A replication in an outpatient sample. *Comprehensive Psychiatry*, **33**, 73–77.

Ingram, I.M. (1961). Obsessional illness in mental hospital patients. *Journal of Mental Science*, **107**, 382–402.

Inouye, E. (1965). Similar and disimilar manifestations of obsessive-compulsive neurosis in monozygotic twins. *American Journal of Psychiatry*, **121**, 1171–1175.

Inscl, T.R. & Akiskal, H.S. (1986). Obsessive compulsive disorder with psychotic features: A phenomenological analysis. *American Journal of Psychiatry*, **143**, 1527–1533.

Insel, T.R., Donelly, E.F., Lalakea, M.L., Alterman, I.S. & Murphy, D.L. (1983a). Neurological and neuropsychological studies of patients with obsessive-compulsive disorder. *Biological Psychiatry*, **18**, 741–751.

Insel, T.R., Donnelly, E.F., Lalaken, M.L., et al. (1983b). Neurological and neurological studies of patients with obsessive compulsive disorder. *Biological Psychiatry*, **18**, 741–751.

Insel, T.R., Gillin, J.C. Moore, A., Mendelson, W.B., Lavenstein, R.J. & Murphy, D.L. (1982). Sleep in obsessive compulsive disorder. *Archives of General Psychiatry*, **39**, 1372–1377.

Insel, T.R., Mueller, E.A., Alterman, I., Linnoila, M. & Murphy, D.L. (1985). Obsessive-compulsive disorder and serotonin: Is there a connection? *Biological Psychiatry*, **20**, 1174–1185.

Insel, T.R., Murphy, D.L., Cohen, R.M., et al. (1983) Obsessive-compulsive disorder. A double-blind trial of clomipramine and clorgyline. *Archives of General Psychiatry*, **40**, 605–612.

Insel, T.R., Zahn, T. & Murphy, D.L. (1985). Obsessive-compulsive disorder: an anxiety disorder? In A.H. Tuma & J.D. Maser (eds), *Anxiety and the Anxiety Disorders*. Hillsdale, NJ: Erlbaum.

Insel, T.R. & Winslow, J.T. (1990). Neurobiology of obsessive-compulsive disorder. In M.A. Jenike, L. Baer, & W.E. Minichiello (eds), *Obsessive-Compulsive Disorders: Theory and Management*, second edition. London: Mosby Year Book.

Institute of Psychiatry and Maudsley Hospital (1987). *Psychiatric Examination: Notes on Eliciting and Recording Clinical Information in Psychiatric Patients*. Oxford: Oxford University Press.

Jackson, D.N. (1984). *Multidimensional Aptitude Battery Manual*. London, Ontario: Research Psychologists Press.

Jacobson, E. (1929) *Progressive Relaxation*. Chicago: University of Chicago Press.

Jacobson, N.S., Follette, W.C. & Ravensdorf, D. (1984). Psychotherapy outcome research: methods for reporting variability and evaluating clinical significance. *Behavior Therapy*, **15**, 336-352.

Jacobson, N.S. & Truax, P. (1991). Clinical significance: a statistical approach to defining meaningful change in psychotherapy research. *Journal of Consulting and Clinical Psychology*, **59**, 12-19.

Jakes, I. (1992). An experimental investigation of obsessive compulsive disorder. Unpublished PhD thesis. London University.

James, W. (1890). *Principles of Psychology*. London: Macmillan.

Janet, P. (1903) *Les Obsessions at la Psychaesthenie*. Paris: Alcan.

Jellife, S.E. (1929). Psychologic components in postencephalitic oculogyric crises. *Archives of Neurology and Psychiatry*, **21**, 491-532.

Jenike, A.J. & Brotman, A.W. (1984). The EEG in obsessive compulsive disorder. *Journal of Clinical Psychiatry*, **45**, 122-124.

Jenike, M. Hyman, S. Baer, & L. (1990). A controlled trial of fluvoxamine for obsessive compulsive disorder: implications for a serotonergic theory. *American Journal of Psychiatry*, **147**, 1209-1215.

Joffe, R.T. & Swinson, R.P. (1990). Tranylcypromine in primary obsessive compulsive disorder. *Journal of Anxiety Disorders*, **4**, 365-367.

Jones, R. (1966). A factorial measure of Ellis' irrational beliefs system with personality maladjustment correlated. Unpublished doctoral disertation. Texas Technological University.

Junginger, J. & Head, A. (1991). Time series analysis of obsessional behavior and mood during self-imposed delay and response prevention. *Behaviour Research and Therapy*, **29**, 521-530.

Junginger, J. & Turner, S. (1987). Spontaneous exposure and self control in the treatment of compulsive checking. *Journal of Behavior Therapy and Experimental Psychiatry*, **18**, 115-119.

Kahneman, D. & Tversky, A. (1982). The simulation heuristic. In D. Kahneman, P. Slovic, & A. Tversky (eds), *Judgement Under Uncertainty: Heuristics and Biases*. Cambridge: Cambridge University Press.

Karno, M., Golding, J.M., Sorenson, S.B. & Burnham, M.A. (1988). The epidemiology of obsessive compulsive disorder in five US communities. *Archives of General Psychiatry*, **45**, 1094-1099.

Kasvikis, Y. & Marks, I.M. (1988). Clomipramine, self-exposure, and therapist-accompanied exposure in OCD: two year follow-up. *Journal of Anxiety Disorders*, **2**, 291-298.

Kayton, L. & Borge, G.F. (1967). Birth order and obsessive compulsive character. *Archives of General Psychiatry*, **17**, 751-754.

Keller, B.B. (1989). Cognitive assessment of obsessive compulsive children. In J. Rapoport (ed.), *Obsessive-Compulsive Disorder in Children and Adolescents*. Washington DC: American Psychiatric Press Inc.

Kelly, D. (1980). The limbic system, sex, and emotions. In *Anxiety and Emotions: Physiologic Basis and Treatment*. Springfield, Ill: Charles C. Thomas.

Kelly, G.A. (1955). *The Psychology of Personal Constructs*. New York: Norton.

Kenny, F.T., Mowbray, R.M. & Lalam, S. (1978). Faradic disruption of obsessive ideation in the treatment of obsessive neurosis. *Behavior Therapy*, **9**, 209-221.

Kenny, F.T., Solyom, L. & Solyom, C. (1973). Thought stopping: a useful treatment in phobias of mental stimuli. *British Journal of Psychiatry*, **119**, 305–307.

Kettle, P.A. & Marks, I.M. (1986). Neurological factors in obsessive-compulsive disorder: two case reports and a review of the literature. *British Journal of Psychiatry*, **149**, 315–319.

Khanna, S., Rajendra, P.N., Channabasavanna, S.M. et al. (1988). Life events and onset of obsessive compulsive disorder. *International Journal of Social Psychiatry*, **34**, 305–309.

Kiloh, L. & Garside, R. (1963). The independence of neurotic depression and endogenous depression. *British Journal of Psychiatry*, **109**, 451–63.

Kimura, D. (1963). Right temporal lobe damage. *Archives of Neurology*, 8, 264–271.

Kirk, J. (1983). Behavioural treatment of obsessional-compulsive patients in routine clinical practice. *Behaviour Research and Therapy*, **21**, 57–62.

Knight, G. (1964). The orbital cortex as an objective in the surgical treatment of mental illness: the results of 450 cases of open operation and the development of the stereotactic approach. *British Journal of Surgery*, **51**, 114–124.

Kohlberg, L. (1980). *The Meaning and Measurement of Moral Development*. Worcester, MA: Clark University Press.

Koopman, P.C., Sanderman, R., Timmerman, I. & Emmelkamp, P.M.G. (in press). The irrational beliefs inventory: development and psychometric evaluation. *European Journal of Psychological Assessment*.

Kraaimat, F. & Van Dam-Baggen, C. (1976). Ontwikkeling van een Selfbeoordelingslijst voor obsessief-compulsief gedrag. *Nederlands Tijdschrift voor de Pschologie*, **31**, 201–211.

Kringlen, E. (1965). Obsessional neurotics: A long-term follow up. *British Journal of Psychiatry*, **111**, 709–722.

Kugler, K. & Jones, W.H. (1992) On conceptualizing and assessing guilt. *Journal of Personality and Social Psychology*, **62**, 318–327.

Kugler, K.E., Murray, J. & Jones, W.H. (1988, April). Guilt and interpersonal factors. Paper presented at the Southwestern Psychological Association, Tulsa, Oklahama.

Lader, M. & Wing, L. (1966). *Physiological Measures, Sedative Drugs and Morbid Anxiety*. Maudsley Monograph. London: Oxford University Press.

Laing, R.D. (1964). Is schizophrenia a disease? *International Journal of Social Psychiatry*, **87**, 333–340.

Lang, P.J. (1970). Stimulus control, response control, and the desensitization of fear. In D.J. Levis (ed.), *Learning Approaches to Therapeutic Behaviour*. Chicago: Aldine Press.

Lang, P.J. (1977). Fear imagery: an information-processing analysis. *Behaviour Therapy*, **8**, 862–886.

Lang, P.J. (1979). A bio-informational theory of emotional imagery. *Psychophysiology*, **16**, 495–512.

Langinvaino, H., Kapiro, J., Koskenvuo, M. & Lonnqvist, J. (1984). Finnish twins reared apart, III: Personality factors. *Acta Genticae Mediacae et Gemmellologiae*, **33**, 259–267.

Lansdell, H. & Donnelly, E.F. (1977). Factor analysis of the Wechler Adult Intelligence Scale subtests and the Halstead-Reitan Category and Tallping tests. *Journal of Consulting and Clinical Psychology*, **45**, 412–484.

La Plane, D., Widlocher, D., Pillon, B., Baulac, M. & Binoux, F. (1981). Comportement compulsif d'allure par necrose circonscite bilaterale pallido-stritale. *Revue Neurologie*, **137**, 269–276.

Lavy, E. & van den Hout, M. (1990). Thought suppression induces intrusions. *Behavioural Psychotherapy*, **18**, 251–258.

Lazarus, R.S. (1964). A laboratory approach to the dynamics of psychological stress. *American Psychologist*, **19**, 400–411.

Lazarus, R.S. (1966). *Psychological Stress and the Coping Process*. New York: McGraw-Hill.

Leckman, J.F. & Chittenden, E.H. (1990). Gilles de la Tourette's syndrome and some forms of obsessive-compulsive disorder may share a common genetic diathesis. *Encephale*, **16** (Spec. No. 1), 321–323.

Lees, A.J., Robertson, M., Trimble, M.R. & Murry, N.M.F. (1989). A clinical study of Gilles de la Tourette's syndrome in the United Kingdom. *Journal of Neurology, Neurosurgery, and Psychiatry*, **47**, 1–8.

Legrand du Saulle, H. (1875). *La Folie du Doute (Avec Delire du Toucher)*. Paris: Delahaye.

Lenane, M.C., Swedo, S.E., Leonard, H., Pauls, D.L., Cheslow, D.L. & Rapoport, J.L. (1990) Psychiatric disorders in first degree relatives of children and adolescents with obsessive-compulsive disorder. *Journal of the American Academy of Child and Adolescent Psychiatry*, **29**, 407–412.

Leonard, H., Goldberger, E., Rapoport, J., Cheslow, D. & Swedo, S. (1990). Childhood rituals: normal development or obsessive-compulsive symptoms? *Journal of the American Academy of Child and Adolescent Psychiatry*, **29**, 17–23.

Levi, A.S. & Pryor, J.B. (1987). Use of the availability heuristic in probability estimates of future events: the effects of imagining outcomes vs imagining reasons. *Organizational Behaviour and Human Decision Processes*, **40**, 219–234.

Lewis, A. (1936). Problems of obsessional illness. *Proceedings of the Royal Society of Medicine*, **29**, 325–336.

Lewis, A. (1966). Obsessional disorder. In Price's *Textbook of the Practice of Medicine*, 10th edn, edited by R. Scott. London: Oxford University Press.

Lewis, A. (1967). *Inquiries in Psychiatry: Clinical and Social Investigations*. London: Routledge & Kegan Paul.

Lewis, H.B. (1984). *Freud and Modern Psychology. Vol 2. The Emotional Basis of Mental Illness*. New York: Plenum.

Lezak, M. (1983). *Neuropsychological Assessment*. Oxford: Oxford University Press.

Lhermitte, F. (1983). Utilization behaviour and its relation to lesions of the frontal lobes. *Brain*, **106**, 237–255.

Linnoilla, M., Vikkunen, M., Scheinin, M. et al. (1983). Low cerebrospinal fluid 5-HIAA concentration differentiates impulsive from non-impulsive violent behavior. *Life Science*, **33**, 2609–2614.

Lloyd, G.G. & Lishman, W.A. (1975). Effect of depression on the speed of recall of pleasant and unpleasant experiences. *Psychological Medicine*, **5**, 173–180.

Lo, W.H. (1967). A follow up study of obsessional neurotics in Hong Kong Chinese. *British Journal of Psychiatry*, **113**, 823–832.

Ludlow, C.L., Bassaich, C.J., Coner, N.P. & Rapoport, J.L. (1989). Psycholinguistic testing in obsessive-compulsive adolescents. In J.L. Rapoport (ed.), *Obsessive Compulsive Disorder in Children and Adolescents*. Washington, DC: American Psychiatric Press.

Luxenberg, J.S., Swedo, S.E., Flament, M.F. et al. (1988). Neuroanatomical abnormalities in obsessive compulsive disorder determined with quantitative x-ray computed tomography. *American Journal of Psychiatry*, **145**, 1089–1093.

Luxenberger, H. (1930). Hereditat und Familientypus der Zwangsneurotiker. *Archiv fur Psychiatrie*, **91**, 590–594.

Macdonald, A.M. & Murray, R.M. (1989). A twin study of Obsessive Compulsive neurosis. Presented at the 6th International Congress on Twin Studies, Rome, 28-31 August.

Macdonald, A.M., Murray, R.M. & Clifford, C.A. (1992). The contribution of heredity to obsessional disorder and personality: a review of family and twin study evidence. In M.T. Tsuang, K.S. Viendler & M.J. Lyons (eds), *Genetic Issues in Psychosocial Epidemiology*. New Brunswick: Rutger's University Press.

Machlin, S.R., Harris, G.J., Pearlson, G.D. et al. (1991). Elevated medial-frontal cerebral blood flow in obsessive-compulsive patients: A SPECT study. *American Journal of Psychiatry*, **148**, 1240-1242.

Mackintosh, N.J. (1983). *Conditioning and associative learning*. New York: Oxford University Press.

MacLean, P.D. (1978). Effect of lesions of globus pallidus on species-typical display behavior of squirrel monkeys. *Brain Research*, **149**, 175-196.

MacLeod, A.K. (1994). Worry and explanation based pessimism. In G.C.L. Davey & F. Tallis (eds), *Worrying: Perspectives on Theory, Assessment and Treatment*. Chichester: Wiley.

MacLeod, A.K., Williams, J.M.G. & Bekerian, D.A. (1991). Worry is reasonable: The role of explanations in pessimism about future personal events. *Journal of Abnormal Psychology*, **100**, 478-486.

Maher, B. (1988). Anomalous experience and delusional thinking: The logic of explanations, In T.F. Oltmanns & B.A. Maher (eds), *Delusional Beliefs*. New York: Wiley.

Mahoney, M.J. (1971). The self management of covert behavior: a case study. *Behavior Therapy*, **2**, 575-578.

Malloy, P. (1987). Frontal lobe dysfunction in obsessive compulsive disorders. In E. Perecman (ed.), *The Frontal Lobes Revisited*. IRBN Press.

Marks, I. (1987). *Fears, Phobias, and Rituals: Panic, Anxiety, and Their Disorders*. Oxford: Oxford University Press.

Marks, I.M. (1990). Behavioural self-treatment for OCD. Paper for workshop on OCD. Tucson, Arizona, 30 October 1990.

Marks, I.M., Crowe, M., Drewe, E., Young, J. & Dewhurst, W.G. (1969). Obsessive-compulsive neurosis in identical twins. *British Journal of Psychiatry*, **115**, 991-998.

Marks, I.M., Hallam, R.S., Connolly, J. & Philpott, R. (1977). *Nursing in Behavioural Psychotherapy. An Advance of Clinical Role for Nurses*. London: Royal College of Nursing of the United Kingdom. White Friars Press.

Marks, I.M., Hodgson, P. & Rachman, S. (1975). Treatment of obsessive-compulsive neurosis by in-vivo exposure. A two year follow-up and issues in treatment. *British Journal of Psychiatry*, **127**, 349-364.

Martin, J.H. (1989). *Neuroanatomy: Text and Atlas*. Englewood Cliffs, NJ: Prentice Hall International.

Martinot, J.L., Allilaire, J.F., Mazoyer, B.M. et al. (1990). Obsessive-compulsive disorder: a clinical, neuropsychological and positron emission tomography study. *Acta Psychiatrica Scandanavica*, **82**, 233-242.

Maudsley, H. (1895). *The Pathology of Mind*, revised edn. London: Macmillan.

Mawson, D., Marks, I.M. & Ramm, L. (1982). Clomipramine and exposure for chronic obsessive-compulsive rituals: two year follow-up and further findings. *British Journal of Psychiatry*, **140**, 11-18.

McFall, M.E. & Wollersheim, J.P. (1979). Obsessive-compulsive neurosis: a cognitive-behavioural formulation and approach to treatment. *Cognitive Therapy and Research*, **3**, 333-348.

McGeogh, J.A. & McDonald, W.T. (1931). Meaningful relation and retroactive inhibition. *American Journal of Psychology*, **43**, 579–588.

McGuire, P.K., Bench, C.J., Frith, C.D. et al. (1994). Functional anatomy of obsessive-compulsive phenomena. *British Journal of Psychiatry*, **164**, 459–468.

McKeon, J.P. (1983). Aetiological aspects of obsessive compulsive neurosis. MD Thesis, University College Dublin.

McKeon, J., McGuffin, P. & Robinson, P. (1984). Obsessive compulsive neurosis following head injury: a report of four cases. *British Journal of Psychiatry*, **144**, 190–192.

McKeon, P. & Murray, R.M. (1987). Familial aspects of obsessive-compulsive neurosis. *British Journal of Psychiatry*, **151**, 528–534.

McNally, R.J. & Kohlbeck, P.A. (1993). Reality monitoring in obsessive-compulsive disorder. *Behaviour Research and Therapy*, **31**, 249–253.

Mena, I., Marik, O., Fuenzalida, S. & Cotzias, A.C. (1967). Chronic manganese poisoning. *Neurology*, **17**, 128–136.

Merkelbach, H., Muris, P., van den Hout, M. & de Jong, P. (1991). Rebound effects of thought suppression: instruction dependent? *Behavioural Psychotherapy*, **19**, 225–238.

Mettler, F.A. (1955). Perceptual capacity, functions of the corpus striatum and schizophrenia. *Psychiatry Quarterly*, **29**, 89.

Meyer, V. (1966). Modification of expectations in cases with obsessional rituals. *Behaviour Research and Therapy*, **4**, 273–280.

Meyer, V., Levy, R., Schnurer, A. (1974). The behavioural treatment of obsessive-compulsive disorders. In H.R. Beech (ed.), *Obsessional States*. London: Methuen.

Miceli, G., Caltagirone, C., Gainotti, G., Masullo, C. & Silveri, M.C. (1981). Neuropsychological correlates of localized cerebral lesions in nonasphasic brain damaged patients. *Journal of Clinical Neuropsychology*, **3**, 53–63.

Mikulincer, M., Kedem, P. & Paz, D. (1990). The impact of trait anxiety and situational stress on the categorisation of natural objects. *Anxiety Research*, **2**, 85–101.

Milby, J.B., Meredith, R.L. & Rice, J. (1981). Videotaped exposure: a new treatment for obsessive-compulsive disorders. *Journal of Behaviour Therapy and Experimental Psychiatry*, **12**, 249–255.

Milner, B. (1963). Effects of different brain lesions on card sorting. *Archives of Neurology*, **9**, 90–100.

Milner, B. (1964). Some effects of frontal lobectomy in man. In J.M. Warren & K. Akert (eds), *The Frontal Granular Cortex and Behaviour*. New York: McGraw Hill.

Milner, B. (1965). Visually-guided maze learning in man: effects of bilateral hippocampal, bilateral frontal, and unilateral cerebral lesions. *Neuropsychologia*, **3**, 317–338.

Milner, B. (1969). Residual intellectual and memory deficits after head injury. In A.E. Walker, W.F. Caveness & M. Critchly (eds), *The Late Effects of Head Injury*. Springfield Ill: C.C. Thomas.

Milner, B. (1971). Interhemispheric differences in the localisation of psychological processes in man. *British Medical Bulletin*, **27**, 272–277.

Milner, B. & Teuber, H.L. (1968). Alterations of perception and memory in man: reflections in methods. In L. Weiskrantz (ed.), *Analysis of Behaviour*. New York: Harper & Row.

Minichiello, W.E., Baer, L. & Jenike, M.A. (1987) Schizotypal personality disorder: a poor prognostic indicator for behavior therapy in the treatment of obsessive-compulsive disorder. *Journal of Anxiety Disorders*, **1**, 273–276.

Modell, J.G., Mountz, J.M., Curtis, G.C. et al. (1989). Neurophysiologic dysfunction in basal ganglia/limbic striatal and thalamocortical circuits as a pathogenetic mechanism of obsessive-compulsive disorder. *Journal of Neuropsychiatry*, **1**, 27–36.

Molliver, M.E. (1987). Serotonergic neuronal systems: what their anatomic organization tells us about function. *Journal of Clinical Psychopharmacology*, **7**, 3S–23S.

Money, J. (1976). *A Standardized Road Map Test of Direction Sense: Manual*. San Rafael, California: Academic Therapy Publications. Chicago.

Monserrat-Esteve, O. (1971). Patologia obsesiva. In S. Monserrat-Esteve, J.M. Costa Molinari, and C. Ballus (eds), *XI Congreso Nacional de Neuropsiquiatrica*, Chap 1, p. 21, Malaga (Spain): Graficassa.

Monteiro, W., Marks, I.M., Noshirvani, H. & Checkley, S. (1986). Normal dexamethasone suppression test in obsessive-compulsive disorder. *British Journal of Psychiatry*, **148**, 326–329.

Morel, B. (1866). Du delire emotif. Nevrose du systeme nerveux Ganglionaire visceral. *Archives of General Medicine*, **7**, 385–402.

Morris, P.E. (1992). Cognition and consciousness. *The Psychologist*, **5**, 3–8.

Morris, P.E., Jones, S. & Hampton, P. (1978). An imagery mnemonic for the learning of people's names. *British Journal of Psychology*, **69**, 335–336.

Morris, P.E. & Reid, R.L. (1970). The repeated use of mnemonic imagery. *Psychonomic Science*, **20**, 337–338.

Mosher, D.L. (1966). The development and multi-trait-multi-method matrix analysis of three measures of three aspects of guilt. *Journal of Consulting Psychology*, **30**, 25–39.

Mosher, D.L. (1979). The meaning and measurement of guilt. In C.E. Izard (ed.), *Emotions in Personality and Psychopathology*, pp. 105–129. New York: Plenum Press.

Mosher, D.L. (1988). Revised Mosher Guilt Inventory. In C.M. Davis & W.L. Yarber (eds), *Sexuality Rated Measures: A Compendium*. Lake Mills, IA: Graphic Publications.

Moulton, R.W., Bernstein, E., Liberty, P.G. & Altucher, N. (1966). Patterning of paternal affection and disciplinary dominance as a determinant of guilt and sex typing. *Journal of Personality and Social Psychology*, **4**, 356–363.

Mowrer, O.H. (1947). On the dual nature of learning — a reinterpretation of 'conditioning' and 'problem solving'. *Harvard Educational Review*, **17**, 102–148.

Murphy, M.R., MacLean, P.D. & Hamilton, S.C. (1981). Species-typical behavior of hamsters deprived from birth of the neocortex. *Science*, **213**, 459–461.

Myers, J., Weissman, M., Tischler, G., Holzer, C., Leaf, P., Ovaschel, H., Anthony, J., Boyd, J., Burke, J., Kramer, M. & Stoltzman, R. (1984). Six-month prevalence of psychiatric disorders in three communities. *Archives of General Psychiatry*, **41**, 959–967.

Nauta, W.J.N. (1973). Connections of the frontal lobe with the limbic system. In L.V. Laitman & K.E. Livington (eds), *Surgical Approaches in Psychiatry. Proceedings of the Third International Congress of Psychosurgery*. Cambridge, England: Medical and Technical Publishing Co.

Nelson, H.E. (1976). A modified card sorting test sensitive to frontal lobe defects. *Cortex*, **12**, 313–324.

Newcombe, F. (1969). *Missile Wounds of the Brain*. London: Oxford University Press.

Neziroglu, F. & Yaryura-Tobias, J.A. (1979). NYT Obsessive-Compulsive Questionaire. Cited in Yaryura-Tobias, J. & Neziroglu, F. (1983). *Obsessive-Compulsive Disorders: Pathogenesis-Diagnosis-Treatment*. Marcel Dekker Inc: New York.

Niler, E.R. & Beck, S.J. (1989). The relationship among guilt, dysphoria, anxiety and obsessions in a normal population. *Behavior Research and Therapy*, **27**, 213–220.

Nordahl, T.E., Benkelfat, C., Semple, W.E. et al. (1989). Cerebral glucose rates in obsessive-compulsive disorder. *Neuropsychopharmocology*, **3**, 261–273.

Norman, D.A. & Shallice, T. (1980). Attention to action: willed and automatic control of behaviour. Center for Human Information Processing (Technical report No. 99). (Reprinted in revised form in: *Consciousness and Self-regulation. Advances in Research and Theory*, Vol 4, 1986, R.J. Davidson, G.E. Schwartz & D. Shapiro (eds), New York and London: Plenum Press, pp. 1–18).

Noshirvani, H.F., Kasvikis, Y., Marks, I., Tsakiris, F. et al. (1991). Gender-divergent aetiological factors in obsessive compulsive disorder. *British Journal of Psychiatry*, **158**, 260–263.

Orly, J. & Wing, J.K. (1979). Psychiatric disorders in two African villages. *Archives of General Psychiatry*, **36**, 513.

Ostereith, P.A. (1944). Le test de copie d'une figure complexe. *Archives de Psychologie*, **30**, 206–356.

O'Sullivan, G. & Marks, I. (1991). Follow-up studies of behavioural treatment of phobic and obsessive compulsive neuroses. *Psychiatric Annals*, **21**, 368–373.

O'Sullivan, G., Noshirvani, H., Monteiro, W. & Marks, I.M. (1991). Clomipramine and exposure for chronic obsessive-compulsive rituals: six year follow-up. *Journal of Clinical Psychiatry*, **52**, 150–155.

Otterbacher, J.R. & Munz, D.C. (1973). State-trait measure of experiential guilt. *Journal of Consulting and Clinical Psychology*, **40**, 115–121.

Parker, N. (1964). Twins: a psychiatric study of a neurotic group. *Medical Journal of Australia*, **2**, 735–742.

Paterson, R.J. & Neufeld, R.W.J. (1987). Clear danger: situational determinants of the appraisal of threat. *Psychological Bulletin*, **2**, 404–416.

Pato, M.T., Zohar-Kadouch, R., Zohar, J. & Murphy, D. (1988). Return of symptoms after discontinuation of clomipramine in patients with obsessive compulsive disorder. *American Journal of Psychiatry*, **145**, 1521–1527.

Pauls, D. (1992). The genetics of obsessive compulsive disorder and Gilles de la Tourette's syndrome. *The Psychiatric Clinics of North America*, **15**, 759–766.

Pavlov, I.P. (1928). *Lectures on Conditioned Reflexes*. New York: International Publishers.

Payne, R. (1960). Cognitive abnormalities. In H.J. Eysenck (ed.), *Handbook of Abnormal Psychology*. London: Pitmans.

Pazos, A., Cortes, R. & Palacios, J. (1985). Quantitative autoradiographic mapping of serotonin in rat brain II. Serotonin II receptors. *Brain Research*, **356**, 231–249.

Pazos, A. & Palacios, J. (1985). Quantitative autoradiographic mapping of serotonin receptors in rat brain I. Serotonin I receptors. *Brain Research*, **346**, 205–230.

Pedersen, N.L., Friberg, L., Floderus-Myrhed, B., McClearn, G.E. & Plomin, R. (1984). Swedish early separated twins: identification and characterization. *Acta Genticae Mediacae et Gemmellologiae*, **33**, 243–254.

Peeke, H.V.S. & Petrinovich, L. (1984). *Habituation, Sensitization and Behaviour*. London: Academic Press.

Pendleton, M.G. & Heaton, R.K.A. (1982). A comparison of the Wisconsin Card Sorting Test and the Category Test. *Journal of Clinical Psychology*, **38**, 392–396.

Perret, E. (1974). The left frontal lobe of man and the suppression of habitual responses in verbal categorical behaviour. Neuropsychologia, **12**, 323–330.

Perse, T.L. (1988). Obsessive-compulsive disorder: A treatment review. *Journal of Clinical Psychiatry*, **49**, 48–55.

Perse, T.L., Greist, J.H., Jefferson, J.W. et al. (1987). Fluvovoxamine treatment of obsessive-compulsive disorder. *American Journal of Psychiatry*, **144**, 1543–1548.

Persons, J. & Foa, E. (1984). Processing of fearful and neutral information by obsessive compulsives. *Behaviour Research and Therapy*, **22**, 259–265.

Philpott, R. (1975). Recent advances in the behavioural measurement of obsessional illness: difficulties common to these and other instruments. *Scottish Medical Journal*, **20** (Suppl), 33–40.

Pirozzolo, F., Hansch, E., Mortimer, J., Webster, D. & Kuskowski, M. (1982). Dementia in Parkinson's disease: a neuropsychological analysis. *Brain and Cognition*, **1**, 71–81.

Pitman, R. (1987a). Pierre Janet on obsessive compulsive disorder. *Archives of General Psychiatry*, **44**, 226–232.

Pitman, R. (1987b). A cybernetic model of obsessive-compulsive psychopathology. *Comprehensive Psychiatry*, **28**, 334–343.

Pollak, J. (1979). Obsessive-compulsive personality: A review. *Psychological Bulletin*, **86**, 225–241.

Pollitt, J. (1957). Natural history of obsessional states. *British Medical Journal*, **1**, 194–198.

Pollitt, J. (1969). Obsessional states. *British Journal of Hospital Medicine*, **2**, 1146–50.

Prasad, A. (1984). A double blind study of imipramine versus zimelidine in treatment of obsessive compulsive neurosis. *Pharmacopsychiatry*, **17**, 61–72.

Price, L.H., Goodman, W.K., Charney, D,S., Rasmussen, S.A. & Heninger, G.R. (1987). Treatment of severe obsessive compulsive disorder with fluvoxamine. *American Journal of Psychiatry*, **144**, 1050–1061.

Rabavilas, A.D., Boulougouris, J.C., Perissaki, C. & Stefanis, C. (1979). The effect of peripheral beta-blockade on psychophysiologic responses in obsessional neurotics. *Comprehensive Psychiatry*, **20**, 378–383.

Rachman, S. (1968). *Phobias: Their Nature and Control*. Springfield, Ill: Charles C. Thomas.

Rachman, S. (1973). Some similarities and differences between obsessional ruminations and morbid preoccupations. *Canadian Psychiatric Association Journal*, **18**, 71–74.

Rachman, S. (1974). Primary obsessional slowness. *Behaviour Research and Therapy*, **11**, 463–471.

Rachman, S. (1976a). Obsessive-compulsive checking. *Behaviour Research and Therapy*, **14**, 269–277.

Rachman, S. (1976b). The modification of obsessions: a new formulation. *Behaviour Research and Therapy*, **14**, 437–443.

Rachman, S. (1980). Emotional processing. *Behaviour Research and Therapy*, **18**, 51–60.

Rachman, S. (1981). Unwanted intrusive cognitions. *Advances in Behaviour Research and Therapy*, **3**, 89–99.

Rachman, S. (1985). An overview of clinical and research issues in obsessional-compulsive disorders. In M. Mavissakalian, S.M. Turner & L. Michelson (eds), *Obsessive-Compulsive Disorder; Psychological and Pharmacological Treatment*. New York: Plenum Press.

Rachman, S. (1993). Obsessions, responsibility, and guilt. *Behaviour Research and Therapy*, **31**, 149–154.

Rachman, S. (1994). Pollution of the mind. *Behaviour Research and Therapy*, **32**, 311–314.

Rachman, S. & de Silva, P. (1978). Abnormal and normal obsessions. *Behaviour Research and Therapy*, **16**, 233–248.

Rachman, S. and Hodgson, R. (1980). *Obsessions and Compulsions*. New Jersey: Prentice-Hall.

Rachman, S., Hodgson, R. & Marks, I.M. (1972). The treatment of chronic obsessive-compulsive neurosis. *Behaviour Research and Therapy*, **9**, 237–247.

Radford, E. & Radford, M.A. (1969). *Encyclopedia of Superstitions*. Westport, CT: Greenwood Press.

Rapoport, J.L. (1989a). *Obsessive-Compulsive Disorder in Childhood and Adolescents*. Washington DC: American Pscyhiatric Press Incs.

Rapoport, J.L. (1989b). *The Boy who Couldn't Stop Washing: The Experience and Treatment of Obsessive-compulsive Disorder*. New York: E.P. Dutton.

Rapoport, J.L. (1991). Basal ganglia dysfunction as a proposed cause of obsessive-compulsive disorder. In Bernard J. Carroll & James E. Barrett (eds), *Psychopathology and the Brain*. New York: Raven Press Ltd.

Rapoport, J., Elkins, R. & Mikkelsen, E. (1980). Clinical controlled trial of chlomipramine in adolescents with obsessive-compulsive disorder. *Psychopharmacological Bulletin*, **16**, 61–63.

Rasmussen, S.A. (1984). Lithium and tryptophan augmentation in clomipramine resistant obsessive-compulsive disorder. *American Journal of Psychiatry*, **141**, 1283–1285.

Rasmussen, S. & Eisen, J. (1990). Epidemiology and clinical features of Obsessive-Compulsive Disorder. In M.A. Fenike, L. Baer & W. Minichiello (eds), *Obsessive-Compulsive Disorders: Theory and Management*, 2nd edn. London: Mosby Year Book.

Rasmussen, S. & Eisen, J. (1991). Phenomenology of OCD: Clinical subtypes, heterogeneity and coexistence. In J. Zohar, T. Insel, & S. Rasmussen (eds), *The Psychobiology of Obsessive Compulsive Disorder*. New York: Springer Publishing Company.

Rasmussen, S. & Eisen, J. (1992). The epidemiology and clinical features of obsessive compulsive disorder. *The Psychiatric Clinics of North America*, **15**, 743–758.

Rasmussen, S.A., Goodman, W.K., Woods, S.W., Heninger, G.R. & Charney, D.S. (1987). Effects of yohimbine on obsessive compulsive disorder. Psychopharmacology, **93**, 308–313.

Rasmussen, S.A. & Tsuang, M.T. (1984). Epidemiology of obsessive-compulsive disorder: A review. *Journal of Clinical Pychiatry*, **45**, 450–457.

Rasmussen, S.A. & Tsuang, M.T. (1986). Clinical characteristics and family history in DSM-III obsessive-compulsive disorder. *American Journal of Psychiatry*, **143**, 317–322.

Raven, J.C. (1958). *Mill-Hill Vocabulary Scale*, 2nd edn. London: H.K. Lewis.

Reed, G.F. (1968). Some formal qualities of obsessional thinking. *Psychiatria Clinica*, **1**, 382–392.

Reed, G.F. (1969a). 'Underinclusion' — a characteristic of obsessional personality disorder: I. *British Journal of Psychiatry*, **115**, 781–785.

Reed, G.F. (1969b). 'Underinclusion' — a characteristic of obsessional personality disorder: II. *British Journal of Psychiatry*, **115**, 787–790.

Reed, G.F. (1977). Obsessional personality disorder and remembering. *British Journal of Psychiatry*, **130**, 184-185.

Reed, G.F. (1985). *Obsessional Experience and Compulsive Behaviour. A Cognitive-Structural Approach.* London: Academic Press Inc.

Reed, G.F. (1991). The cognitive characteristics of obsessional disorder. In P. A. Magaro (ed.), *Cognitive Bases of Mental Disorders. Annual Review of Psychopathology.* Vol. 1. London: Sage.

Rettew, D.C., Cheslow, D.H., Rapoport, J.L., Leonard, H.L. & Lenane, M.C. (1991). Neuropsychological test performance in trichotillomania: a further link with obsessive compulsive disorder. *Journal of Anxiety Disorders*, **5**, 225-235.

Rey, A. (1941). L'examen psychologique dans les cas d'encephalopathie traumatique. Archives de Psychologie, **112**, 286-340.

Rey, A. (1970). *L'examen Clinique en Psychologie.* Paris: Presses Universitaires de France.

Reynolds, M. & Salkovskis, P.M. (1991). The relationship among guilt, dysphoria, anxiety and obsessions in a normal population: An attempted replication. *Behaviour Research and Therapy*, **29**, 259-265.

Ricciardi, J.N., Baer, L., Jenike, M.A., Fischer, S.C., Sholtz, D. & Buttloph, M.L. (1992). Changes in DSM III-R Axis II diagnoses following treatment of obsessive compulsive disorder. *American Journal of Psychiatry*, **149**, 829-831.

Rickels, K. (1978). Use of anti-anxiety agents in anxious outpatients. *Psychopharmacology*, **58**, 1-17.

Riperre, V. (1984). Can hypoglycemia cause obsessions and ruminations? *Medical Hypotheses*, **15**, 3-13.

Robertson, J.A. (1979). Controlled investigation of the treatment of obsessive-compulsive disorders. MD dissertation. Middlesex Hospital, London.

Robins, L., Helzer, J., Weissman, M., Ovaschel, H., Gruenberg, E., Burke, J. & Reiger, D. (1984). Lifetime prevalance of specific psychiatric disorders in three sites. *Archives of General Psychiatry*, **41**, 949-958.

Robinson, A.L., Heaton, R.K., Lehman, R.A.W. & Stilson, D.W. (1980). The utility of the Wisconsin Card Sort Test in detecting and localizing frontal lobe lesions. *Journal of Consulting and Clinical Psychology*, **48**, 614.

Roper, G., Rachman, S. & Marks, I. (1975). Passive and participant modelling in exposure treatment of obsessive-compulsive neurotics. *Behaviour Research and Therapy*, **13**, 271-279.

Rosen, I. (1957). The clinical significance of obsessions in schizophrenia. *Journal of Mental Science*, **103**, 773-786.

Rosen, K.V. & Tallis, F. (1995). Investigation into the relationship between personality traits and OCD. *Behaviour Research and Therapy*, **33**, 445-450.

Rosen, K.V., Tallis, F. & Davey, G. (submitted). Obsessive compulsive disorder and guilt.

Rosen, M. (1975). A dual model of obsessional neurosis. *Journal of Consulting and Clinical Psychology*, **43**, 453-459.

Rosenberg, B.J. (1953). Compulsiveness as a determinant in selected cognitive-perceptual performances. *Journal of Personality*, **21**, 506-516.

Rosenberg, C.M. (1967). Familial aspects of neurosis. *British Journal of Psychiatry*, **113**, 405-413.

Rosenberg, C.M. (1968) Complications of obsessional neurosis. *British Journal of Psychiatry*, **114**, 477-478.

Rubenstein, C.F., Peynircioglu, Z.F., Chambless, D.L. & Pigott, T.A. (1993). Memory in sub-clinical obsessive-compulsive checkers. *Behaviour Research and Therapy*, **31**, 759–765.

Rubin, R.T., Villanueva-Meyer, J., Ananth, J. et al. (1992). Regional xenon 133 cerebral blood flow and cerebral technetium 99m HMPAO uptake in unmedicated patients with obsessive-compulsive disorder and matched control subjects. *Archives of General Psychiatry*, **49**, 695–702.

Rudin, E. (1953). Ein beitrag zur frage der zwangskrankheit insebesondere ihrere hereditaren beziehungen. *Archives Psychiatrische Nervenkrankheit*, **191**, 14–54.

Rutter, M. (1989). Pathways from childhood to adult life. *Journal of Child Psychology and Psychiatry*, **30**, 23–51.

Salkovskis, P.M. (1983). Treatment of an obsessional patient using habituation to audiotaped ruminations. *British Journal of Clinical Psychology*, **22**, 311–313.

Salkovskis, P. (1985). Obsessional-compulsive problems: a cognitive-behavioural analysis. *Behaviour Research and Therapy*, **25**, 571–583.

Salkovskis, P.M. (1989a). Obsessional disorders. In K. Hawton, P.M. Salkovskis, J. Kirk and D.M. Clark (eds), *Cognitive Behaviour Therapy for Psychiatric Problems: A Practical Guide*. Oxford: Oxford Medical Publications.

Salkovskis, P.M. (1989b). Cognitive-behavioural factors and the persistence of intrusive thoughts in obsessional problems. *Behaviour, Research and Therapy*, **27**, 677–682.

Salkovskis, P.M. (in press). Cognitive factors in obsessional problems. In R. Rapee (ed.), *Current Controversies in the Anxiety Disorders*. New York: Guilford press.

Salkovskis, P.M. & Campbell, P. (1994). Thought suppression induces intrusion in naturally occurring negative intrusive thoughts. *Behaviour Research and Therapy*, **32**, 1–8.

Salkovskis, P.M. & Harrison, J. (1984). Abnormal and normal obsessions: a replication. *Behaviour Research and Therapy*, **22**, 549–552.

Salkovskis, P.M. & Warwick, H.M.C. (1986). Morbid preocccupations, health anxiety, and reassurance: A cognitive-behavioural approach to hypochondriasis. *Behaviour Research and Therapy*, **24**, 597–602.

Salkovskis, P.M. & Warwick, H.M.C. (1988).Cognitive therapy of obsessive-compulsive disorder. In C. Perris, I.M. Blackburn & H. Perris (eds), *The Theory and Practice of Cognitive Therapy*. Heidelberg: Springer.

Salkovskis, P.M. & Westbrook, D. (1989). Behaviour therapy and obsessional ruminations: can failure be turned into success?, *Behaviour Research and Therapy*, **27**, 149–160.

Sanavio, E. (1988). Obsessions and compulsions: the Padua Inventory. *Behaviour Research and Therapy*, **26**, 169–177.

Sandler, J. & Hazari, A. (1960). The obsessional: on the psychological classification of obsessional character traits and symptoms. *British Journal of Medical Psychology*, **33**, 113–122.

Sawle, G., Hymas, N., Lees, A. et al. (1991). Obsessional slowness. Functional studies with positron emission tomography. *Brain*, **114**, 2191–2202.

Schneider, J.S. (1984). Basal ganglia role in behavior: Importance of sensory gating and its relevance to psychiatry. *Biological Psychiatry*, **19**, 1693–1709.

Schneider, K. (1958). *Psychopathic Personalities*. Trans. J.W. Hamilton. London: Cassell.

Seibyl, J.P., Krystal, J.H., Googman, W.K. & Price, L.H. (1989). Obsessive-compulsive symptoms in a patient with right frontal lobe lesion. *Neuropsychiatry, Neuropsychology, and Behavioural Neurology*, **1**, 295–299.

Shafran, R. & Tallis, F. (submitted). Obsessive Compulsive Hoarding: Three cases suggesting the primacy of cognition.

Shagass, C., Roemer, R.A., Straumanis, J.J. & Josiassen, R.C. (1984). Distinctive somatosensory evoked potential features in obsessive compulsive disorder. *Biological Psychiatry*, **19**, 1507–1524.

Shallice, T. (1982). Specific impairments in planning. *Philosophical Transactions of the Royal Society of London*, **298**, 199–209.

Shallice, T. & Burgess, P.W. (1991). Deficit in strategy application following frontal lobe damage in man. *Brain*, **114**, 727–741.

Sher, K., Frost, R., Kushner, M., Crews, T. & Alexander, J. (1989). Memory deficits in compulsive checkers: replication and extension in a clinical sample. *Behaviour Research and Therapy*, **27**, 65–69.

Sher, K., Frost, R. & Otto, R. (1983). Cognitive deficits in compulsive checkers: an exploratory study. *Behaviour Research and Therapy*, **21**, 357–363.

Sher, K., Mann, B. & Frost, R. (1984). Cognitive dysfunction in compulsive checkers: further explorations. *Behaviour Research and Therapy*, **22**, 493–502.

Sherman, S.J., Skov, R.B., Hervitz, E.F. & Stock, C.B. (1981). The effects of explaining hypothetical future events: from possibility to probability to actuality and beyond. *Journal of Experimental Social Pychology*, **17**, 142–158.

Shields, J. (1962). *Monozygotic Twins*. Oxford: Oxford University Press.

Skinner, B.F. (1953). *Science and Human Behaviour*. New York: Macmillan.

Snowdon, J. (1980). A comparison of written and postbox forms of the Leyton obsessional inventory. *Psychological Medicine*, **10**, 165–170.

Solomon, R.L., Kamin, L.J. & Wynne, L.C. (1953). Traumatic avoidance learning: several extinction procedures with dogs. *Journal of Abnormal and Social Psychology*, **48**, 291–302.

Spielberger, C.D., Goruch, R.L., Lushene, R., Vagg, P.R. & Jacobs, G.A. (1980). Manual for the State-Trait Anxiety Inventory. Palo Alto, Calif.: Consulting Psychology Press.

Spitzer, R.L., Williams, J.B.W., Gibbon, M. et al. (1987). Structured clinical interview for DSM-III-R (SCID). New York: New York Psychiatric Institute. *Biometric Research*, 1987.

Steketee, G.S. (1993). *Treatment of Obsessive Compulsive Disorder*. London: The Guilford Press.

Steketee. G.S. & Freund, B. (1993). Psychometric properties of the Compulsive Activity Checklist. *Behavioural Psychotherapy*, **21**, 13–25.

Steketee, G., Grayson, J.B. & Foa, E.B. (1987). A comparison of characteristics of obsessive compulsive disorder and other anxiety disorders. *Journal of Anxiety Disorders*, **1**, 325–335.

Steketee, G. Quay, S. & White, K. (1991). Religion and guilt in OCD patients. *Journal of Anxiety Disorders*, **5**, 359–367.

Stengel, E. (1945). A study on some clinical aspects of the relationship between obsessional neurosis and psychotic reaction types. *Journal of Mental Science*, **91**, 166–87.

Stern, R. (1970). Treatment of case of obsessional neurosis using a thought-stopping technique. *British Journal of Psychiatry*, **117**, 441–442.

Stern, R.S. & Cobb, J.P. (1978). Phenomenology of obsessive-compulsive neurosis. *British Journal of Psychiatry*, **132**, 233–239.

Stern, R., Lipsedge, M. & Marks, I. (1973). Obsessive ruminations: a controlled trial of thought stopping technique. *Behaviour Research and Therapy*, **11**, 659–662.

Sternberger, L.G. & Burns, G.L. (1990a). Maudsley Obsessional-Compulsive Inventory: obsessions and compulsions in a nonclinical sample. *Behaviour Research and Therapy*, **28**, 337–340.

Sternberger, L.G. & Burns, G.L. (1990b). Obsessions and compulsions: psychometric properties of the Padua Inventory with an American college population. *Behaviour Research and Therapy*, **28**, 341–345.

Sturgis, E.T. & Meyer, V. (1981). Obsessive compulsive disorders. In S.M. Turner, R.S. Calhoun, and H.E. Adams (eds), *Handbook of Clinical Behaviour Therapy*. New York: Wiley.

Stuss, D.T. & Benson, D.F. (1986). *The Frontal Lobes*. New York: Raven Press.

Stuss, D.T., Benson, D.F., Kaplan, E.F., Weir, W.S., Naeser, M.A., Lieberman, I. & Ferrill, D. (1983). The involvement of orbitofrontal cerebrum in cognitive tests. *Neuropsychologia*, **21**, 135–148.

Stroop, J.R. (1935). Studies of interference in serial verbal reactions. *Journal of Experimental Psychology*, **18**, 643–662.

Suess, L. & Halpern, M.S. (1989). Obsessive compulsive disorder: The religious perspective. In J. Rapoport (ed.), *Obsessive-Compulsive Disorder in Children and Adolescents*. Washington DC: American Psychiatric Press Inc.

Swedo, S.E., Lenane, M.C., Leonard, H.L. & Rapoport, J.L. (1990, November). Drug treatment of trichotillomania: Two year follow up. Paper presented at the meeting of the Association for Advancement of Behaviour Therapy, San Francisco.

Swedo, S., Leonard. H. & Rapoport, J. (1992a). Childhood obsessive compulsive disorder. *The Psychiatric Clinics of North America*, **15**, 767–775.

Swedo, S.E., Pietrini, P., Leonard, L.H. et al. (1992b). Cerebral glucose metabolism in childhood-onset obsessive-compulsive disorder. Revisualisation during pharmacotherapy. *Archives of General Psychiatry*, **49**, 690–694.

Swedo, S.E. & Rapoport, J.L. (1989). Phenomenology and differential diagnosis of obsessive-compulsive disorder in children and adolescents. In J.L. Rapoport (ed.), *Obsessive Compulsive Disorder in Children and Adolescents*. Washington, DC: American Psychiatric Press.

Swedo, S.E., Rapoport, J.L., Cheslow, B.S. et al. (1989a). High prevalence of obsessive-compulsive symptoms in patients with Sydenham's chorea. *American Journal of Psychiatry*, **146**, 246–249.

Swedo, S.E., Schapiro, M.B., Grady, C.L. et al. (1989b). Cerebral glucose metabolism in childhood onset obsessive-compulsive disorder. *Archives of General Psychiatry*, **46**, 518–523.

Tallis, F. (1992). *Understanding Obsessions and Compulsions*. London: Sheldon Press.

Tallis, F. (1993) Doubt reduction using distinctive stimuli as a treatment for compulsive checking: an exploratory investigation. *Clinical Psychology and Psychotherapy*, **1**, 45–52.

Tallis, F. (1994) Obsessions, responsibility, and guilt: two case reports suggesting a common and specific aetiology. *Behaviour Research and Therapy*, **32**, 143–145.

Tallis, F. (1995). The characteristics of obsessional thinking; Difficulty demonstrating the obvious? *Clinical Psychology and Psychotherapy*, **2**, 24–39.

Tallis, F. & de Silva, P. (1992). Worry and obsessional symptoms: A correlational analysis. *Behaviour Research and Therapy*, **30**, 103–105.

Tallis, F. & Eysenck, M. (1994). Worry: mechanisms and modulating influences. *Behavioural Psychotherapy*, **22**, 37–56.

Tallis, F., Eysenck, M.W. & Mathews, A. (1991). Elevated evidence requirements and worry. *Personality and Individual Differences*, **12**, 21–27.

Taylor, J.G. (1963). A behavioural interpretation of obsessive-compulsive neurosis. *Behaviour Research and Therapy*, **1**, 237–244.

Taylor, L.B. (1979). Psychological assessment of neurosurgical patients. In T. Rasmussen & R. Marino (eds), *Functional Neurosurgery*. New York: Raven Press.

Thines, G. (1987). Phenomenology. In R. L. Gregory (ed.), *The Oxford Companion to the Mind*. Oxford University Press: Oxford.

Thoren, P., Asberg, M., Bertilsson, L., Mellstrom, B., Sjoqvist, F. & Traskman, L. (1980a). Clomipramine treatment of obsessive-compulsive disorder II: biochemical aspects. *Archives of General Psychiatry*, **37**, 1289–1294.

Thoren, P., Asberg, M., Cronhom, B. et al. (1980b). Clomipramine treatment of obsessive compulsive disorder I: a controlled clinical trial. *Archives of General Psychiatry*, **37**, 1281–1285.

Toates, F. (1990). *Obsessional Thoughts and Behaviour*. Wellingborough: Thorsons.

Tonkonogy, G.A. & Barriera, P. (1989). Obsessive-compulsive disorder and caudate-frontal lesion. *Neuropsychiatry, Neuropsychology and Behavioural Neurology*, **2**, 203–209.

Torgersen, S. (1990). Genetics of anxiety and its clinical implications. In G.D. Burrows, M. Roth, and R. Noyes (eds), *Handbook of Anxiety, Vol 3: The Neurobiology of Anxiety*. Amsterdam: Elsevier.

Tryon, G.S. (1979). A review and critique of thought stopping research. *Journal of Behavior Therapy and Experimental Psychiatry*, **10**, 189–192.

Tsuang, M.T. (1966). Birth order and maternal age of psychiatric inpatients. *British Journal of Psychiatry*, **112**, 1131–1141.

Turner, S.M., Beidel, D.C. & Stanley, M.A. (1992). Are obsessional thoughts and worry different cognitive phenomena? *Clinical Psychology Review*, **12**, 257–270.

Tynes, L.L., White, K. & Steketee, G.S. (1990). Toward a new nosology of OCD. *Comprehensive Psychiatry*, **31**, 465–480.

Underwood, B.J. (1957). Interference and forgetting. *Psychological Review*, **64**, 49–60.

Upadhyaya, A.K., Abou-Salehm M.T., Wilson, K., Grime, S.J. & Critchley, M. (1990). A study of depression in old age using single photon emission computerised tomography. *British Journal of Psychiatry*, **157** (suppl. 9), 76–81.

Vaisaner, E. (1975). Psychiatric disorders in Finland. *Acta Psychiatrica Scandinavica*, **62** (suppl. 263), 27.

van den Broek, M.D., Bradshaw, C.M. & Szabadi, E. (1993). Utility of the Modified Wisconsin Card Sorting Test in neuropsychological assessment. *British Journal of Clinical Psychology*, **32**, 333–343.

van Oppen, P. (1992). Obsessions and compulsions: dimensional structure, reliability, convergent and divergent validity of the Padua Inventory. *Behaviour Research and Therapy*, **30**, 631–637.

van Oppen, P. (1994). Obsessive compulsive disorder: issues in assessment and treatment. Unpublished PhD thesis, Vrije Universiteit, Amsterdam.

van Oppen, P. & Arntz, A. (1994). Cognitive therapy for obsessive compulsive disorder. *Behaviour Research and Therapy*, **32**, 79–87.

van Oppen, P., Haan, E. de, Balkan, A.J.L.M. van, Spinhoven, Ph., Hoogduin, C.A.L. & Dyck, R. (in press). Cognitive therapy and exposure in vivo in the treatment of obsessive-compulsive disorder. *Behaviour Research and Therapy*.

van Oppen, P., Hoekstra, R.J. & Emmelkamp, P.M.G. (in press). The structure of obsessive compulsive symptoms. *Behaviour Research and Therapy*.

Veale, D. (1993). Classification and treatment of obsessional slowness. *British Journal of Psychiatry*, **162**, 198–203.

Veale, D.M., Sahakian, B.J., Owen, A.M. & Marks, I.M. (submitted). *Cognitive Deficits in Tests Sensitive to Frontal Lobe Dysfunction in Obsessive Compulsive Disorder*.

Vingoe, G. (1980). The treatment of chronic obsessive condition via reinforcement contingent upon success in response prevention. *Behaviour Reserach and Therapy*, **18**, 212–217.

Vinogradova, O.S. (1975). Functional organization of the limbic system in the process of registration of information: facts and hypotheses. In R.L. Isaacson & K.H. Pribram (eds), *The Hippocampus, Vol. 2, Neurophysiology and Behavior*. New York: Plenum Press.

Visset, S., Hoekstra, R.J. & Emmelkamp, P. (in press). Long term follow-up study of obsessive compulsive patients after exposure treatment.

Walsh, K.W. (1978). Frontal lobe problems. In G.V. Stanley & K.W. Walsh (eds), *Brain Impairment: Proceedings of the 1976 Brain Impairment Workshop*. Parkville, Victoria: Neuropsychology Group, University of Melbourne.

War Department (1944). *Army Individual Test Battery Manual of Directions and Scoring*. Washington D.C: Adjutant General's Office.

Warren, R. & Zgourides, G.D. (1991). Anxiety Disorders: A Rational-Emotive Perspective. Elmsford, NY: Pergamon Press.

Watson, J.P. & Marks, I.M. (1971). Relevant and irrelevant fear in flooding: a crossover study of phobic patients. *Behavior Therapy*, **2**, 275–293.

Watts, F. (submitted). *An Information-Processing Approach to Compulsive Checking*.

Waxman, D. (1977). A clinical trial of clomipramine and diazepam in the treatment of phobic and obsessional illness. *Journal of International Medical Research*, **5**, 99–109.

Wechsler, D. (1955). *Wechsler Adult Intelligence Scale: Manual*. New York: Psychological Corporation.

Wechsler, D. (1981). *WAIS-R Manual*. New York: Psychological Corporation.

Wechsler, D. & Stone, C. (1945). *Manual for the Wechsler Memory Scale*. New York: The Psychological Corp.

Wegner, D. (1989). *White Bears and Other Unwanted Thoughts: Suppression, Obsession, and the Psychology of Mental Control*. New York: Viking Penguin.

Weilberg, J.B., Mesulam, M.M., Weintraub, S. et al. (1989). Focal striatal abnormalities in a patient with obsessive-compulsive disorder. *Archives of Neurology*, **46**, 233–235.

Welch, G. (1979). The treatment of compulsive vomiting and obsessive thoughts through graduated response delay, response prevention, and cognitive correction. *Journal of Behavior Therapy and Experimental Psychiatry*, **10**, 77–82.

Wells, A. (1990). Panic disorder in association with relaxation induced anxiety: an attentional training approach to treatment. *Behavior Therapy*, **21**, 273–280.

Wells, A. (1994). Attention and the control of worry. In G.C.L. Davey & F. Tallis (eds), *Worrying: Perspectives on Theory, Assessment and Treatment*. Chichester: Wiley.

Wells, A. & Mathews, G. (1994). *Attention and Emotion: A Clinical Perspective*. Hillsdale, NJ: Lawrence Earlbaum Associates.

Westphal, K. (1877). Uber Zwangsvorstellungen. *Arch Psychiatr. Nervenkrankheiten*, **8**, 734–750.

Whitty, C.W.M., Duffield, J.E., Tow, P.M. et al. (1952). Anterior cingulectomy in the treatment of mental disease. *Lancet*, **1**, 475–481.

Willingham, W.W. (1956). The organization of emotional behaviour in mice. *Journal of Comparative and Physiological Psychology*, **49**, 345–348.

Wilner, A., Reich, T., Robins, I., Fishman, R. & van Doren, T. (1976). Obsessive-compulsive neurosis. *Comprehensive Psychiatry*, **17**, 527–539.

Wise, S.P. & Rapoport, J.L. (1989). Obsessive-compulsive disorder: is it basal ganglia dysfunction? In J. Rapoport (ed.), *Obsessive-Compulsive Disorder in Children and Adolescents*. Washington DC: American Psychiatric Press Inc.

Wolpe, J. (1958). *Psychotherapy by Reciprocal Inhibition*. Stanford, CA: Stanford University Press.

Wolpe, J. (1982). *The Practice of Behavior Therapy*. New York: Pergamon Press.

Woodruff, R. & Pitts, F.N. (1964). Monozygotic twins with obsessional illness. *American Journal of Psychiatry*, **120**, 1075–1080.

World Health Organisation (1992). *The ICD-10 Classification of Mental and Behavioural Disorders: Clinical Descriptions and Diagnostic Guidelines*. Geneva: WHO.

Yaryura-Tobias, J.A., Bebirian, R.J., Neziroglu, F. & Bhagavan, H.N. (1977). Obsessive-compulsive disorders as a serotonin defect. *Res. Comm. Psychol. Psychiatry Behav.*, **2**, 279–286.

Yaryura-Tobias, J.A. & Bhagavan, H.N. (1977). L-tryptophan in obsessive compulsive disorders. *American Journal of Psychiatry*, **134**, 1298–1299.

Yaryura-Tobias, J. & Neziroglu, F. (1983). *Obsessive-Compulsive Disorders: Pathogenesis-Diagnosis-Treatment*. New York: Marcel Dekker Inc.

Zielinski, C.M., Taylor, M.A. & Juzwin, K.R. (1991). Neuropsychological deficits in obsessive compulsive disorder. *Neuropsychiatry, Neuropsychology and Behavioural Neurology*, **4**, 110–126.

Zitrin, C.M., Klein, D.F., Woerner, M.G. & Ross, D.C. (1983). Treatment of phobias: I. Comparison of impipramine hydrochloride and placebo. *Archives of General Psychiatry*, **40**, 125–138.

Zohar, J., Insel, T.R., Berman, K.F., Foa, E.B., Hill, J.L. & Weinberger, D.R. (1989). Anxiety and cerebral blood flow during behavioral challenge: Dissociation of central from peripheral subjective measures. *Archives of General Psychiatry*, **46**, 505–510.

Zohar, J., Insel, T.R., Zohar-Kadouch, R.C. et al. (1988). Serotonergic responsivity in obsessive-compulsive disorder: Effects of chronic clomipramine treatment. *Archives of General Psychiatry*, **45**, 167–172.

Zohar, J., Klein, E.M., Mueller, E.A., Insel, T.R., Uhde, T. & Murphy, D.L. (1987a). 5HT obsessive compulsive disorder and anxiety. *Proceedings*, American Pychiatric Association, 140th Annual Meeting, Chicago, p. 175.

Zohar, J., Mueller, E.A., Insel, T.R. et al. (1987b). Serotonergic responsivity in obsessive-compulsive disorder: comparison of patients and healthy controls. *Archives of General Psychiatry*, **44**, 946–951.

Zohar, J. & Zohar-Kadouch, R. (1991). Is there a specific role for serotonin in obsessive compulsive disorder? In S. Brown & H.M. van Praag. *The Role of Serotonin in Psychiatric Disorders* (eds), New York: Brunner Mazel.

APPENDIX

Names and addresses of charitable organisations in the USA and UK.

The OCD Foundation Inc.
PO Box 9573
New Haven
Connecticut 0635
USA

Obsessive Action
PO Box 6097
London
W2 1WZ

INDEX

The Wiley Series in

CLINICAL PSYCHOLOGY

Related titles of interest from Wiley...

Current Insights in Obsessive Compulsive Disorder

Edited by **E. Hollander, J. Zohar, D. Marazziti** and **B. Oliver**

A wide-ranging, authoritative and comprehensive coverage of the most recent and significant advances in the basic research and clinical investigation of obsessive compulsive disorder

0-471-95142-0 312pp 1994 Hardback

Psychological Management of Schizophrenia

Edited by Max Birchwood and Nicholas Tarrier

Offers a practical guide for mental health professionals wanting to develop and enhance their skills in these new treatment approaches. Core chapters have been selected and updated for this volume, including coverage of family interventions and network support; early warning systems to anticipate and control relapse, strategies to control distressing symptoms and improving recovery from acute psychosis.

0-471-95056-4 176pp 1994 Paperback

Panic Disorder

Theory, Research and Therapy

Edited by Roger Baker

A valuable resource for the range of professions engaged in providing psychological treatment for patients presenting with anxiety and panic disorders.

0-471-93317-1 364pp 1991 Paperback

Panic Disorder

Clinical, Biological and Treatment Aspects

Edited by Gregory M. Asnis and Herman M. Van Praag

Reviews recent biological and genetic research on the causes and mechanisms of panic disorder.

0-471-08999-0 368pp 1995 Hardback